DEFENDING THE BRAND

DEFENDING THE BRAND

*Aggressive Strategies
for Protecting Your Brand
in the Online Arena*

Brian H. Murray

AMERICAN MANAGEMENT ASSOCIATION

*New York • Atlanta • Brussels • Chicago • Mexico City • San Francisco
Shanghai • Tokyo • Toronto • Washington, D.C.*

This publication is designed to provide accurate and authoritative information in regard to the subject matter covered. It is sold with the understanding that the publisher is not engaged in rendering legal, accounting, or other professional service. If legal advice or other expert assistance is required, the services of a competent professional person should be sought.

Library of Congress Cataloging-in-Publication Data

Murray, Brian H., 1968-
    Defending the brand : aggressive strategies for protecting your brand in the online arena / Brian H. Murray.
        p.   cm.
    Includes index.
    ISBN 0-8144-0754-4
    1. Brand name products.   2. Trademark infringement.   3. Electronic commerce.   4. Product management.   I. Title.

HD69.B7M79   2003
658.8'27—dc22

                                                                    2003014924

Printing number

10   9   8   7   6   5   4   3   2   1

Dedicated to the memory of Edmund R. Fischer

Contents

Preface   xiii

Acknowledgments   xv

Introduction   1

Section One   Digital Brand Abuse   **5**

Chapter 1   The Dark Side   7
             Objectionable Content   8
             Pornography   8
                 Adult Entertainment   9
                 Child Pornography   11
             Hate, Violence, and Extremism   12
             Gambling   13
             Parody   14
             Defining "Objectionable"   18
             Who's at Risk?   21
             What to Do   21
             The Business Case   24
             The Board Room Summary   26

Chapter 2   The Opportunities and Threats of Online
             Commentary   27
             The Rumor Mill   28
                 Financial Earnings   30
                 Early Warning   31
             Information Security   32
                 Other Security and Liability Threats   33
             The World's Largest Focus Group   34
                 Activism and "Sucks" Sites   36
                 Nobody Is Immune   39
             Managing Risk   40
             Buried Treasure   40
             The Business Case   41
             The Board Room Summary   42

Chapter 3   Customer Diversion   44
             Customer Capture   45
                 Cybersquatting   45
                 Typo-Piracy   47
                 Domain Name Administration   50
                     Arbitration   52
                 Search Engine Manipulation   52
                     Invisible Seeding   54
                     Visible Seeding   54
                     Spoofing   54
                     Managing Seeding and Spoofing Issues   55
                 Paid Placement   56
                 Adware   58
                 Mislabeled Links   60
                 Unsolicited E-Mail   61
             Keeping the Customer   62
             Bringing the Customer Back   66
             The Motive   67
             Scope of the Problem   68
             The Future   69
             The Business Case   70
             The Board Room Summary   71

Section Two   Online Partners and Distribution Issues   73

Chapter 4   Managing Partner Compliance   75
             The Customer Experience   76

Changing Dynamics 77
Online Partners 77
  Affiliates 79
  Suppliers 80
  Distributors 84
  Third Parties 90
Monitoring Partners 93
  Step 1: Prioritization 93
  Step 2: Brand Management 94
  Step 3: Enforcement 95
The Business Case 95
The Board Room Summary 97

Chapter 5   **Counterfeits and Gray Markets** 98
Gray Markets 99
  Combating Gray Market Activity 101
Counterfeiting 102
  Copier Supplies 103
  Pharmaceuticals 103
Online Monitoring 104
  Criteria That May Signal a Suspect Distributor 105
  Testing Authenticity 108
The Business Case 109
The Board Room Summary 110

Chapter 6   **Defending Against Digital Piracy** 111
Music 112
  Sales Leads 114
Video 116
  Cease and Desist 118
  Customer Convenience 119
  Copy Protection and Digital Rights Management 120
Software 121
Text and Images 125
  E-Books 125
    The Stephen King Experiment 126
  News Services 127
Criteria for Identifying Licensing Revenue Opportunities 127
  Market Data 129
The Business Case 131
The Board Room Summary 132

Section Three   Trust   **133**

Chapter 7	The Costs of Compromised Privacy and Security	135
	Information Collection Technologies	136
	Cookies	137
	Web Beacons	137
	Information Security	140
	Customer Information Collection	141
	Customer Information Storage	142
	Corporate Identity Theft	144
	Managing Privacy and Security	147
	The Business Case	149
	The Board Room Summary	150

Section Four   Competitive Intelligence   **151**

Chapter 8	Using Online Competitive Intelligence to Outmaneuver Competitor Brands	153
	The Internet as a Competitive Intelligence Source	154
	Brand Presence	155
	Brand Reach	156
	Competitor Brand Abuse	158
	Competitor Absence	158
	Linking Relationships	159
	Partnerships	159
	Recruiting Competitor Partners	160
	Online Commentary	162
	Collecting the Data	164
	Counterintelligence	164
	Actionable Information	165
	The Business Case	166
	The Board Room Summary	167

Section Five   Taking Action   **169**

Chapter 9	How to Use Online Monitoring to Control Your Brand and Capture Revenue	171
	The What-Where-How Approach	172
	What to Search For	172
	Where to Search	173

	How to Search	175
	Stakeholders	175
	Customer Eyes	177
	False Positives	178
	Detecting Objectionable Associations	178
	Allocation of Resources	181
	When to Outsource	182
	How to Outsource	184
	Company Background	184
	Security	185
	Scope of Services	186
	Partnerships	187
	Experience and Qualifications	187
	The Business Case	188
	The Board Room Summary	189
Chapter 10	Constructing Your Plan of Attack	190
	Designing an Effective Approach	191
	Step 1: Categorize Incidents by Offender	191
	Step 2: Categorize the Abuse	192
	Step 3: Prioritize the Incidents	193
	Step 4: Determine Whether the Incidents Warrant Action	194
	Step 5: Assign Responsibilities for Taking Action	196
	Step 6: Select the Communication	196
	Step 7: Secure Approval	199
	Step 8: Contact the Offender	200
	Step 9: Revisit the Incident	201
	Step 10: Take Follow-up Action	201
	Best Practices in Action	202
	Objectionable Content	202
	Cybersquatting	203
	Unauthorized Brand/Logo Use	203
	Partner Noncompliance	203
	The Business Case	203
	The Board Room Summary	204
Chapter 11	Mobilizing the Forces	206
	State of Affairs	206
	Raising Awareness	207
	Build a Business Case	207
	Manage Risk	207

Adopt Experiential Learning   208
Develop a Plan   208
Apathy Is the Enemy   208
Who's Responsible?   209
Stepping Up   210
The Business Case   211
The Board Room Summary   212

Glossary   213

Appendix A: Top-Level Domains   221

Appendix B: Sample Affiliate Guidelines   225

Appendix C: Sample Guidelines for Managing Partner Compliance   231

Appendix D: Overview of Peer-to-Peer (P2P) Networks   235

Appendix E: Sample RFP Scope of Work   239

Appendix F: Sample Cease-and-Desist Letters   243

Notes   249

Index   259

Preface

I never cease to be amazed by the bold, clever, and unscrupulous behavior that is so common on the Internet. Through my experience defending brands, I can say with confidence that anything that you thought would never happen online is probably already going on, and anything you think couldn't possibly exist on the Internet is almost certainly there. Though it's an overused cliché, the Internet really is the Wild West of the new millennium.

For brand owners, the implications of uninhibited online activity are frightening. The rules of the game have changed, and it certainly hasn't made things easier. There is a dark side to managing a brand in the twenty-first century, and few companies have stepped up to the challenge of dealing with it. As a result, criminals and overly aggressive competitors are often two steps ahead.

This book provides an inside view of the unique issues that companies face related to brand abuse and piracy in the digital age. It also introduces strategies that have been used successfully to combat assaults, and provides the knowledge and insights necessary to take control of your brand and capture revenue.

Defending the Brand is different from most branding books in that there is limited discussion of abstract theories or unproven methodologies. This is meant to be a practical book, providing a glimpse at real-life matters that affect brands in today's world—valuable lessons from the "digital trenches."

The issues and solutions presented are rarely cut-and-dry. Part of the challenge that companies face is that online brand problems are messy and do not fall into neat buckets. Unfortunately, brand abusers aren't considerate enough to align their exploits with existing corporate organizational structures, so it's often unclear who should act and react in defense of the brand. Responsibilities for detecting and countering brand abuse are often murky or spread among various departments. The content of the book reflects this fact. While defending the brand remains the central theme, the subjects discussed are not always confined to pure "brand" issues because the dynamics are more complex than that. Defending the brand must be a concerted, cross-departmental effort supported by a champion at the executive level who can readily recognize the overall implications.

Wherever possible, real-life examples are used to illustrate the issues covered in this book. *All specific incidents mentioned in the text and shown in figures are real.* Many of the referenced abuses are no longer present, and that is good. The offender has probably either been caught in the act or decided to move on. This should not be surprising—the pace of change online is torrid and criminals take full advantage of mobility and anonymity to evade enforcement efforts. Consider the examples provided herein to be snapshots of moving targets.

Each chapter of *Defending the Brand* includes at least one business case to demonstrate the potential financial implications. These cases are not intended to be exact; they are meant to be illustrative in nature, outlining the basic logic by which issues translate to a company's bottom line. While the numbers and approaches used in the cases are drawn from experience, each company is different, and you are encouraged to customize the business cases to make them your own.

The primary goal of the early chapters of *Defending the Brand* is to help you gain familiarity with the types of threats and opportunities that may exist online. Later chapters offer additional insights on how to tackle the challenge of online monitoring and take action. Throughout the book, each chapter concludes with a Boardroom Summary where key points are reiterated, both for the sake of reinforcement and future reference. At the end of *Defending the Brand* you will find a glossary that defines technical terms used throughout.

Through my experience protecting brands and digital assets, I have seen dozens of global companies fight back and gain control, preserving brand equity and capturing millions of dollars in incremental revenue. It is my sincere hope that *Defending the Brand* arms you with the knowledge necessary to duplicate these results.

Acknowledgments

O ver the past four years at Cyveillance, Inc., I have had the privilege to lead a team of professionals that aggressively defends brands and digital assets for some of the most prestigious companies in the world. *Defending the Brand* is based on that experience. I would therefore like to acknowledge the entire client services department at Cyveillance, whose commitment to excellence is only matched by their dedication to the serving the customer.

I would also like to thank Cyveillance's clients, without whom the writing of *Defending the Brand* would not have been possible. These clients were some of the first companies to realize the importance of defending their brands online. Their prescience has paved the way for others, and this book reflects the lessons learned from their challenges and successes.

Defending the Brand also draws heavily on Cyveillance projects, studies, and white papers, for which I would like to acknowledge everyone who has contributed. In particular, I would like to thank Alvin Allen, Mark Bayer, Laura Cooper, James Cowart, Rick Grand, James Green, Robeson Jennings, Jonathan Lee, Meghan McNamara, Amanda Monier, Eric Olson, Beth Sanville, and Paul Tierney.

On an individual level, I would like to thank Rich Moore, chief marketing officer at Cyveillance, who provided the guidance and encouragement to launch this endeavor, and Panos Anastassiadis, president and CEO, for his unwavering support. I would also like to thank Gary McClain for helping me get started, my agent David Fugate of Waterside Productions for his advice and assistance, and both Ellen Kadin of AMACOM and Karen Brogno for helping to make this book the best it could be.

For taking time out of their extremely busy schedules to do peer reviews, I would like to thank Patrick and Stephanie Fox, Mark Fischer, Todd Bransford, Sue Deagle, Meghan McNamara, Dipankar and Rini Sen, and James Cowart. *Defending the Brand* reflects their thoughtful insights.

Finally, I would like to acknowledge you, the reader, for your interest in learning more about the unique challenges of defending a brand in the new millennium. Growing awareness and a thirst for knowledge on the issues covered in *Defending the Brand* can no longer be ignored.

DEFENDING THE BRAND

Introduction

Digitalization and the convergence of networked communication mediums have forever changed the way we live and conduct business. Broadband and wireless technologies, networked appliances, and multipurpose consumer devices promise to embed digital networks even deeper into our everyday routines. Unfortunately, while such technological advances have created fantastic opportunities, they have also facilitated new, unscrupulous business tactics and provided a haven for criminals who thrive on the victimization of corporations and consumers alike.

Few people are aware of the extent to which brands and digital assets are exploited online through practices such as piracy, counterfeiting, deceit, and fraud—all in blatant fashion. And the level of abuse is rapidly escalating, costing companies millions of dollars annually in lost business and goodwill. Fierce competition and economic pressures have exacerbated the situation as ethics fall by the wayside in the struggle for profits and survival. The situation is further aggravated when brand owners fail to protect their assets.

Just ask Nintendo about the importance of defending brands in the new millennium. Imagine how shocked the company was to discover that pornographic websites were using Nintendo's popular character names to lure unsuspecting web surfers. The last thing Nintendo wants is for a young fan of online games to inadvertently end up at a raunchy porn site. The problem had become so severe that Nintendo knew it had to take action. "The Nintendo brand is synonymous with high-quality entertainment, and we are very concerned about sites that are using our popular icons, such as Mario Bros. and Pokémon, to promote explicit adult content," said Richard Flamm, general counsel of Nintendo of America.[1]

Nintendo now aggressively tracks down the porn sites that are abusing its brand and hijacking its customers. "We are continuously working to have all Nintendo content removed from URLs, metatags, and web pages of the inappropriate sites identified . . .," spokeswoman Beth Llewelyn said. The video game company takes legal action if the website operators don't cooperate.[2] Nintendo's diligent attention to the issue and commitment to action has been a model of best practices—allowing the company to successfully combat the online assault on its brands.

The post–New Economy era comes replete with unique, Internet-specific risks as well as "old economy" risks that have been morphed or amplified by this ever-changing and expanding digital medium. For example, the abuse of digital assets goes well beyond the threat to brand names and includes the piracy of text, audio, video, and software. Piracy has always been an issue, but the Internet's ability to provide unparalleled reach, anonymity, and mobility has raised piracy and other online criminal activity to unprecedented levels.

Microsoft Corp. knows this better than most companies as it wages an aggressive global war against software piracy, a problem that threatens to undermine the company's entire business model. Microsoft has shut down hundreds of thousands of online auctions and Internet sites offering pirated or counterfeit Microsoft software worldwide. According to Microsoft corporate attorney Tim Cranton, test purchases made by Microsoft indicate that over 90 percent of the Microsoft software sold online is counterfeit or infringes upon the company's intellectual property rights. "The anonymity and broad access of the Internet makes online fraud a serious issue worldwide that causes both consumer and economic harm," said Cranton.[3]

Aside from outright fraud and theft, there are scores of other abuses that threaten brands in the twenty-first century. Propagation of false rumors, the online sale of counterfeit products, privacy violations, unauthorized claims of affiliation, and misrepresentation by partners are just a few examples. Left unchecked, all these activities undermine the customer experience and destroy brand equity.

Ruthless competitors and criminals alike are becoming more aggressive and the situation is rapidly deteriorating. Abusive tactics don't take long to do damage in this high-speed, connected world, and the explosion of digital content has outpaced most companies' ability to remain abreast of cyberactivity. If not managed effectively, this risk can threaten the revenue and value of any business. Aggressive tactics are widely employed on the Internet to hijack the consumer experience, capture customers, and grow revenue—and all major brands are being leveraged to some extent. The question is, *Who's cashing in on the value of your brand? Is it you? Or is it somebody else?*

Forrester Research estimates that online transactions will reach $7 trillion in the U.S. by 2006.[4] With two-thirds of the U.S. population, three-quarters of our children, and a rapidly growing share of the world population now online, companies have a lot at stake. Even those few remaining companies with no online strategy must take note that millions of customers are going online everyday to shop and conduct research.

Smart companies regain control by gathering intelligence and taking action to defend their brands and digital assets. By proactively managing its brands, a company's influence extends beyond its own domain, which helps maintain the integrity of distribution channels, establishes a higher level of branding consistency, drives revenue, increases market share, and improves customer loyalty. How aggressively a company defends its brands may ultimately be the difference between failure and success.

Section 1

Digital Brand Abuse

"Now, it don't seem to me quite so funny,
What some people are gonna do for money"
Bob Dylan,
"Talking Bear Mountain Picnic Massacre Blues," 1962

Chapter 1

The Dark Side

For many companies, a powerful brand is the foundation upon which the business is built—it provides differentiation and commands a premium that ultimately translates into incremental cash flow. A brand does this by associating a product or service with desirable values, qualities, or other attributes in the mind of the consumer. This is why successful companies across the globe make it their mission to "defend the brand."

In the digital world, the value of a brand is magnified because a brand can help compensate for the limitations of the online medium. While it is possible to see and hear things online, for example, a customer cannot try something on, feel its weight and texture, or smell and taste it. People also lose intangible aspects of the customer experience, such as "atmosphere" or the subtleties of face-to-face interactions.

An established, reputable brand can help overcome gaps in the online experience by conveying qualities that might otherwise be indistinguishable. A customer's previous experience and exposure to the brand can suggest qualities such as durability, fit, style, comfort, or other characteristics not easily conveyed through a digital medium, such as a feelings of stability, goodwill, or trust. This is one reason e-commerce vendors elect to claim or imply affiliation with respected brands.

Because familiar brands can engender feelings of goodwill in the consumer, websites often use others' brand names, logos, and slogans for the express purpose of diverting unsuspecting people to their site. This is particularly evident when the content of the site is entirely unrelated to the brand names the site is using. A common tactic is to incorporate brand names into various elements of website or e-mail design in an attempt to attract attention and generate site traffic by tricking customers or outmaneuvering the search engines people rely on to find relevant sites (see Chapter 3).

As criminals and businesses compete aggressively for revenue, they have every incentive to use and abuse a famous brand. This is why hundreds of thousands of online merchants—from legitimate partners to porn peddlers—make liberal use of popular brands.

Objectionable Content

Like it or not, digital networks have resulted in the proliferation of websites dealing in sexual and extremist material that can be highly objectionable to many customers. These sites blatantly abuse leading brand names in every way imaginable and some you couldn't have dreamed of. While website operators are usually the primary offenders, exploitation of brands also occurs in online environments such as chat rooms, newsgroups, message boards, peer-to-peer (P2P) networks, streaming media, and e-mail. Such abuse is common, and it undermines hard-earned brand equity by exposing consumers to offensive content in association with the brand.

This is the dark side of brand management—dealing with sites that feature violence, hate, or deviant sexual themes. Repulsive sites that prey on brands are a digital economy hazard that can propagate when left to their own devices. While managing this kind of abuse can be frustrating and distasteful, it can be a costly mistake not to defend your brand.

Individual consumers can be deeply affected by exposure to a trusted brand in association with objectionable content, and with large segments of the population online, the impact on a company is significant. Material associated with a brand—whether authorized and endorsed by the company or not—affects consumer perceptions of brands, influences their purchasing decisions, and can spread virally among networks of friends, families, and coworkers.

Pornography

The porn industry is often considered a media pioneer, credited with expanding acceptance and use of VCRs and the Internet. Analysts estimate that more than one-third of all Internet users visit an adult content site every month, and most are paying customers. Tracking revenue from adult Internet sites has proved to be difficult because of the sheer number of sites, but conservative estimates put adult entertainment-industry revenue at anywhere from $1 billion to $10 billion.[1] Here's another measure of how popular online pornography is: The combined monthly unique visitors for the top five porn sites exceeded the television audience for Super Bowl XXXVI.[2]

With so much at stake, porn merchants are technologically sophisticated. Porn website designers know how people navigate the Web, so they employ numerous tactics that use well-known brands to lure people to their sites.

The dangers are real. There are now hundreds of thousands of porn sites online catering to every conceivable preference and fetish. In fact, internal Cyveillance studies have shown that approximately one in four of the top 300,000 most-visited domains on the Internet contain pornography. Some of these sites can be extremely offensive, particularly for unsuspecting visitors.

Pornography is also rapidly pushing its way into the realm of wireless communications. A survey conducted by British consultancy MobileStreams Ltd. found that European carriers have identified adult entertainment as one of the top drivers fueling the growth of multimedia messaging services. Several carriers in Europe and Asia already offer adult content to their subscribers on a pay-per-view or subscription basis, and some have even appointed adult content managers to help build this profitable segment of their business.

Adult Entertainment

Adult entertainment sites comprise the largest segment of online pornography. The sites range from the mildly explicit to those promoting perverse and illegal sexual activity. To gauge how much brand abuse is perpetrated by these sites, branding consultancy Prophet commissioned a study in 2002 that included a detailed analysis of 20,000 pornographic websites. The study determined which consumer brands appeared most frequently on the analyzed sites. Even after excluding Internet brands, entertainment brands, and celebrity names, the results of the exercise revealed that ninety popular consumer brands appeared in excess of 1,000 times each. The results also demonstrated that nobody is immune—abused brands were diverse and ranged from Avis to Zippo.

> *"Having a globally recognized brand name like Zippo makes us a prime target of other businesses who want to gain brand awareness on the Internet by falsely claiming affiliation with us."*
>
> —MICHAEL MARTIN, VICE PRESIDENT OF SALES
> AND MARKETING AT ZIPPO MANUFACTURING CO.[3]

BARBIE'S PLAYPEN

Visitors to the Internet site Barbiesplaypen.com may have been expecting to find Barbie dolls. The site, which prominently displayed the Barbie brand name, actually solicited users with lurid photos and offers for "hot naked women as they enjoy every possible sex act"—definitely not the image Mattel, Inc. has worked hard to build over many years, and not what moms and dads want little Susie to find when she's looking for the Barbie Dream House.

Figure 1-1. *Internet sites use the Barbie name and image to solicit customers.*

The world's largest toy, game, and doll manufacturer, Mattel has sold more than a billion Barbie dolls since 1959. In a lawsuit filed against Internet Dimensions Inc., owner of Barbiesplaypen.com, Mattel stated that it exerts great efforts to preserve the image of its Barbie products. A Mattel spokesperson said the company will defend its brand names. "For us, it really is about enforcing our rights," said Lisa Marie Bongiovanni. "We have incredible equity in our brands." Bongiovanni said Mattel won't risk a customer thinking it sponsors a porn site, or any non-Mattel site. The company will go after anyone who uses a Mattel trademark, she said.[4]

The judge ordered the pornographic website to stop using Mattel's trademark, issued a cease-and-desist order, and effectively shut down the site. "The Barbie dolls, with their long blonde hair and anatomically improbable dimensions, are ostensibly intended to portray wholesomeness to young girls," wrote Judge Harold Baer in his decision. "The 'models' on the Barbiesplaypen.com site, although many have long hair and anatomically improbable dimensions, can in no way be described as engaging in 'wholesome' activities. The obvious intent of the defendants is to cash in on the favorable public image of the Barbie doll," Baer wrote.[5]

Mattel has a history of aggressively protecting the Barbie image. While the company was successful in shutting down the Barbie's Playpen site, the victory was one battle in an ongoing war against brand abuse (see Figure 1-1). The Barbie brand name has been used by hundreds of porn and escort sites. Examples include such sites as www.busty-barbies.de, www.teenbarbies.com, www.escortbarbie.com, and www.barbiexxx.com.

Child Pornography

A *Red Herring* magazine investigative report uncovered highly organized child porn e-commerce generating revenue through the unwitting support of credit card firms and major advertisers. The logos of MasterCard and Visa are prominently displayed on the subscription page of nearly all child porn sites. The *Red Herring* investigation further noted that Sexteens, a Yahoo! Geocities child porn site, included sponsorship ads from Chevron, Continental Airlines, ArtistDirect, and other leading corporations.

"We didn't even think to ask if our ads were running in unregulated areas. We're horrified," said Chevron spokesperson Bonnie Chaikind. Chevron's banner advertisement appeared beside explicit child porn images. "There is no way we would ever be tied to any subject like this," said Chaikind. "We were never told that appearing on pornographic content was a possibility."[6] Consider yourself told.

The repercussion of this unwitting involvement in child pornography is more than just a brand management nightmare. Depending on the degree of knowledge and complicity of involved parties, nearly everyone associated with the creation, transmission, and distribution of online child pornography could be prosecuted. And the problem is widespread. According to *Business Week,* complaints about child porn in cyberspace have grown sixfold since 1998. The U.S. Customs Service estimates that there are more than 100,000 websites offering child pornography—which is illegal worldwide.

Any executive would agree that it is better to make sure the brand is not associated with child pornography websites or e-mail (see Figure 1-2) before it is viewed by potential customers, and certainly before it is exposed through an investigative report. Yet surprisingly, few companies take proactive steps to manage this type of risk. Specific approaches to monitoring online branding and taking action will be covered later in this chapter, as well as in Chapters 9 through 11.

Hate, Violence, and Extremism

While the porn industry may be a leading offender, there are many other associations that can diminish a brand in the eyes of a consumer. The broad reach and anonymity of the Internet have fostered the growth of communities and markets that were previously discreet, repressed, or even illegal. The fear of getting caught typically prevented most people from acting out on their predilections, but "the Internet breaks down inhibitions to violate the law because the risks are much lower," says Kevin A. Delli-Colli, who heads the U.S. Customs Service CyberSmuggling Center in Fairfax, Virginia. "You can contact the

Figure 1-2. *Example of pornographic e-mail that includes popular brands.*

seller anonymously, click on the product, and it's in your house."[7] Examples of growing online communities include the hundreds of thousands of websites dedicated to illegal and perverse activities and controversial subject matter. They include sites affiliated with extremist organizations and terrorists, hate sites, and sites dedicated to unsavory subjects such as death, torture, rape, defecation, incest, or extreme violence.

"North of 70 percent of all e-commerce is based on some socially unacceptable, if not outright illegal, activity."

—Jeffrey Hunker, dean of the
H. John Heinz III School of Public Policy and Management,
Carnegie Mellon University[8]

Why are these organizations and vendors moving online? One reason is the unparalleled sales potential; in addition, global digital networks allow groups to recruit, network, and plan events more easily. And since fringe and extremist communities tend to conduct business according to their own set of rules, their unrestrained use of brand names and logos is an alarming prospect for trademark owners around the globe.

Even Apple Computer, a company that has always fostered a somewhat rebellious image, was disturbed to find its brand prominently displayed on the Church of Satan's website. When Apple threatened legal action, the "Think different" slogan and "Made with Macintosh" web badge were subsequently removed from the website.[9]

Gambling

Gambling is another type of online content that may be considered offensive, or at least inconsistent with desired brand image. Like porn, hate, extremism, and terrorist sites, gambling sites abuse popular brands. While online gambling trails the porn industry by a considerable margin, it is still one of the most pervasive, profitable, and technologically advanced industries online.

Interactive gambling, including online casinos, sports books, and lotteries, represents one of the only industries where profitability is almost assured. The ease and anonymity of online gambling have contributed to explosive growth rates. Gambling sites are accessible to anyone, anywhere, anytime. London-based Merrill Lynch analyst Andrew Burnett says online gambling could generate more than $150 billion in revenues by 2015.[10]

Despite its popularity, gambling has always been shrouded in controversy.

There have been numerous studies citing the negative impact of gambling on individuals, families, and communities. It is recognized as a potentially addictive activity that can damage personal relationships and undermine financial security. There are also legal issues swirling around the gambling industry in some countries, including the United States. Despite legal hurdles, Internet gambling continues to grow as tax-hungry countries see it as a boon.

Given the controversies and generally unwholesome image of the interactive gaming industry, association with gambling can pose a substantial risk to brand equity. Since gaining consumer trust is a top priority, gaming sites prominently display established brands, oftentimes to the detriment of the rightful brand owner. Some sites, such as Ibmcasino-one.com and Microsoft-casino.net, have made unauthorized use of proprietary brands right in their domain names. This is particularly alarming since the domain name is often the first thing a customer sees and is generally used to identify a site.

Gambling sites employ many of the same tactics used by porn sites, including aggressive spamming and using leading brands for their own benefit. Depending on the specific brand, gambling sites can be a greater threat than porn sites, particularly if the desired brand messaging centers on risk aversion and stability.

Parody

More and more often brand owners are encountering their trademarks in association with objectionable content on parody sites. What is parody? Princeton University's WorldNet defines parody as "a composition that imitates somebody's style in a humorous way; humorous or satirical mimicry." The courts, on the other hand, have defined parody as a "simple form of entertainment conveyed by juxtaposing their irreverent representation of the trademark with the idealized image created by the mark's owner."[11]

The nature of parody abuse varies widely, and while it can sometimes be mildly amusing, it can also be extremely damaging. Common abuses include alterations to brand logos, distorted advertisements, or depictions of mascots and other trademarked characters engaged in unwholesome activities. Children's characters and cartoon characters are popular targets for exploitation, which is particularly disturbing since some of the images could be traumatic if viewed by children (see Figure 1-3).

Brand abuse perpetrated under the cloak of parody can be a tricky situation to address. In the United States, for example, the courts have protected parody as free speech under the First Amendment. Even the Anticybersquatting Consumer Protection Act specifies that parody is a form of fair use that must be

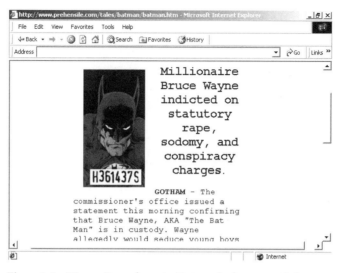

Figure 1-3. *Warner Bros. character Batman is the target of abuse.*

considered by a court as a mitigating factor for any defendant sued under the statute.[12]

Companies are not without recourse. Depending on the situation, use of images in parody settings has not always received protection from the courts. As far back as the early 1970s, for example, Walt Disney Co. successfully sued a publisher for portraying Mickey Mouse as a gun-toting, drug-running airplane pilot. The judge found that the publisher infringed Disney's copyrights and ordered all existing copies be destroyed.

In more recent cases, some guidelines have emerged that must be followed by anybody who decides to parody a brand. For example, the courts have said a parody must "convey two simultaneous—and contradictory—messages: that it is the original, but also that it is not the original and is instead a parody."[13] To the extent that an alleged parody conveys only the first message, "it is not only a poor parody but also vulnerable under trademark law, since the customer will be confused." While a parody necessarily must engender some initial confusion (see Figure 1-4 for examples), an effective parody will diminish the risk of consumer confusion "by conveying [only] just enough of the original design to allow the consumer to appreciate the point of parody."[14]

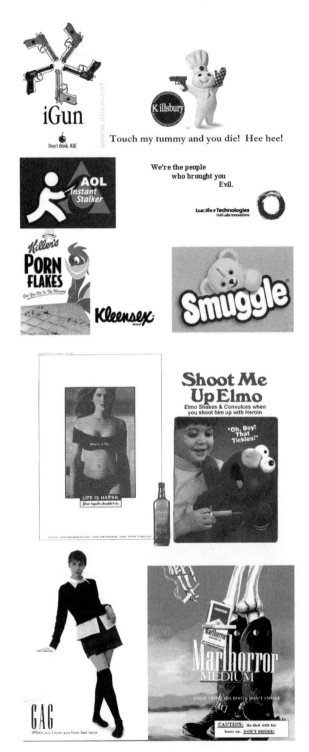

Figure 1-4. *Examples of altered company logos and potentially offensive advertisements found on self-proclaimed parody sites.*

BERT IS EVIL

The nonprofit Sesame Workshop faced a brand abuse problem with its Muppet character Bert. The "Bert Is Evil" parody website first appeared in the mid-1990s and offered "compelling photographic evidence of the Muppet consorting with Hitler, the KKK, and of course, Jerry Springer."[15] Other photos showed him posing with O. J. Simpson, smoking dope at Woodstock, and making love to Pamela Anderson. The image that would come back to haunt Sesame Workshop, however, was a doctored photo showing an angry Bert with terrorist Osama bin Laden (see Figure 1-5).

Figure 1-5. *The original doctored image of Sesame Street character Bert and Osama bin Laden, from the parody website "Bert Is Evil."*

Incredibly, in the wake of the September 11, 2001 terrorist attacks, the Bert-Osama image was lifted from the Internet and used for posters held aloft at a violent anti-American protest in Bangladesh—an image that was subsequently captured by photographers and widely reported in the mainstream media (see Figure 1-6).

In response to the broad circulation of this offensive image, Sesame Workshop issued the following statement: "Sesame Street has always stood for mutual respect and understanding. We're outraged that our characters would be used in this unfortunate and distasteful manner. This is not humorous. The people responsible for this should be ashamed of themselves." The producers also vowed to take action to keep this from happening again.

Figure 1-6. *An image of Bert appears just to the right of Osama bin Laden (AP Wide World.)*

"We are exploring all legal options to stop this abuse and any similar abuses in the future," Sesame Workshop producers said.[16]

Defining ''Objectionable''

Unfortunately, defending a brand is made more complicated by the fact that not all people find the same material offensive. What is considered objectionable varies widely and depends on factors such as age, religion, culture, and other demographics. It also depends on personal preference.

Pornography, for example, has wider acceptance in Europe than in North America or Asia, where a higher percentage of the population is apt to find it offensive. This is evidenced by the fact that the online publication of pornographic material is illegal in India, punishable by up to ten years in jail,[17] while sexually provocative images may be readily found on mainstream sites in Germany and Spain, where leading Internet service providers (ISPs) have content-licensing agreements with providers of hardcore pornography.[18]

Illustrating that associations need to be approached in an objective manner, some brand managers have decided that pornography is consistent with their desired brand image. In categories like beer, clothing, and footwear, consumers have shown tolerance for more sexually explicit advertising. The shoe company Pony, for example, has used porn film stars as models in its advertising campaigns.[19]

Besides pornography, other types of content that may sometimes be offensive to customers include sites devoted to controversial subject matter such as abortion, tobacco, drugs (see Figures 1-7 and 1-8), alcohol, firearms, and capital punishment. According to the U.S. Justice Department, the Internet is to blame for the explosion of the billion-dollar illegal drug paraphernalia industry.[20]Association of a brand with notorious criminals, hostilities, or historical events could also be troubling, depending on the specific audience, the nature of the content, and the values that the brand is intended to communicate.

Brand managers and trademark lawyers must take such factors into account when deciding on what boundaries to establish for limiting brand usage, weighing such considerations as the nature of the product or service in ques-

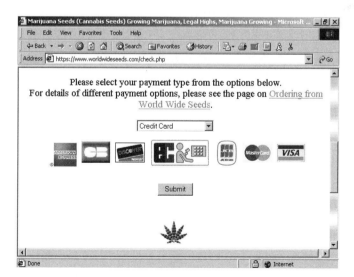

Figure 1-7. *This site displays logos for payment types accepted for the purchase of marijuana seeds.*

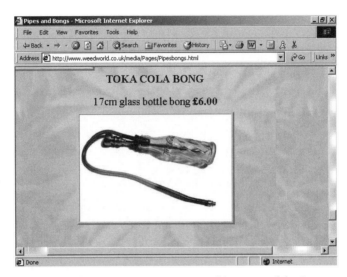

Figure 1-8. *This site generates revenue at the expense of the Coca-Cola brand.*

tion and the demographics of the target market. While online content might not conform to an individual's personal preferences, it may align with a target market segment. Sound judgment is required, followed by swift action when appropriate.

SPAM, SPAM, SPAM . . .

Hormel Foods Corp. has battled a brand association problem since the mid-1990s, when one of its most valuable brand names, SPAM, started to appear online as a slang term for mass online postings and junk e-mail. Use of the term "spam" in this manner was adopted from the Monty Python skit in which a group of Vikings sang a chorus of "SPAM, SPAM, SPAM . . ." in an increasing crescendo, drowning out all other conversation.

"Next to your employees and your physical assets, what holds the most value for a company is your brand," said Hormel spokesperson Julie Craven. "And part of your responsibility is to protect that and make sure it's used correctly and consistently."[21]

Unfortunately, Hormel's belated attempts to protect the brand from association with unsolicited e-mail were futile—the slang use of the term "spam" had already spiraled out of control. In an online policy statement, Hormel now takes the position that the slang term doesn't affect the strength of its brand. They support this conclusion by citing a Federal District Court case involving the Star Wars brand owned by LucasFilms Ltd., where the court refused to stop use of the slang term in reference to the Strategic Defense Initiative on the basis that it did not weaken the trademark.

While Hormel downplays the problem, its experience illustrates that negative brand associations can take many different forms and can spread rapidly online. It also shows that the perpetuation of the association can be as concerning as its offensiveness. For example, while a brand's presence in conjunction with child pornography is alarming, having your brand name become synonymous with something like junk mail could be just as damaging.

Who's at Risk?

As the examples in this chapter indicate, the popularity of a brand makes it an enticing target. In general, the more renowned the brand, the more likely it is to be victimized, regardless of the industry. Since they are more widely known, consumer brand names are usually at the highest risk for abuse, as are other popular icons such as celebrities and politicians.

Despite perceptions to the contrary, companies whose business is confined to brick-and-mortar operations are not immune. In fact, to some extent just the opposite is true—pervasive brand abuse is frequently experienced by companies that do business entirely offline, usually as a result of their failure to acknowledge the issue and protect themselves. This lack of vigilance gives free reign to offenders and heightens the risks and costs associated with brand abuse.

While online brand abuse can affect any company, certain business models and industries may be more vulnerable as a result of their image. Unregulated brand abuse can be particularly damaging to consumer perceptions of innocence, trust, security, stability, and quality. As a result, brands targeted at children and family should exercise particular care (see Figure 1-9), as should companies in the financial services and insurance industries.

The consequences of brand abuse can be particularly dire for financial services and insurance companies for other reasons as well. Consumers are conducting more and more research online and making their decisions based on this experience. Once a mistake is made, it can continue to cost both the consumer and the company dearly for a long period of time.

What to Do

While each company should make its own decisions and always seek the advice of an attorney, insights can be gleaned from how other companies have elected

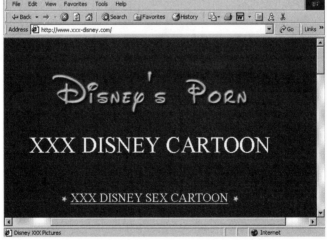

Figure 1-9. *Examples of pornography sites abusing Disney brands.*

to defend their brands against common types of abuse. You can improve your likelihood of success with insights into the most common approaches that businesses have used and lessons they have learned in the battle to defend their brands against specific types of abuse.

When brands are associated with objectionable content, most companies draft a strongly worded cease-and-desist letter informing the site that they are using a trademark/brand in a way that is inconsistent with their company's Internet policies. The brand owners request that the site immediately remove the brand from its metatags, page title, hidden text, or other element of the website or e-mail.

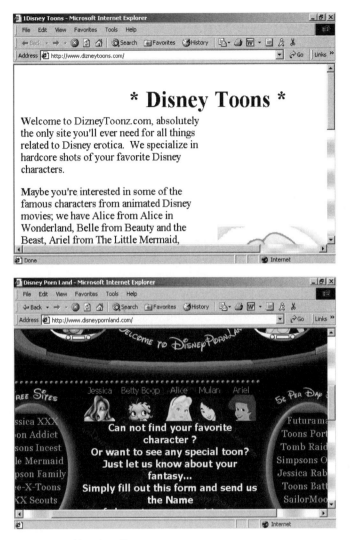

Figure 1-9. *(Continued).*

The correspondence is typically prepared by legal departments or outside counsel. While some companies prefer to send paper letters, others have found that it takes them less time and they receive quicker responses if they send the letter via e-mail or, when there are high volumes of incidents, through a workflow management utility that allows for batch processing.

Many companies reference the site IP address and paste the URL into the subject. Some even insert a screen capture of the violation into their letter. While the added detail is helpful, the benefits of including additional information need to be weighed against the additional level of effort required.

It is not uncommon for companies that use the cease-and-desist approach for adult sites to receive responses within a week. This is because most of the sites in question would rather avoid attracting unnecessary attention, prefer-ring just to have the issue go away. Brand owners can use this information to their advantage. While compliance rates vary according to a number of factors, success rates of 85 percent or better are not uncommon.

One large family-oriented company has been very successful following this approach in its war on brand abuse by pornographic sites. Since many of the company's brands are targeted at children, association with objectionable con-tent takes the highest priority. Considering the target market, the company takes a hard-line approach from the start. The legal team sends a cease-and-desist letter to the site owner, and then offending sites are revisited three months later. If the violation has not been addressed to the company's satisfac-tion, the site is rechecked monthly until the incident is resolved. Sites that do not comply receive additional legal notifications or action, depending on the seriousness of the offense. The company has found this tiered approach to be successful about 90 percent of the time.

Even though sending cease-and-desist letters may seem straightforward, the challenge of effectively monitoring online activity and taking appropriate ac-tion should be approached in a calculated fashion. There are many issues to consider, including how to isolate relevant activity, how to prioritize incidents, and what forms of communication to use when responding.

The first step to defend your brand is to gain familiarity with the types of threats and opportunities that may exist online. The first eight chapters of *Defending the Brand* should help you with that, as well as provide you with some issue-specific advice on taking action. Once you understand what you're up against, Chapters 9 through 11 arm you with the additional knowledge necessary to achieve the best results and maximize your return on investment in brand protection.

THE BUSINESS CASE ▸ To approximate the cost of a brand's association with ob-jectionable content, conventional advertising metrics can be applied. The negative impression caused by association with objectionable content can be conservatively expected to cause as much damage to a brand as a positive impres-sion creates goodwill. As such, you can assign a value to each negative impres-sion made by assuming that for every person exposed to a brand associated with objectionable content, the cost to the company is equal to but opposite the effects of an advertisement.

Here's a way to quantify the impact of brand abuse: Brand owners can expect that there are about 600 sites associating the average brand with objectionable content. The figure is far higher for popular brands. Association with objectionable content costs most companies somewhere between $100,000 and $2 million per year, with the average falling at approximately $700,000.[22] The following example illustrates how brand abuse might translate into lost brand equity.

Example

The brand manager for a household consumer product has discovered that adult entertainment and hate sites are abusing one of the company's premier brands. This is of particular concern since the product is family-oriented and the target end-users spend a significant amount of time online. To put a dollar value on lost equity, the company used the following step-by-step assumptions and calculations:

Step	Assumption
1	Number of sites where abuse is present: 600
2	Average annual number of visitors to each site: 100,000
3	Average number of impressions per visitor per year: 2
4	Total number of impressions = (1) × (2) × (3) = 120,000,000
5	Cost per impression: $0.01
6	Total cost = (4) × (5) = $1,200,000

Note that this approach to estimating lost brand equity does not account for the fact that shocking material may have a more powerful impact on consumers than conventional advertising. Images of extreme violence, or of a company mascot engaged in lewd behavior, for example, can make an indelible impression. There is also the risk that the negative association might gain further exposure by attracting the attention of the media.

Any business case should include best-case, worst-case, and most-likely scenarios to help provide a better feel for the potential impact of the problem. Checking the results across a wider range of inputs will also allow you to evaluate the sensitivity of your calculation to each assumption.

Finally, the immediate impact on the bottom line may not always be the overriding factor when determining whether to attack an issue like brand abuse. Many companies are committed to defending their brand regardless, particularly when the abuse is an affront to the core values of the company. It is usually in the best long-term interest of the stakeholders to combat abuse, even in those cases where it might not give a near-term boost to the bottom line.

····················▶

*THE
BOARD
ROOM
SUMMARY*

····················▶

Association with objectionable material threatens to undermine brand equity. Brand managers must be aware that:

➤ The value of a brand is heightened online, making it a target for abuse.

➤ The pornography industry is an online pioneer and the worst offender, though sites dedicated to topics such as gambling, hate, and violence also pose a threat.

➤ Defining what is considered objectionable is not always straightforward, and often depends on the values of your target market.

➤ All companies with recognizable brands are at risk, regardless of whether they conduct business online.

➤ Strongly worded cease-and-desist letters can be an effective way to combat abuses.

➤ The financial impact of association with offensive material can be estimated, and it is substantial.

➤ Beyond the financial implications, there may be moral reasons to defend a brand.

Chapter 2

The Opportunities and Threats of Online Commentary

New technologies and digital communication networks have put the world at our fingertips. We are interconnected via tens of millions of websites, Usenet newsgroups, message boards, chat rooms, instant messaging, short messaging service (SMS), weblogs, streaming media, peer-to-peer (P2P) networks, and e-mail. Wireless and broadband technologies have extended networks well beyond personal computers to handheld consumer devices.

The speed and reach of this new connectivity puts vast amounts of information, both accurate and erroneous, at a customer's disposal. It also provides an audience for anyone with an agenda. In such an environment, any organization that isn't paying attention to what's being published and broadcast about its brands could find itself in serious trouble.

Slanted, malicious, or libelous messages can spring out of nowhere and blindside an organization. In addition, more and more customers are conducting research online, so content regarding your brand—published by you or anyone else—influences customers' purchasing decisions. Statements about products, customer service, financial performance, and other aspects of business can spread even further through viral marketing.

As digital networks become more ubiquitous, shrewd organizations vigilantly monitor online environments to remain cognizant of the context in which their brands appear. Early detection of rumors, product misrepresentations, or leaks of confidential information makes it possible for a company to take counteractions before it's too late, thereby protecting customers, brand equity, corporate image, sales, and stock value.

Online environments can also be a valuable source of customer feedback. Understanding how your brand is being represented through online commentary can provide insights into the customers' experience and purchasing decisions. Such market intelligence can create a competitive advantage by allowing you to fine-tune positioning and enhance product offerings.

In addition, monitoring for online brand name mentions can further mitigate corporate risk by uncovering potential threats, boycotts, and lawsuits. From a corporate security, legal, and public relations perspective, intelligence gathered from cyberspace is critical to contain any issues that may arise online because rapid response is often the only way to avoid lasting damage.

The Rumor Mill

"Tommy Hilfiger said that blacks and Asians shouldn't wear his clothes." "Purchasers of Gerber baby foods are entitled to a $1,400 savings bond." "Colonel Sanders bequeathed money to the KKK." "Children have died of snakebites while playing in Burger King ball pits." "Mountain Dew causes testicles to shrink." All of these statements are false rumors that propagated online, causing confusion and tarnishing brand image.

As powerful as the Internet has become in delivering corporate spin and reinforcing branding messages, so too is its ability to cast a shadow upon a brand. Online rumors are easily posted and rapidly disseminated. The effects of a well-timed or well-placed allegation or comment can be staggering, regardless of whether or not it's true.

"Dubbed the information superhighway in its infancy, the Internet has in many ways fulfilled its early promise of providing unprecedented access to information and communication. But for all its shady characters and dangerous alleys, the Net might just as well have been called the disinformation superhighway."[1]

The problem is not a new one, yet such rumors and fictitious product information continue to catch organizations off-guard and hurt sales. This was the case when erroneous warnings were posted on the Internet that Febreze Fabric Spray, a Procter & Gamble (P&G) fabric deodorizer, was harmful to pets. Unfortunately, the rumor was not addressed quickly enough to keep it from spreading out of control by e-mail, word-of-mouth, and Internet message posts, such as the one shown in Figure 2-1.

To ensure retention of its customer base of 40 million households, P&G responded by launching a costly marketing campaign that promoted Febreze as an environmental and pet-safe product. The Febreze website now includes a page dedicated to promoting the product as safe for pets. The site also specifically refutes the Internet rumor (see Figure 2-2). According to the manufacturer, "of all the veterinarians we've talked to, not one believes that Febreze was a factor in the death of a pet."

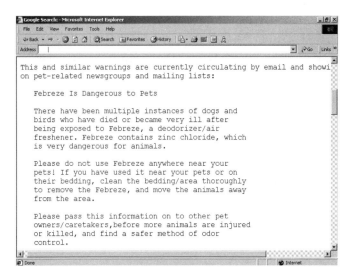

Figure 2-1. *Usenet newsgroup posting about Febreze rumor.*

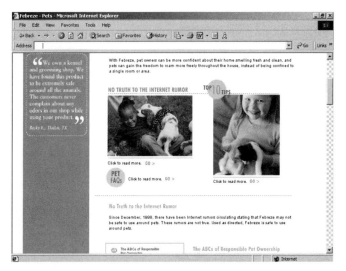

Figure 2-2. *The official Febreze website refutes the Internet rumor.*

Financial Earnings

The rise of do-it-yourself investing has created great interest in stocks among a broader range of people, including investors with less experience and higher expectations for returns. Such investors often go online for news, advice, and tips. Unfortunately, in the digital world there is no easy way to distinguish someone with real knowledge from an imposter spreading rumors to manipulate stock prices for a short-term profit.

Corporate financial earnings are one of the more notorious subjects of false rumors, frequently in the form of a fake press release. In the infamous "Emulex stock hoax," a bogus press release caused Emulex Corp. stock to plummet 62 percent in one day, wiping out $2.5 billion of market value.[2] Though the stock later rebounded, much damage was done. Even in cases where a stock's price recovers, such incidents can cast doubt and shake investor confidence.

Another doctored press release posted online announced far lower than expected earnings for E*TRADE. The release appeared realistic enough that many investors thought it was real. "It is not on the radar screen until you get hit right between the eyes," said Henry Carter, vice president of compliance for E*TRADE Group. "I don't think people fully appreciate the power of the Internet. I don't think people realize that people read these things and believe them."[3]

Companies that are diligent in tracking rumors can manage this risk and protect their reputation by responding when necessary. Oracle Corp. demonstrated this when it successfully deflected an Internet rumor. Oracle stock came under attack when stories started circulating online that the business was troubled and key executives would soon resign.

Fortunately, Oracle was monitoring the message boards and took prompt action by notifying the trading desks at Morgan Stanley and Goldman Sachs that the rumors were not true. At the same time, Oracle's press office was quelling speculation by speaking directly to reporters who got the word out. The stock stabilized and recovered later that same day.[4]

INTEL

A rumor can be even more damaging to a brand when there is a kernel of truth to it. One of the first examples of the risk associated with online commentary dates back to 1994, when a math professor in Virginia went online to post his findings regarding flaws in the Intel Pentium processor. Rumors spread online and then articles began to appear in print and were reported on radio and television. Some of the reports were incomplete, incorrect, or slanted in such a way as to cause panic, despite the fact that the flaw was virtually insignificant.

While Intel Corp. had been aware of the imperfection for some time, the actual consumer impact of the flaw was so negligible that Intel did not anticipate a problem. In fact, Intel later disclosed that an average spreadsheet user would encounter the flaw "once in every 27,000 years of use." But that didn't matter. By the time Intel decided to act, the situation had spiraled out of control—eventually forcing the chipmaker to announce a costly, no-questions-asked return policy.

When flaws were discovered in future versions of Pentium processors, Intel was much more forthcoming, stating up-front that the glitch could generate wrong answers in some cases. Intel called on its major hardware and software partners, including IBM and Microsoft, to share their assessment of the defect publicly. In doing so, Intel averted the need for another costly recall.[5]

Not only does Intel's experience demonstrate that a kernel of truth can make a rumor more damaging, but it also shows that such a rumor is more likely to be picked up by the mainstream media, adding fuel to the fire.

Early Warning

The Internet can also sometimes serve as a good way to spot burgeoning public relations issues, provided you can filter out the noise. Complaints related to the highly publicized Firestone and Ford recalls, for example, gained momentum online well before the issue became a favorite press topic. Inside information related to the Enron scandal also first appeared online.

The New York Times reported that on April 12, 2001, with the stock at $57.30, an online message posted on Yahoo! predicted Enron's fate with uncanny accuracy. "The Enron executives have been operating an elaborate con scheme that has fooled even the most sophisticated analysts," the message said. "The first sign of trouble will be an earnings shortfall followed by more warnings. Criminal charges will be brought against ENE executives for their misdeeds. Class-action lawsuits will complete the demise of ENE."[6]

On March 1, 2000, with the stock at $69, another online message advised: "Dig deep behind the Enron financials and you'll see a growing mountain of off-balance-sheet debt which will eventually swallow this company. There's a reason they layer so many subsidiaries and affiliates. Be careful."

For companies that are proactive, the online environment can be used to their advantage by serving as an early-warning system. If you monitor what is being said about your brand online, you are in a much better position to take countermeasures that will ultimately lower the cost of response and mitigate the effect on brand image.

Information Security

Every company has its secrets. Confidential information ranges from proprietary product details to internal litigation to financial earnings. Some of these corporate secrets, if divulged, can taint or jeopardize the value of a brand. Businesses are also entrusted with the responsibility of safeguarding customer and client information that, if leaked, could undermine consumer trust.

Here are a few examples of the types of information leaks that have the potential to damage a brand:

➤ Legal (e.g., attorney-client or work product privileged information, details of internal litigation or ongoing investigations)

➤ Product (e.g., confidential product details, new product development or marketing strategies such as planned pricing changes and promotions)

➤ Financial (e.g., earnings data, indications of insider trading or stock manipulation)

➤ Consumer (e.g., private customer or client information, especially medical history and credit card information)

➤ Internal Communications (e.g., information considered confidential such as internal memos, e-mails, or employee manuals)

➤ Security (e.g., details of corporate security or compromises in system security)

Unfortunately, a trend toward opening corporate networks to partners and customers has made information security more challenging than ever before. The Internet has provided a new port of entry to the inner sanctum of a corporation. It also offers skilled hackers the anonymity and mobility they need to compromise corporate systems with little fear of reprisal.

The apparent ease with which cybercriminals breached the security of Microsoft Corp. and accessed unannounced product details sent alarms throughout the world. Many feel that if this could happen to Microsoft, then no company is safe. According to a report prepared by the Center for Strategic and International Studies in Washington, D.C., "whoever stole proprietary secrets at the heart of the ubiquitous Windows program can hack into any PC in the world that uses it and is connected to the Internet."[7]

The speed and reach of the Internet has also heightened the risk that leaked or stolen information will be widely distributed in a short period of time. It is now simple for even technology-challenged individuals to send mass e-mails or launch their own websites. As a result, there is an ever-present risk that a disgruntled employee, contractor, vendor, partner, or anyone else with access to sensitive information will broadly disseminate confidential information that can threaten a brand. Even positive comments and well-intentioned people pose a risk if they disclose information not available to the public.

Well-known companies are often the subjects of message boards, weblogs, and websites devoted to discussing company developments. It is not unusual for such sites to disclose proprietary information ahead of a scheduled launch, and media outlets sometimes report that information. Apple Computer, for example, filed a lawsuit against an employee who leaked secret product information. The employee posted photos and specifications online for several Apple products, including the iBook, the Power Mac G4, and the Pro Mouse months before the products were released.[8] "Innovation is in Apple's DNA, so the protection of trade secrets is crucial to our success," said an Apple spokesperson. "Our policy is to take legal actions where necessary to preserve the confidentiality of our intellectual property."[9]

Whenever trade secrets are posted online, investors are put at risk financially and the company is left at a competitive disadvantage. Such occurrences can also taint the brand in the eyes of the consumer, particularly if security and trust are part of the desired brand image.

Managing this risk requires a two-pronged approach involving information security and an aggressive online monitoring program (see Chapter 7 and Chapter 9, respectively). Proactively monitoring your brand better positions your company to take countermeasures that will lower the cost of response and mitigate damage.

"There are no secrets. The networked market knows more than companies do about their own products. And whether the news is good or bad, they tell everyone."[10]

—CHRISTOPHER LOCKE, *The Cluetrain Manifesto*, Thesis 12

Other Security and Liability Threats

Monitoring for online brand abuse can inadvertently uncover a host of other security-related issues aside from leaks of proprietary product information. It's not uncommon for large companies to find angry customers organizing a boycott or posting the CEO's private home address and phone number. Managers should therefore be prepared to forward these incidents to the appropriate individuals within their organization for follow-up action.

Hint: Online monitoring can further mitigate risk by uncovering information such as leaks, threats, boycotts, and lawsuits.

The following list demonstrates the breadth of issues that may surface online during the course of brand monitoring:

➤ Physical and Cyberspace Attacks (e.g., threats or other indications of planned physical attacks against executives, employees, and facilities, or cyberattacks in the form of hacks, denial of service, etc.)

➤ Events (e.g., planned boycotts, pickets, or protests)

➤ Fraud (e.g., facilitation or promotion of fraud against the company)

➤ Legal (e.g., planned legal action against the company, such as class-action lawsuits or statements made by employees)

The World's Largest Focus Group

Online commentary represents an opportunity that is just as great as the risks it can pose. Millions of consumers are online talking about every major company right now—on message boards, e-mail distribution lists, chat rooms, blogs, and more. As more and more consumers go online to conduct research, talk about their favorite brands, or complain about a product or service, the available feedback becomes more valuable for those able to extract it. Monitoring and interpreting customer commentary online can provide important insights into products; consumer perceptions, satisfaction, and sentiment; and market trends.

"Faster than focus groups, cheaper than consultants, and more analytical than random customer engagements, the collected information [from online discussions] can play a pivotal role in gauging a company's presence and success."[11]

Hint: Analyzing commentary is an opportunity to gain insights into products, consumer perceptions, and market trends.

There are clearly drawbacks to using an unstructured, uncontrolled environment to collect consumer feedback, though some might say it's less biased and of greater value than traditional methods. Since feedback is direct from the consumer and unsolicited, you're likely to get honest opinions. Types of feedback include:

➤ What people are discussing and overall sentiment about the brands and marketplace

➤ Firsthand accounts of customer experiences

➤ Current product usage and satisfaction levels

➤ Consumer commentary on products or services related to price, quality, and other characteristics

➤ Factors that are influencing purchasing decisions

➤ Consumer reaction to promotions, new offerings, and changes

➤ Discussion of new competitive offerings, and side-by-side comparisons

Benefits of this feedback include:

➤ Better understanding of consumer perception of brands and marketplaces

➤ Additional intelligence on which to base marketing and sales projections

➤ Insights into what information is influencing customers' purchasing decisions

➤ Better ability to fine-tune positioning against customers' needs, experiences, and perceptions

➤ Opportunities to proactively enhance product offerings

➤ Improved ability to align brands and products with evolving customer needs

➤ More advance warning to counteract competitive moves (see Chapter 8)

Activism and "Sucks" Sites

Activist sites, or so-called "sucks" sites, erected by passionate people with an agenda are an offshoot of online customer commentary forums. Many times these sites are born of frustration or philosophical differences with the way a company conducts business. In today's networked world, revenge for perceived corporate wrongs is always just a few keystrokes away.

Sometimes, the commentary on these sites can be vulgar, one-sided, and not representative of the brand's overall image. On many of these sites, brands, slogans, and logos are attacked or distorted (see Figure 2-3). Even though you may consider the content to be distasteful or offensive, these sites need to be tracked and evaluated as objectively as possible.

A company has limited legal recourse when such a site uses its brands in

Figure 2-3. *Altered brand logos found on "sucks" sites.*

the context of sharing opinions (see Figure 2-4), unless it could be confusing to the public or is leveraging the brand for commercial purposes. This doesn't mean that a site can't cross the line. Some sites get pretty aggressive about their abuse of a brand, and if they don't make it clear that they have no affiliation with the brand owner, companies should be very concerned. Sites that claim or imply a relationship with the brand owner merit swift legal action. Such sites pose a genuine threat to the brand and can undermine customer loyalty, if left unchallenged.

More often, the site is clearly not affiliated with the brand owner. While the abuse may be disturbing, or even infuriating, companies need to exercise discretion. Hate sites are quick to post cease-and-desist letters from corporate

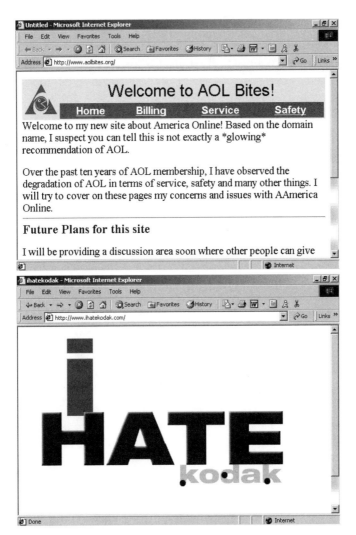

Figure 2-4. *Examples of consumer complaint sites.*

attorneys because it appears to validate their cause. They see it as an opportunity to cast the company in a negative light.

Burke Stinson, senior public relations director for AT&T, prefers to just set the record straight. "If something is being said that's malicious or dead wrong, we will jump in and say something very brief and very pointed. We don't use adjectives and adverbs and we don't use legal jargon," Stinson says. "Rattling legal sabers is not the way to go. Clearing the air is much better," he says. "Even if you do stamp out a website, it's certain that a dozen more will rush in to take its place."

In one case, AT&T found that its employees were complaining about company policy online. AT&T counteracted the negative half-truths by creating its own site. The site addressed the concerns and explained AT&T's side of the story.

Stinson cautions that it's important for marketers to start taking notice of online activity. "Companies that ignore this phenomenon are ignoring [it] at the risk of their reputation. Maybe in the last century you could take a week or month or season to respond, but not anymore."[12]

Oftentimes, the best recourse is to stay on top of the issues and promptly address complaints before the offending site gains a following and assumes a life of its own. Protest site Pepsibloodbath.com, for example, declared victory and closed itself down after PepsiCo quit advertising Pepsi at bullfights.[13]

BALLY TOTAL FITNESS

Drew Faber, a customer who felt he had been misled regarding the terms of his health club membership, erected a "Bally's Total Fitness Sucks" site. "I thought a website would be the easiest way to get a response from Bally's," Faber said. Unfortunately, Bally didn't respond until five months later, by which time the site was a popular destination for other dissatisfied customers. If Bally had contacted him right away, Faber said, he probably would have let the site die a quiet death.[14]

Bally later sued Faber for trademark infringement in an attempt to compel him to discontinue use of the Bally brand. In its complaint, Bally asserted that the defendant's actions constituted trademark infringement, dilution, and unfair competition. The court disagreed and, on the defendant's motion for summary judgment, dismissed the complaint.

According to the court, "Faber's site states that it is 'unauthorized' and contains the words 'Bally sucks.' No reasonable consumer comparing Bally's official website with Faber's would assume Faber's site to come from the same source, or thought to be affiliated with, connected with, or sponsored by, the trademark owner."[15]

Nobody Is Immune

Bally, PepsiCo, and AT&T are most certainly not alone in their struggles with complaint sites. Some companies such as Ford Motor Co. (see Figure 2-5) and

Figure 2-5. *Examples of logo abuse found on Ford "sucks" sites.*

Microsoft have networks of dozens of "sucks" sites erected in their honor. "Some of them are so completely over the edge, in our opinion, that it seems pointless to even try to counterpoint what they say," notes a Nike spokesperson. "Some are actually very well thought out and have offered us a different point of view."[16]

ROYAL DUTCH/SHELL

The Netherlands-based Royal Dutch/Shell Group of Companies has received acclaim for taking online commentary seriously enough to provide an uncensored forum for complaints and open communication on its own website. People use the forum to say all kinds of things—posts run the gamut from compliments and mild complaints to accusations of murder.

Shell's innovative approach has served the company well. Not only does Shell benefit from valuable feedback, but it can proactively head off potential issues and misunderstandings before they spiral out of control. In addition, Shell allows employees to directly respond to the messages. The personal approach creates a more compassionate image for Shell.

Commercial sites have used a similar approach to generate a feeling of community among customers. A study by McKinsey & Co. found that at some sites, regular users of message forums and feedback areas generated two-thirds of sales, although they accounted for just one-third of all visitors. "Even people who don't directly contribute, but do read those message boards, are more likely to come back and to buy," noted McKinsey analyst Shona Brown. "If they feel a connection, they're more likely to take the next step and become buyers."[17]

Managing Risk

The key to managing risk associated with online complaints and customer commentary is to be proactive, monitor relevant sites regularly, and use them to your advantage. The posts can bring issues to your attention that you were not previously aware of, some of which may offer the opportunity to improve the business.

Most sites of interest can be found through common search engines. Consumer opinion and financial message boards such as Epinions.com or Yahoo! Finance include their own proprietary search utilities. In general, brand commentary can be found through methods similar to those used for monitoring brand abuse (which is covered in more depth in Chapter 9).

Buried Treasure

The value to be gained from harvesting online customer commentary—particularly for consumer-facing brands—hasn't gone unnoticed by Internet entrepreneurs. Some Internet forums specifically cater to customers looking to share their product or service experience with others. The complaint sites are "filling a void," says Martin Petersen, director of public affairs at Playtex Products. "People want to reach companies and don't know how to do it."[18]

Businesses such as Intelliseek have sprouted up to assist corporations in mining consumer feedback and in responding to posts when necessary. Monitoring services usually specialize in either consumer feedback or editorial commentary, though an effective monitoring program will cover both. For small to medium-size companies, service providers such as eWatch and Cyberalert can help monitor for online brand mentions through economical, automated "clipping" services that issue daily reports and can cost as little as a few hundred dollars a month.

"Disgruntled consumers are a hot commodity on the Internet, where a dozen or more sites have been competing to become the virtual soapbox of choice for tens of thousands of angry customers."[19]

Whether monitoring is handled in-house or through a vendor, taking action and actively communicating responses through online channels allows a company to harness the power of viral marketing to strengthen a brand.

THE BUSINESS CASE

Regardless of the sales strategy a company employs, when customers are influenced by online commentary it can result in captured or lost revenue, depending on what they are exposed to. The impact of brand commentary varies according to a host of factors, such as the nature of a comment, the perceived authority of the commentator, the topic or object of the opinion, the timing of the posting, the logic or strength of the comment, and other qualitative factors.

When online commentary is monitored, the intelligence can be used to avert losses or take action that result in incremental value. While each case is different, the potential savings can be enormous.

For negative commentary, one way to assess the financial impact is to estimate the number of customers who ultimately change their mind and either purchase elsewhere or not at all. Once you have estimated the number of lost customers, you then multiply by the average lifetime value of a customer. For a far more conservative estimate, you can limit the damage to one transaction and use the average purchase size.

Example One

An employee at a large software company encounters an online post detailing the presence of a security flaw in the company's newest software release. A careful check of the software reveals that there are no security flaws, but a search online reveals that the rumor has already appeared on several message boards and newsgroups. The commentary further reveals that because of a recent hacking incident, security is perceived to be an increasingly important factor in the buyer's decision-making process. To estimate how many customers the software maker might lose because of this rumor, the company applied this step-by-step calculation and assumptions:

Step	Assumption
1	Number of negative posts identified: 20
2	Average number of customers who read each post: 10,000
3	Total potential customers exposed to post = (1) × (2) = 200,000

Step	Assumption
4	Percent of buyers influenced by posts: 1%
5	Total number of customers lost = (3) × (4) = 2,000
6	Average lifetime value of a customer: $800
7	Total cost = (5) × (6) = $1,600,000

Had the software company been actively monitoring online commentary, the results may have been much different. The software company could have reacted by immediately contacting the people who posted the rumor, posting a concise response online, and even launching a timely campaign to promote how secure the product is. In the process, the software maker would also be differentiating itself from the competition. As a result, the rumors would be stifled and the company could even gain market share in a $1.5 billion industry.

Example Two

The brand manager for a line of consumer dairy products monitors online commentary and finds that environmentalists are posting negative statements and facts related to the amount of packaging waste the products generate. The source of the statistics appears to be well informed and shows that the waste is disproportionate to competitors' products.

The brand manager works with packaging designers and finds a mutually acceptable way to reduce packaging. The initiative saves on raw material costs, curbs further environmental protest, and even gains some environmentalist favor, resulting in a slight gain in market share.

THE BOARD ROOM SUMMARY

The speed and reach of the online environment puts vast amounts of information, both accurate and erroneous, at a customer's disposal. It also provides an audience for anyone with an agenda. Brand owners should be aware that:

➤ Slanted, malicious, or libelous messages can propagate quickly online, causing confusion, influencing purchasing decisions, and tarnishing brand image.

➤ Shrewd organizations vigilantly monitor online environments to remain cognizant of the context in which their brands appear.

➤ By proactively monitoring your brand, you are better positioned to take countermeasures that will lower the cost of response and mitigate damage.

➤ Monitoring online brand usage can further mitigate corporate risk by uncovering information leaks, threats, boycotts, and lawsuits.

➤ Analyzing customer commentary is an opportunity to gain valuable insights into products, consumer perceptions, and market trends.

Chapter 3

Customer Diversion

Deceitful technology tactics that once confined themselves to gaming and adult sites have now become mainstream. These days, your competitors and other companies may be luring your customers away using your own brands, and a lack of corporate vigilance has allowed such practices to propagate nearly unchecked.

Some website designers have perfected the art of using the trademarks of others for their own profit. As a result, online shoppers are confronted with more intrusive and sophisticated "capture" tactics. There is ample evidence of this practice. When you type a word or term into a search engine, have you ever noticed that you don't always get back what you expected? Or have you ever made a typo when entering a web address and ended up on a porn site? Most people have already experienced the chicanery that is pervasive online, even if they didn't realize why it was occurring.

The tactics that web designers employ to divert customers range from spamming and blatantly mislabeling "links" to literally taking over control of the user's computer. Every aspect of a customer's online experience comes under assault as sites fight aggressively for revenue. Left unmanaged, the brand abuse diverts customers from their intended destination, wreaks havoc on the customer experience, and undermines brand equity.

Customer Capture

On the Internet, there are numerous ways that people can reach their intended destination. The three most common methods are to use a search engine, click on a link within a web page or e-mail message, or directly enter the destination URL into the browser. All of these vehicles come under attack, and clever coders are constantly thinking up new ways to capture and manipulate customers, often at the expense of a popular brand. Figure 3-1 shows some of the ways that criminals and aggressive competitors prey on customers as they go online to conduct research or make a transaction.

Cybersquatting

Cybersquatting is the registration of a domain name because it is desirable to a third party that's already doing business under that name. It is also a form of brand abuse that can mislead and divert customers (see Figure 3-2). Cunning sites know that the presence of a brand within the domain can improve placement in search results, help gain consumer confidence, and sometimes attract visitors seeking the legitimate brand owner's home page.

An example of cybersquatting occurred when a porn company called "The Net" launched a site at www.foradodge.com, attracting substantial Internet traffic from surfers whose intended destination was the heavily promoted

Customer Navigation Method	Divert Them to Drive Up Traffic	Hold Them to Convert	Bring Them Back Again	The Payoff
Directly Type Address in Browser	Cybersquatting and Typo-Piracy	Spawning, Mouse-Trapping, Framing, Re-directing	Insert Address as Customer Home or Start Page, Add Address to "Favorites"	Increased Referral Fees and Commissions, Better Advertising Metrics, and Increased Sales
Search Engine	Seeding, Spoofing, Paid Placement, and Browser Utilities			
Links	Mislabeled or Misleading Links			
E-mail	Spam			

Figure 3-1. *The hijacker's guide to customer acquisition.*

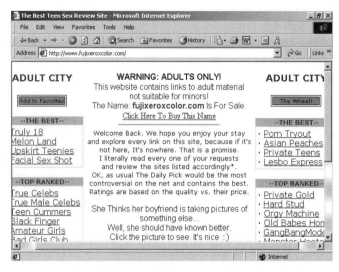

Figure 3-2. *This adult site used the Fuji Xerox brand in the domain name.*

Chrysler automotive site www.4adodge.com. "The Net is clearly using one of the most identifiable brand names in the automotive industry to make money dispensing pornography," said Chrysler in a statement.[1] Other sites registered by the same cybersquatter included www.cnn.net and www.nasa.com.

V E R I Z O N

When Bell Atlantic and GTE merged to form Verizon Communications, the company tried to get a jump on cybersquatters, registering more than 500 domain names to protect their brands. Despite this effort, within four weeks of the merger, 400 domains were registered by outsiders using the name Verizon or one of its other brands. One of these sites was www.verizonreallysucks.com, which sports a distorted logo (see Figure 3-3) and bills itself as "The official website for Verizon Grievances . . . a place where the customers and employees of Verizon can voice their complaints."

Figure 3-3. *Altered logo from www.verizonreallysucks.com.*

> "Generally, we are dealing with cases where we're trying to protect our customers against consumer fraud and confusion or [from] people who are otherwise just stealing our brand to divert traffic" for commercial purposes, says Sarah Deutsch, vice president and associate general counsel at Verizon.[2]

It is not uncommon for derivations of a popular brand name to show up in thousands of registered domains, most of which are not held by the brand's legitimate owner. Querying a domain search engine demonstrates that the brand name Toyota, for example, is present in more than 5,000 registered domains, and AOL appears in about 12,500 (see Figure 3-4). Some of these domains may have been registered with the brand owner's blessing, though most were not.

Cybersquatting can also involve a third party registering a brand name in a different top-level domain than the official site, such as .net, .com, or .org. A frequently cited example is when people looking for the U.S. government site www.whitehouse.gov mistakenly enter www.whitehouse.com and end up on an adult site, or www.whitehouse.net, which is a parody site.

Typo-Piracy

Everybody makes a typo or spelling mistake once in a while, and typo versions of brand names account for a considerable amount of traffic. Some of the more sneaky sites take advantage of these slipups to divert customers. Typo-piracy, or typo-squatting, is the practice of registering domain names that consist of popular trademarks with minor typographical errors, thereby capturing traffic from users who inadvertently mistype the domain name of their intended destination.

For example, the publishers of the Spiegel catalog filed a complaint against an entrepreneur who registered the misspelled speigels.com, spiegals.com, and spiegles.com, all of which took users to websites offering music CDs or Internet answering machines.[3] This type of abuse is experienced by most popular brands. Visitors who accidentally add an extra *t* to Hyatt.com, for example, will find themselves automatically redirected to a porn site. Inadvertently typing an extra letter *n* in JCPenney.com will send an unsuspecting customer to an online travel agent, as will adding an extra *r* to Marriott.com (see Figure 3-5).

As another example, a discount travel agent attracted visitors through affiliates who registered typo-piracy domains, which would redirect customers to the agent's own website. The travel agent now manages its affairs through an affiliate network that prohibits such practices.

Figure 3-4. *Sites used the AOL brand in their domain name.*

Examples of typo-piracy domains registered by the discount travel site include:

➤ sheroton.com

➤ aavis.com

➤ alamocarrental.com

➤ travekocity.com

➤ brithishairways.com

➤ wwwmytravelco.com

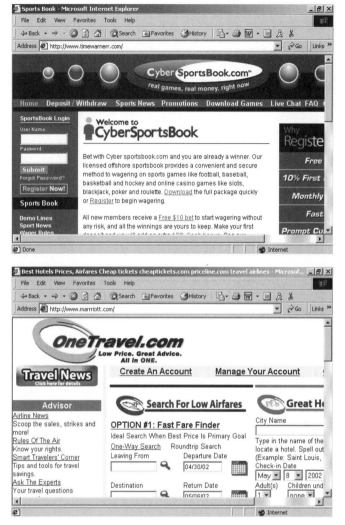

Figure 3-5. *Typo-piracy: a discount travel site owned Marrriott.com and a gambling site registered Timewarnerr.com.*

➤ heaptickets.com

➤ dollarrent.com

➤ travleosity.com

➤ americanairlnes.com

➤ ryonair.com

➤ wwwradisson.com

➤ wwwnwa.com

➤ wyndamhotels.com

Another common typo-piracy trick is to register domains that capture traffic from people who inadvertently leave out the "dot" that typically follows www or precedes com, net, or org. The software will interpret this as part of the domain name and then add another www before the one you entered. The result may look something like wwwqwest.net or wwwqwest.com, which were sites registered to people with no apparent legitimate affiliation with Qwest Communications. Other examples are shown in Figure 3-6.

Domain Name Administration

Attacking the cybersquatters and typo-pirates of the world is not a simple task. The introduction of new top-level domains (TLDs) such as .us, .info, and .biz

Figure 3-6. *Both wwwhondamotorcycle.com and Ibmcom.com attracted visitors who accidentally left a "dot" out when typing the site address.*

complicate domain name management efforts. Beyond these generic TLDs (gTLDs), there are hundreds of individually administered country code domains (ccTLDs) that make it even more difficult. (A list of gTLDs and ccTLDs is included in Appendix A for reference purposes.) Examples of ccTLDs are .de for sites registered in Germany and .jp for sites registered in Japan.

Multinational corporations that own thousands of domains are waging a constant battle against brand abuse on the domain name front. This effort can be time-consuming and complex as disputes may fall under multiple international jurisdictions. Because of the domain name mayhem, the position title of "domain name administrator" is becoming more common within large companies. It is generally the full-time responsibility of these people to maintain the necessary registrations and combat cybersquatting for the company.

In cases where partners are not involved, domain name violations such as cybersquatting and typo-piracy are also commonly resolved through cease-and-desist letters. The communication asks the site to transfer domain ownership and may offer to reimburse the site owner's registration fee. A cease-and-desist notice may be delivered by e-mail or more traditional mail methods, and success rates are generally over 90 percent. In rare instances, when this approach is not effective, arbitration can be pursued to resolve the issue.

A HOTEL CHAIN DEFENDS ITS DOMAINS

A leading international hotel group identified numerous cybersquatters, including a number of competing travel and hotel sites. To manage the issue, the hotel group designated one person in the general counsel's office to take responsibility for acting upon the intelligence they collect. Among other things, this point person reviews all sites delivered to assess whether the hotel group has any preexisting relationships. If not, the site is contacted by outside counsel that sends a hard copy letter on the outsourced law firm's letterhead. The correspondence requests the site owner to transfer domain ownership to the hotel group.

If there is a partner relationship between the hotel group and the offender, the matter is handled by business development. While the communication is less formal, the direction is clear and, when appropriate, cites the relevant provisions of the partner agreement.

In most circumstances, the hotel group will reimburse registration costs. To date, all but two of the sites identified have transferred their domain ownership to the hotel group. The hotel group pursued legal options through the ICANN (Internet Corporation for Assigned Names and Numbers) mediation process against the two remaining sites.

Arbitration. To help address the cybersquatting problem, the Internet Corporation for Assigned Names and Numbers (ICANN) adopted the Uniform Domain Name Dispute Resolution Policy (UDRP) in 1999. If brand owners believe that they are the victims of abuse, the UDRP permits complainants to file a case with a resolution service provider, such as the World Intellectual Property Organization (WIPO).

As a result of arbitration, a domain name can be canceled or transferred, or the respondent may be allowed to keep the domain name. According to WIPO, factors that guide the decision of the arbitration panelists include:

➤ Whether the domain name is identical or confusingly similar to a trademark or service mark in which the complainant has rights

➤ Whether the respondent has any rights or legitimate interests in the domain name (e.g., legitimately offers goods and services under the same name)

➤ Whether the domain name was registered and is being used in bad faith[4]

Unfortunately, while WIPO has begun providing dispute resolution services for some ccTLDs, many of them have not adopted the UDRP policies. It can also be difficult to track down offenders since many top-level domain registries do not have effective processes in place to confirm whether the information provided at the time of registration is accurate. Arbitration has proved to be a successful approach to brand defense for some companies. One company that used arbitration to its benefit is The Dream Merchant, owner of the famous Cirque du Soleil mark. The domain at issue was cirquedusoleil.com, which is similar to the Cirque du Soleil brand (the difference being the transposition of the letters *e* and *i*). The disputed domain name pointed to a pornographic website entitled "Tina's Free Live Cam." In 2003, the National Arbitration Forum found that the domain was registered in bad faith and the domain name was transferred to The Dream Merchant.[5] Google had similar success in challenging the owner of Googel.com.

There are many cybersquatting and domain name services that have been launched to make the whole process more manageable. Domain name registrars such as VeriSign, Register.com, and others offer a range of economical solutions to help companies monitor domain registration activity, combat cybersquatters, and monitor for other types of brand abuse.

Search Engine Manipulation

Search engines sometimes return seemingly random, irrelevant pages. Poor search results are often caused by "traffic diversion" or "search optimization" tactics—the unauthorized incorporation of popular trademarks in the design elements of a site to fool search engines and increase the number of visitors. It's the digital equivalent to hanging popular logos and slogans outside of your store to trick shoppers into coming inside.

As a result of search engine manipulation, studies have shown that nearly one in five of all search engine users never reach their intended destination.[6] With a substantial percentage of the online population using search engines for navigation, customer diversion creates a significant issue for any company with a recognized brand.

Search engines work by sending out software "spiders" or "crawlers" that visit pages on the Internet to download and index online content. When a user enters search words, the search engine then analyzes its database to determine what sites are most relevant to the user's query. To lure more traffic, website designers implement a host of tricks and tactics to optimize their placement in search results, creating the appearance that they have content relevant to popular search terms, even though they may not.

While no search engine is perfect, the most popular ones tend do the best job of filtering out irrelevant results. Maintaining an acceptable level of relevancy in top search returns is a constant battle—it requires highly advanced algorithms that continuously evolve to stay one step ahead of clever web designers who are constantly attempting to optimize their site's placement. Only the top search engines have the resources to effectively curb this kind of manipulation. Unfortunately, there are still many unsophisticated portals online. Some of these second-tier search engines attract high levels of traffic and can be manipulated.

While sometimes the offending site may be innocent and the web designers unaware of the implications of their transgression, traffic diversion is also a common, aggressive tactic intentionally employed by competitors to steal customers. Should a competitor employ such tactics successfully, the diverted customer may decide to switch to the competitive offering—if for no other reason than the fact that they are already there and it is more convenient.

Unfortunately, porn sites are some of the most aggressive, sophisticated offenders when it comes to search manipulation. While diverted customers are apt to discern when a website is not actually affiliated with your brand, it probably is not part of your carefully crafted customer experience to have them navigating a porn site. Ultimately, a customer that encounters your brand on a seemingly unaffiliated site may just become frustrated and give up.

There is an ongoing battle between search engines, as they struggle to deliver relevant results, and aggressive web designers, as they strive for higher placement within the listings. Some of the more common tricks that have been successfully used to optimize a site's false placement on search returns include invisible and visible seeding, spoofing, and paid placement.

Invisible Seeding. The most common tactic for search engine optimization is the hidden "seeding" of content to get the highest possible placement in search engine returns. This involves the unauthorized incorporation of proprietary content, popular brand names, phrases, or other keywords (unrelated to visible site content) within nonvisible page elements such as the metatags and nonvisible text, including text hidden through slight variations in color shading. While not immediately apparent or even all that effective, this remains a common intellectual property abuse perpetrated against top brands (see Figure 3-7).

Visible Seeding. A more blatant abuse is the seeding of visible, irrelevant text to optimize traffic from search engines. This includes the unauthorized use of proprietary content, popular brand names, slogans, logos, etc. within visible page elements such as the title, URL, or text (see Figure 3-8). This practice can be damaging to shoppers searching the Web for leading brands since it also encompasses claimed affiliations and the potential for association of these brands with objectionable content. The brand presence can range from a prominent display to placement on the very bottom of the page where visitors are unlikely to see it at all.

Spoofing. Highly aggressive and sophisticated sites sometimes use "spoof" pages to optimize search engine traffic. Most variations of spoofing are based

```
www.helmsleyhotels - Notepad
File   Edit   Format   Help
<META name="description" content="The Helmsley Hotels.">
<META name="keywords" content="hotels, hotels, hotels, hotels, hotels,
hotels, hotels, hotels, hotels, hotels, travel, travel, travel, travel,
travel, travel, travel, travel, travel, travel, new york, new york, new york,
new york, new york, new york, new york, new york, new york, new york,
accomodations, accomodations, accomodations, accomodations, accomodations,
accomodations, accomodations, accomodations, accomodations, accomodations,
resort, resort, resort, resort, resort, resort, resort, resort, resort,
resort, vacation, vacation, vacation, vacation, vacation, vacation, vacation,
vacation, vacation, vacation, hotel, hotel, hotel, hotel, hotel, hotel,
hotel, hotel, hotel, hotel, helmsley, helmsley, helmsley, helmsley, helmsley,
helmsley, helmsley, helmsley, helmsley, helmsley, hilton, hilton, hilton,
hilton, hilton, hilton, hilton, hilton, hilton, hilton, ritz carlton, ritz
carlton, ritz carlton, ritz carlton, ritz carlton, ritz carlton, ritz
carlton, ritz carlton, ritz carlton, ritz carlton, five star, five star, five
star, five star, five star, five star, five star, five star, five star, five
star, tourism, tourism, tourism, tourism, tourism, tourism, tourism, tourism,
tourism, tourism, luxury, luxury, luxury, luxury, luxury, luxury, luxury,
luxury, luxury, luxury, fine, fine, fine, fine, fine, fine, fine, fine, fine,
fine, sheraton, sheraton, sheraton, sheraton, sheraton, sheraton, sheraton,
sheraton, sheraton, sheraton, sheraton, radisson, radisson, radisson,
radisson, radisson, radisson, radisson, radisson, radisson, radisson, hyatt
regency, hyatt regency, hyatt regency, hyatt regency, hyatt regency, hyatt
regency, hyatt regency, hyatt regency, hyatt regency, hyatt regency,
manhattan, manhattan, manhattan, manhattan, manhattan, manhattan, manhattan,
manhattan, manhattan, manhattan, central park, central park, central park,
central park, central park, central park, central park, central park, central
park, central park">
<META name="author" content="Jason Inasi">
<META name="date" content="04/23/1996">
<META name="expire" content="04/23/1997">

<TITLE>The Helmsley Hotels</TITLE>

</HEAD>
```

Figure 3-7. *The source code of the Helmsley Hotels website revealed that the firm was making liberal use of competitor brand names.*

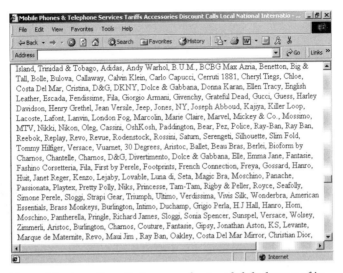

Figure 3-8. *An online cell phone merchant seeded the bottom of its home page with thousands of brand names in an attempt to attract customers.*

on the principle of "cloaking," or showing content to a search engine's crawlers that's different from what a human visitor sees when visiting the same site. Spoof pages can take various forms, including the use of "doorway" or "landing" pages. These are pages that include links into the "real" site but are designed to cater to specific search terms and search engines. The visitor doesn't usually see the content on these pages since upon retrieval of the page, the person is automatically redirected to another location. Some sites may go so far as to "page-jack" content, which happens when offenders copy an entire page from a popular site and paste it on a page of their own.

One advanced approach to spoofing is called "web spamming." Web spamming occurs when designers copy a web page and embed code that directs a search engine's crawlers to revisit the duplicate every day, but without caching (i.e., storing) the page. The false web pages, disguised as legitimate sites, then appear higher in the search results. Another common approach is "link spamming" where web designers erect hundreds or even thousands of bogus sites that point to the same page. This practice is employed with the intent of fooling search engines that evaluate the quantity of links or the content of the pages linking to a site when determining relevancy.[7]

Managing Seeding and Spoofing Issues. Brand managers often send letters to unaffiliated third parties using logos or brand names in various ways that threaten to divert customers. These letters respectfully ask whether those sites have preexisting agreements to use trademarked brands or display logos. If they do not, the third-party sites are asked to remove the logo or brand name.

When contacted parties turn out to have a formal agreement, they are asked politely via letter to correct improper brand representation. Some companies elect to send such sites copies of their Internet guidelines. Often, corporate legal departments would only get involved if the third party is unresponsive.

Though compliance rates vary widely, depending on the industry and the specific issue, sites without preexisting agreements are moderately less responsive. Sites that do have agreements in place are usually quick to rectify the issue.

A major pharmaceutical company follows a methodology that has been very successful in protecting its product brand names from being used to divert customers. The incidents they prioritize are invisible seeding of content in metatags and logo abuse. The highest-priority offenders are unauthorized distributors or websites that promote herbal alternatives to the company's drug brands.

This pharmaceutical company first confirms that the site is not a legitimate distributor of its drug. After it is verified that the site is in violation, the legal team sends the registrant of the site a cease-and-desist letter by fax and registered mail. Approximately 90 percent of the sites notified comply with the request to remove the product name within a month of notification.

In cases where herbal alternatives to its products are being distributed, the pharmaceutical company places an order for the product and analyzes it to ensure that the proprietary chemical compound in its own products is not being used.

Paid Placement

Most search engines now offer paid placement or sponsored links, also known as "pay for play," where they charge a fee to guarantee prominent display or a higher listing in the results provided for specific search terms, including brand names. Oftentimes these paid placements are displayed in a different location than the nonpaid results, though they are frequently the first things searchers see when their query returns are served up. Many of the leading search engines outsource the bidding and placement process to companies such as "pay-for-performance" firm Overture Services, Google, or Findwhat.com (who merged with European "pay-per-click advertising network" Espotting in 2003).

The rapid and broad adoption of paid placement advertising has created a whole new brand management issue as brands and slogans are some of the most popular search terms that companies bid on, regardless of whether they are entitled to do so (see Figure 3-9). Paid placement companies host a kind of virtual auction, where the high bidder's listing will appear in response to a query for that brand. Keeping track of who is bidding on your brand is a

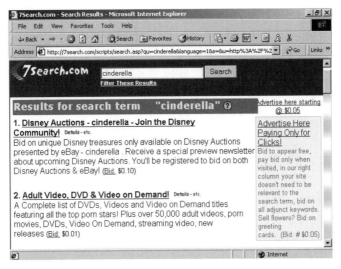

Figure 3-9. *Adult video merchant bids $0.01 for second place in results for "Cinderella."*

challenge as the number of paid placements increases and the variations on a single brand name are practically limitless. For example, somebody trying to manage the Hyatt brand may find competitors and discount travel agents bidding on the following names:

➤ Hyatt Hotels

➤ Hyatt reservation

➤ Hyatt reservations

➤ Hyatt discount

➤ Hyatt Regency

➤ Hyatt website

➤ Hyatt vacations

➤ Hyatt Atlanta

➤ Hyatt New York

➤ Hyatt Minneapolis, etc.

Have you ever noticed that while you're searching, the search engine will also display conventional banner or rich media advertising for a product related to your search terms? In addition to paid placement, some search engines sell more conventional advertising that is served up in response to specific user queries, including trademarks. Sometimes searching on a brand name will trigger competitive advertising, a practice that has been successfully challenged in the courts by companies such as Esteé Lauder.

When you need to take action against a third party that is buying search engine placement or advertising in response to queries for your brand, there are several approaches that you can take. The first option is to take the case up with the company selling the placement. Some companies are more responsive than others. Google, for example, prohibits this type of abuse and also removes advertisers that don't maintain a high enough click-through rate.

A second alternative is to take the case up directly with the bidder. This is particularly effective if the bidder is a partner or distributor. To avoid any misunderstanding, policies and procedures regarding paid placement should be included in partner Internet guidelines.

Should all other approaches fall short, there are two other options at your disposal:

1. Pay the "ransom" and maintain the highest bid on your own trademarks. Note that this approach can be less costly if you keep partners out of the bidding process.

2. Seek the advice of counsel regarding legal action against either the bidder or the company facilitating the abuse.

Adware

Companies like The Gator Corporation and WhenU have generated even more controversy by providing a means by which companies can advertise to people visiting competitors' websites. Gator and WhenU offer free utilities users can download to their computers that provide services such as e-wallets, digital clocks, or weather bars. In exchange for giving users these utilities, the companies reserve the right to launch ads as their users navigate the Internet. The ads are displayed to the users by opening a new window on top of the viewed page.

One of the reasons that adware has generated so much controversy is that the companies offering these utilities will often sell advertising to the direct competitor of the site where the ad is launched. A computer with WhenU's WeatherCast software, for example, may launch a Delta Airlines advertisement when one of their 20 million users visits the reservation section on the Southwest Airlines website. The user, who is about to make a reservation on Southwest, may see the advertisement and decide to investigate Delta instead. By targeting someone who is about to buy from a competitor, this practice can divert large numbers of customers.

Hint: Monitoring who is advertising on your site is relatively easy if you download the adware and periodically browse your own website.

United Parcel Service sued Gator for launching FedEx advertisements to users visiting UPS's site. InterContinental Hotels Group, PLC, has also sued Gator, claiming copyright and trademark infringement, unfair competition, and computer trespass. Terence Ross, a partner in the D.C. office of Los Angeles–based Gibson, Dunn & Crutcher, believes that Gator violates copyright law because it "alters the publishers' intended appearance of their sites and because the company is effectively creating an unauthorized derivative work—the website superimposed with a pop-up ad."[8] He also says that the pop-up ads launched by Gator software (see Figure 3-10) violate the Lanham Act, which is the federal trademark law, because viewers may mistakenly believe the ads are associated with the website.

"Gator is selling advertising on web pages not owned by them, doing it without authorization, and then pocketing the profits from those sales."
—TERENCE ROSS, COPYRIGHT LAWYER[9]

While not everyone agrees with Ross's interpretation of Gator's business model, no one disputes that its practices are aggressive and controversial. And despite the potential legal implications and ongoing litigation, the use of these ads is widespread and is a blatant maneuver to steal customers.

In addition to suing, the options for managing this issue are very similar to those at your disposal for paid placement. You can pursue the issue with either the company buying or facilitating the advertising. Some advertisers might not even realize how these free utilities work and will stop using them for target marketing when they find out. For example, when The New York Times Company found out that its ads were appearing over competitor sites without the site publisher's permission, it halted the practice.

Other companies employ technology to combat the issue and have developed software that can detect if visitors to their sites have programs such as Gator's on their computer. You can also buy your way out, though it may be expensive.[10] Extended Stay America, Inc. noted in court papers that if a company buys an ad campaign with Gator, it can avoid having pop-up ads on its own site for a cost upwards of $50,000.

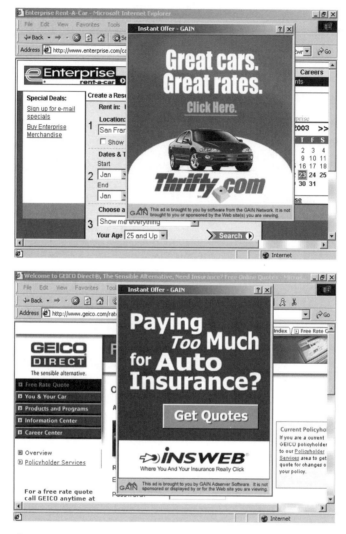

Figure 3-10. *Examples of ads launched by Gator Corporation's eWallet software.*

Mislabeled Links

Some people prefer to navigate the Internet by surfing from one site to the next using hyperlinks. Sites will intentionally mislabel links to send the visitor to a destination other than where the user thought he was going. This practice is more common than most people realize and is another way that unethical sites sometimes use the value of a trusted brand to their own advantage.

Most companies follow the same approach for these sites as they do for unaffiliated sites that use logos or seed their site with brands. The company

Figure 3-10. *(Continued)*.

asks the site to rectify the situation immediately. Success rates are similar to other customer diversion tactics.

Unsolicited E-Mail

Studies show that spam now accounts for more than two-thirds of e-mail traffic, and the volume of unsolicited electronic mail continues to rise.[11] E-mail is easy to use and cheap to send. Uncontrolled distribution and low costs have resulted in message volumes that sour customers and waste their time. Jupiter

Research estimates that Internet users can expect to receive about 3,800 junk messages per year by 2007.[12]

The tactics used to send unsolicited commercial e-mail are becoming more sophisticated as spammers battle to outwit filters designed to keep spam out of your mailbox. As with websites, e-mail has proved to be a haven for fraud. E-mail also serves as a funnel to pull consumers onto questionable Internet sites that cannot otherwise be found. Some e-mails solicit transactions via other channels, including phone, fax, or the U.S. Postal Service.

> *"Spam has become the organized crime of the Internet."*
> —BARRY SHEIN, PRESIDENT OF INTERNET SERVICE PROVIDER THE WORLD[13]

Brand abuse is rampant in junk mail. Figures 3-11 and 3-12 are examples of how upstart e-mail advertisers vie for consumer attention and attempt to engender trust by exploiting popular brands. Con artists and unknown enterprises find a strong brand can help them establish a perception of legitimacy. Almost every major brand is abused by spam and it remains one of the most difficult abuses to monitor and defend against. Chapters 9 and 10 provide some insights into how to monitor and take action against spammers.

Keeping the Customer

The porn industry has long been considered a technology "crystal ball," and the mainstream adoption of a tactic known as "spawning" illustrates that the

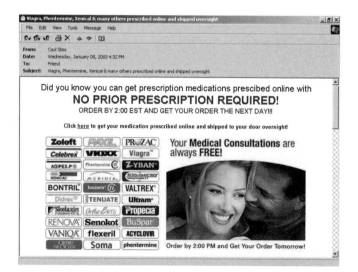

Figure 3-11. *E-mail solicitation for Thailand-based pharmacy uses popular pharmaceutical brands.*

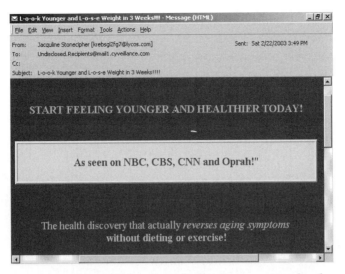

Figure 3-12. *Spam e-mail uses popular brands to promote sales of human growth hormone spray.*

adage still holds true. A by-product of the online porn industry, spawning entails the automatic launch of new browser windows or the opening of hidden "stealth" windows either upon entering or exiting a site, or on delay.

Pop-up and pop-under ads have been widely adopted as a somewhat less intrusive variation of this irksome tactic. These interactive ads take many different forms, sometimes incorporating video and sound clips as advertisers embrace a rich media format. This practice differs from that of companies such as Gator because the advertisements are placed and launched by the site owner.

Advertising crosses the line to spawning when the technology is abused. In some cases, site designers embed code that repeatedly launches scores of new browser windows faster than the shopper can close them, effectively taking over the user's computer screen. The tactic is frequently used in combination with a second trick called "mouse-trapping."

Mouse-trapping is the online equivalent of locking the door behind the customer so she can't leave a website. The offending sites will often set the trap through the manipulation of the browser's "back" or history buttons to prevent the shopper from leaving the site, or the deactivation of browser "exit" or "close" capabilities.

Mouse-trapping is another offspring of the online porn industry that is going more mainstream. "I think it's evil," says Donna Hoffman, a professor at Vanderbilt University specializing in online marketing and consumer behavior. "They're thinking, 'We need to do everything we can to keep users at our site.' It's beyond annoying, it's offensive."[14]

A common variant combines mouse-trapping with spawning by launching a full-screen advertisement window with no visible frame or controls. The only way for a customer to exit the website is to click on a button within the ad to accept the offer, download software, or request further information. Other times the exit or "decline" buttons actually function as "accept" buttons.

"Redirect" pages, or pages that immediately forward the visitor to another page, can also be used to stop the user from leaving a site. Redirect pages are sometimes present for legitimate purposes, such as load balancing or sending visitors to a version of the site catering to the geographic region of the visitor. Redirects are considered mouse-trapping when a site skirts good design etiquette and allows the redirect page to enter the browser history, effectively blocking a shopper from retreating from the site.

Another variation of mouse-trapping occurs when the shopper hits the back button and is sent to the wrong location, for which the offender may be able to collect a referral fee. While shoppers believe they are headed toward the exit, they are actually headed for a door to another store.

"Consumers are being exposed to increasingly sophisticated and aggressive techniques on the Internet that divert shoppers and convert traffic to revenue."
—MICHAEL MALONEY, A DIRECTOR AT NAVIGANT CONSULTING, INC.

Finally, some sites attempt to keep shoppers on a site by "framing" the browser window while they view content from other domains (Figure 3-13). Framing appears to the user as an online version of the picture-in-picture feature available on some television models. The "frame" is sometimes left visible for branding purposes, but more devious sites will purposefully hide it so that shoppers think they have left the site when actually they are still on it, but in a separate frame. Not only is the practice inconvenient, it can compromise shoppers' privacy and leave them more exposed to fraud or identity theft.

An offshoot of framing is "in-lining," where select pieces of content, such as images, are "borrowed" and served up from another site. While in-lining has many legitimate applications, it can also be used as a way to use copyrighted content without authorization.

FTC HALTS INTERNET HIJACKING SCAM

The U.S. government helped discourage nefarious technology tactics, in all their manifestations, almost as soon as they started to appear online. In its

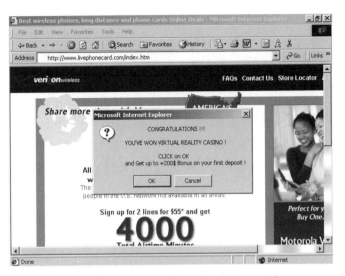

Figure 3-13. *Livephonecard.com frames the Verizonwireless.com website.*

one-hundredth law enforcement action targeting deception on the Internet, the U.S. Federal Trade Commission (FTC) asked a U.S. District Court judge to halt an Internet scam that used "page-jacking" and "mouse-trapping" to lure people to a network of pornographic websites operated out of Portugal and Australia.

"These operators hijacked websites, 'kidnapped' consumers and held them captive," said Jodie Bernstein, former director of the FTC's Bureau of Consumer Protection. "They exposed surfers, including children, to the seamiest sort of material and incapacitated computer close buttons so they couldn't escape. They copied as many as 25 million web pages from sites as diverse as the *Harvard Law Review* and the Japanese Friendship Garden."

According to the complaint, in a practice called "page-jacking," the defendants made exact copies of web pages posted by a wide range of unrelated parties, including the embedded code used by search engines to index the subject matter of the site. When the search engines displayed the bogus pages as search results, surfers assumed from the listings that the defendants' sites contained the information they were seeking. But when they clicked on the listing, the redirect command embedded in the copycat site immediately rerouted consumers to a site that contained sexually explicit material.

Once there, consumers were "mouse-trapped"—that is, their Internet browser's "back" and "close" buttons were incapacitated so that when they tried to exit the site, they were sent to additional adult sites in an unavoidable, seemingly endless loop.

Bernstein speculated that the high rate of traffic generated by the "kidnapped" surfers allowed the defendants to charge premium prices for advertising on their site. In addition, the defendants may have received income from referral or commission fees by diverting surfers to other adult-oriented websites.[15]

Aided in its investigation by The Australian Competition and Consumer Commission and the Portuguese Instituto do Consumidor, the FTC was successful in shutting down the offending sites. In addition, the perpetrators were restrained from copying web pages, using redirect commands, misrepresenting the contents of their sites, overriding a user's browser functions, or registering any new domain names.[16]

Bringing the Customer Back

One more trick up the creative coder's sleeve is to make a change to people's browser that will bring them back to a website at a later point in time. This includes the addition of a site to the shopper's list of favorites or the unauthorized substitution of the shopper's browser "home page." This tactic, known as home-jacking, automatically returns shoppers to the site the next time they launch their browser. Only very knowledgeable surfers are going to realize that they can use their browser tools to reset the address of their home page.

Finally, one of the most treacherous practices is the unauthorized download of software onto the visitor's computer, including viruses or plug-ins, such as spyware that can track the user's keystrokes or provide outside access to the user's computer.

Unauthorized software invades a consumer's privacy and can also expose the individual to fraud or identity theft. Sometimes this tactic is coupled with the mislabeling of buttons so that when the user is prompted to choose whether to download software, the software gets downloaded whether the consumer selects "yes" or "no."

ENTANGLED ON THE WEB

A Cyveillance study audited the use of technology tactics on 100,000 websites. Each tactic was evaluated and ranked according to the criteria of frequency, level of intrusiveness, and potential for damage.[17] Frequency reflected the popularity of the practice, while the level of intrusiveness was defined as the degree to which the technology disrupts the customer's online experience. "Potential for damage" was the degree to which the tactic can present hazards, such as exposing children to objectionable content, compromising security, or exposing the shopper to fraud. The study identified the top-ten technology tactics that are used to entangle customers on the Web:

Top-Ten List

1. Spawning

2. Mouse-trapping

3. Invisible seeding

4. Unauthorized software downloads

5. Spoof pages

6. Typo-piracy and cybersquatting

7. Changing home page or favorites

8. Visible seeding

9. Mislabeling links

10. Framing

The Motive

Simply put, brands are abused through the use of these tactics and others to make money. The payout can come in many forms. The first way to drive revenue is through the acquisition of new customers. This is often the case when competitors abuse your brand. It's also true of many upstart companies attempting to establish trust or legitimacy.

The second major way to make money by diverting and trapping customers is through advertising revenue and affiliate programs. Revenue-sharing programs are often based on certain online advertising metrics, such as the average time somebody spends on a site, the number of repeat visits, or the number of visitors. Affiliate programs will pay out cash for referrals, usually without regard for the tactics employed to capture the traffic.

In May 2002, a U.S. federal court ordered the owner of a website network to pay back more than $1.8 million he earned by luring unsuspecting web surfers to pornography-related websites and then trapping them there. Using tactics such as cybersquatting, mouse-trapping, and spawning, the network of sites generated referral fees from unsuspecting advertising affiliate programs. In addition to forfeiting his illicit revenue, the perpetrator was ordered to refrain from diverting or obstructing online consumers in the future.[18]

While this criminal was caught, most offenders go unpunished. The online environment has fostered a free-for-all mentality, and there is little incentive for unregulated sites to abide by the law or even uphold basic business ethics. In fact, it can be argued that just the opposite is true. Online advertising metrics do not account for the *context* by which the metric was achieved and can thus unwittingly provide incentive for abuse.

As an example, say a credit card issuer rewards affiliates who publish its advertising by paying them a fee for each referral that becomes a cardholder. An affiliate may decide to violate guidelines and use unprincipled capture tactics, such as spam, false promises, and search engine manipulation, because the more visitors it can draw in, the more potential cardholders it can earn a fee from. This approach increases the number of referrals by a factor of 1,000, but the use of underhanded tactics reduces the conversion rate from 1.0 to 0.01 percent. Result? The affiliate fees earned still go up by a factor of ten. However, the negative brand image, quantity of prospective customers tainted, and the cost of fielding all the customer service complaints make this a very bad deal for the bank.

To avoid this situation, the credit card issuer can simply monitor the referring URLs of its top affiliates to make sure they are legitimate pages in compliance with the company's affiliate agreement, which prohibits e-mail marketing. If the credit card company finds instead that the referring URL is just a page that automatically redirects people, it is likely that the affiliate is using e-mail to drive traffic.

Scope of the Problem

According to the study cited previously (see the sidebar "Entangled on the Web"), more than 25 percent of Internet sites use one of these aggressive tactics in an apparent attempt to divert and capture shoppers. The adoption of such tactics by mainstream sites corresponds with economic pressures as companies seek to drive revenue by any means at their disposal. The use of these techniques is highly disruptive to the customer's experience and highlights the shortsightedness, desperation, and inexperience of some online ventures.

> *"Using overly aggressive practices on the Web can severely undermine building a positive brand customer experience and will damage your brand reputation."*
>
> —ALAN SIEGEL, CHAIRMAN AND CEO OF SIEGELGALE,
> A STRATEGIC BRANDING AND INTERNET CONSULTING FIRM

Fortunately, there are ways to manage customer diversion tactics. Chapter 4 is an introduction to managing the issue of compliance within partner networks, such as the credit card affiliate scenario described previously. Chapters 9 through 11 provide deeper insights into both online monitoring and how to take action and protect your customers.

The Future

Every year the Internet penetrates deeper into the average person's life, in some ways that are obvious and many others that are subtle. You can now access the Internet from most new cars, for example, as well as some consumer electronics goods. In 2002, Merloni Elettrodomestici, Europe's third-largest appliance manufacturer, began "giving away" new digitally wired washing machines that are installed in the home and connected to the Internet. The machines then electronically bill the homeowners' bank accounts for each wash.[19] Many treadmills and refrigerators are also going online. Appliances are usually Internet-enabled for convenience, such as to provide online access to the customer or to automatically notify the manufacturer if the device malfunctions.

Criminals and brand abusers can be counted on to stay ahead of the curve and are always developing innovative new tricks. The day may not be far off when instead of mouse-trapping, a clever, invasive online vendor turns off your dishwasher, sends an ad across its digital display face, or generates a false maintenance request!

It's not as far-fetched as you think. Digital trickery has already worked its way from computers to cell phones. In Japan, for example, there was an incident where e-mail messages sent to cell phones contained an Internet link that, when clicked, caused the phones to dial the national emergency number. In Europe, binary code has been mailed to cell phones using short message service, or SMS, which caused the phones to crash, forcing users to detach the battery and reboot.[20]

One thing is for certain—as more and more facets of the customer's daily life become interconnected, online tactics to attract or divert customers will play a greater role in the customer's experience, both while shopping and after purchase. The degree to which these experiences are positive or negative will play a significant role in shaping brand image. Safeguarding customers against the most aggressive and negative tactics will be an increasingly important part of defending the brand.

For companies with established brands, technological practices can divert customers from their intended destination and wreak havoc with the customer experience, causing them to make alternative purchases or just give up in frustration. Left unmanaged, the brand abuse can undermine revenue and brand equity.

The following example illustrates how customer diversion might translate into lost revenue. It also represents the incremental revenue that could be captured by defending the brand.

Example

The brand manager for a luxury hotel and casino chain has discovered that gambling sites and competitors are using its brand name to divert customers online. The methods employed include search engine manipulation, cybersquatting, typo-piracy, and mouse-trapping, among others. The use of these tactics is of particular concern because the content on the offending sites may cause the diverted customers to change their mind about the hotel chain and take their business elsewhere. To calculate how customer diversion could impact the hotel chain's revenue, the brand manager applied this step-by-step formula and assumptions:

Step	Assumption
1	Average monthly visitors to hotel chain site: 300,000
2	Average monthly visitors diverted: 30,000
3	Conversion rate on offending sites: 1.5%
4	Average monthly customers lost to competitors = (2) × (3) = 450
5	Total number of customers lost annually = (4) × 12 = 5,400
6	Average value of a customer: $2,000
7	Total annual cost of online customer diversion = (5) × (6) = $10,800,000

Competitors and other online entities use aggressive tactics to lure your customers away using your own brands. Be mindful that:

➤ Deceitful and intrusive techniques that once confined themselves to adult sites have now become mainstream.

➤ Online shoppers are being confronted with a host of aggressive and sophisticated "capture" tactics that prey on brands, resulting in confusion and frustration.

➤ Every aspect of a consumer's online experience comes under assault as sites fight aggressively for revenue.

➤ Left unmanaged, brand abuse can divert customers, wreak havoc with the customer experience, and undermine brand equity.

➤ Offending sites convert diverted customers into revenue through competitive offerings, the manipulation of advertising metrics, and referral programs.

➤ Regardless of whether a company conducts business online, a portion of diverted customers equates to lost revenue, and the costs can add up quickly, if you don't defend the brand.

Online Partners and Distribution Issues

"This was the unkindest cut of all."
WILLIAM SHAKESPEARE, *Julius Caesar* (Act III, Scene 2)

Chapter 4

Managing Partner Compliance

A strong brand is the cornerstone of customer loyalty and contributes to recurring, higher-margin revenue streams. Knowing this, business strategies are increasingly focused on leveraging the value of the brand to acquire and retain customers. One way to do this is by extending brand reach and reinforcing your branding through partners.

Online partner networks can be effective vehicles to leverage a brand and drive potential customers to a company's site. The down side to partner networks is reduced control over the customer experience and the use of the brand. For example, if partner sites are difficult to navigate, show shoddy quality, engage in underhanded tactics, or divert customers from the brand owner, partner networks can quickly become a liability. This is truer than ever in the digital world, where the distinction between a brand owner and its partners is frequently blurred.

The role of partners often expands online, and incorporating them in branding strategies has become increasingly important—particularly as customers move online not only to make transactions, but also to research their offline purchases. In some cases, partner roles have expanded to the extent that a customer's exposure to a brand is entirely outside the brand owner's direct control, from the point of brand awareness through fulfillment.

In many ways, partners are online "ambassadors" of the brand, so how they choose to represent you shapes your brand image. Your brand presence—be it in the form of a logo, slogan, product description, specifications, or pricing information—is entrusted to a partner, and accurate or inaccurate, what that partner does with your brand plays a significant role in the customer experience. "On the World Wide Web, the brand is the experience and the experience is the brand."[1]

Partners must therefore be considered and managed in any efforts to build a consistent, branded customer experience. Left to their own devices, partner networks can undermine the customer experience, destroy brand equity, and divert revenue to competitors. As such, effective brand defense strategies incorporate online partner management.

The Customer Experience

As Tom Peters states in his book *In Search of Excellence*, "There are only two ways to create and sustain superior performance over the long haul. First, take exceptional care of your customers via superior service and superior quality. Second, constantly innovate." Satisfied and loyal customers are crucial for the success of any business. Unless the customer experience either meets or exceeds expectations, consumers are likely to take their business elsewhere.

Unfortunately, while organizations invest millions of dollars in the development and execution of customer-centric strategies, few are cognizant of the need to manage the customer's total experience—including their interaction with online partners.

Some companies are making it a priority to provide a consistent customer experience across all channels. Retailers Lowe's and Ann Taylor, for example, have taken great pains to get their websites as closely aligned with and supportive of their offline store experience as possible.[2] At the same time, their online strategies limit knowledge and control over the customer's experience to the confines of their own websites, even though their customers also encounter their brands on the broader Internet.

Avis Rent A Car has achieved high levels of customer loyalty by obsessing over every step of the customer experience, though its efforts have been primarily offline. But as Avis customers move online to make their travel plans, third parties such as travel agents increasingly shape the customer experience. Future customer loyalty initiatives must consider the extent to which customers interact online with partners and others claiming a relationship with Avis. In fact, more than 98 percent of the average company's Internet brand presence falls outside of its own domain, much of which typically is on partner sites.[3]

Brand presence on partner sites is no accident as partners are in a position to derive great value from liberally promoting their association with a reputable brand. Unfortunately, if a brand is not actively managed, partners may engage in self-serving tactics that can disrupt the customer experience and dilute the brand.

Changing Dynamics

A number of factors contribute to the need for close attention to partners online. One is channel conflict. While a company's relative position of strength in the value chain remains important, in some cases the Internet has rendered intermediaries less significant or added another level of complexity to already complicated partner relationships.

Nascent online models and metrics can sometimes inadvertently encourage abuse, particularly in the absence of guidelines or enforcement. This situation is exacerbated when partner guidelines are nonexistent, not communicated properly, or not monitored and enforced.

Online Partners

In the drive for market share and customer acquisition, companies are harnessing all their resources in an effort to meet the rising demands of online customers. These customers conduct online research, are influenced by online marketing, and may or may not make online transactions.

Among the most popular strategies aimed at winning these online viewers are affiliate marketing networks—that is, programs designed to extend brand reach through strategic relationships to increase site traffic and grow market share. Companies are learning to leverage the brands of their suppliers as well by developing Internet guidelines and policies that link strategies and noncompete agreements to guide sales through their own channels.

The benefits of online relationships are widely recognized. They lay the framework for operational efficiencies, a dramatic expansion of brand reach, and growth in sales and market share. At the same time, each relationship becomes an extension of an organization—a delegate, so to speak, of the organization's brand positioning, goals, and values. These delegates often make the first impression on the customer, and if not properly managed, they can have a negative effect on a company's bottom line.

Online partners can engage in a wide range of activities that threaten to undermine a branded customer experience. Examples include:

> ➤ Displaying outdated, misleading, altered, or bogus promotions, pricing, and product information

➤ Displaying altered or outdated logos or slogans

➤ Engaging in illegal activities such as the sale of controlled or prohibited products

➤ Engaging in brand abuse (e.g., cybersquatting, search service manipulation, framing, or other tactics) that diverts and retains your customers

➤ Failing to clearly disclose the geographic region served

➤ Displaying potentially objectionable content such as pornography, profanity, or hate speech

➤ Failing to offer security or violating customer privacy

➤ Using spam to drive traffic or mass postings in chat rooms, newsgroups, or message boards

➤ Leaving broken, outdated, or mislabeled links, sometimes referred to as "link rot"

➤ Using "deep links" that send the consumer somewhere further within a site than intended, bypassing important information such as branding and privacy statements or disclaimers

➤ Copying the "look and feel" of your site and confusing the customer

➤ Selling in direct competition, advertising or displaying competing content, or giving preferential positioning and treatment to competitors (see Figure 4-1)

To manage the risks associated with online partner activity, many companies have established guidelines for their partners to follow. To illustrate how partner management concerns are reflected in the contractual terms of actual partner agreements, sample excerpts of license and usage guidelines from affiliate programs are included in Appendix B. The terms of the agreements provide insights into the multitude of issues that can and do arise regularly; usage guidelines cover everything from altered logos to use of the brand in connection with the "glorified consumption of drugs or alcohol."

While on the surface some of the offenses may seem relatively minor, they can have a significant impact—particularly when compounded across large partner networks. For example, consider an affiliate that also participates in a competitor's affiliate network. Both your logo and that of the competitor are side by side, but yours is a broken link that takes users nowhere. Your competitors' link, on the other hand, is functional and readily transports visitors to the

Figure 4-1. *Travel agents use the Disney brand in their domain name while promoting competitive offerings.*

competitor's order screen. Such a scenario is likely to divert customers, if for no other reason than simple convenience.

Affiliates

As a result of their potential to drive significant amounts of revenue, affiliate programs have burgeoned in the online world. An affiliate relationship exists between a merchant of a product or service and a website owner who promotes the merchant's offerings. Affiliates are sometimes also called "publishers" since they will display a logo or other form of advertising. While affiliate program structures vary, the affiliate may earn a small commission from the merchant for each referral that results in a sale. This arrangement motivates affiliates to drive qualified leads. Other times the affiliate may be awarded for traffic referred, regardless of conversion rates.

Depending on the circumstances, a brand may benefit from either offering an affiliate marketing program or joining one. At the same time, affiliate programs can damage a brand. Wherever there is an opportunity to generate revenue online, entrepreneurial sites will find any weaknesses that exist in the system and exploit them. Affiliate programs are no exception.

In an effort to boost referral fees, affiliates sometimes resort to tactics whose offline equivalent would never be tolerated. Examples include displaying exaggerated or false promotions, trapping customers on their site, or sending millions of unsolicited e-mails with misleading messages. Some affiliates subvert the system when they compensate for their lack of ability to attract quality leads by using deceitful tactics to drive as many referrals as possible (see Figure 4-2). Affiliates have even been discovered boosting their fees by generating false sales with stolen credit cards, which are readily available from thieves in Internet chat rooms.

Left unmanaged, affiliate networks can take on a life of their own and mushroom out of control. Unfortunately, while the benefits of an affiliate program are immediately evident in terms of customer acquisition, if the affiliate network is unmonitored, the true price paid for those referrals is not always obvious. Unscrupulous affiliates will use a brand to engage in the same types of customer diversion practices as porn site operators.

For affiliate networks to be effective, corporate branding guidelines must be established and communicated. Affiliate activities must then be monitored and the guidelines enforced. Affiliates are sometimes a customer's first exposure to your brand, so abuses must be taken seriously. Penalties for noncompliance must be severe. If the partners cannot see that the consequences of brand abuse outweigh the potential rewards, problems are likely to arise.

> *"The single most important thing you can do for your customers is to anticipate and eliminate snags and delays in their experience of dealing with you."*
>
> —PATRICIA SEYBOLD, AUTHOR OF *Customers.com*[4]

Suppliers

In general, suppliers are more powerful online because the Internet enhances their ability to integrate forward and sell directly to customers. This is particu-

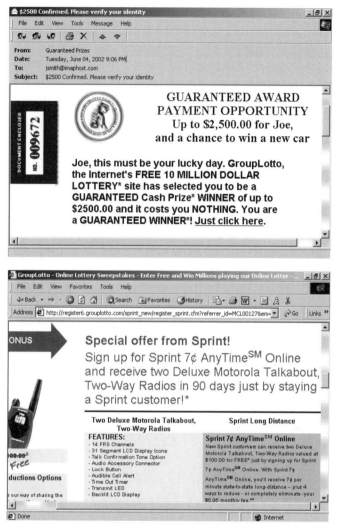

Figure 4-2. *An affiliate uses misleading e-mail (top screen) to drive visitors to a sign-up page for Sprint long-distance service (bottom.)*

larly true for suppliers that have a strong brand of their own and are not dependent on complementary services or large distributors. In addition, suppliers are well positioned to serve as a resource to consumers by maintaining up-to-date, detailed product information and specifications on their offerings. A Yankelovich Partners survey found that 93 percent of consumers polled have researched products online.[5] With increasing research being done online, suppliers play a greater role in the customer's experience.

Properly managed and integrated into the online customer experience, suppliers can be a valuable resource and generate sales referrals. Suppliers can also abuse your brand and use their newfound visibility to experiment with business models and generate new revenue streams at your expense. Examples include referring visitors to competitors or even engaging in direct competition themselves.

THE HOME DEPOT

Like many companies, The Home Depot wrestles with the conflicts and challenges of channel management and supplier guidelines as the Internet completely redefines the relationships among manufacturers, suppliers, distributors, and retailers. The Internet's influence on The Home Depot's business is much greater than the value of online sales in the building materials and home improvement supplies market; it extends to homeowners researching their do-it-yourself projects and contractors researching their supply purchases.

Customers are going online for guidance in lieu of speaking with sales clerks or browsing in a brick-and-mortar store. The implication of this trend is that The Home Depot has less control over the customer shopping experience—an alarming trend for a company that has built its reputation on superior customer service and knowledgeable salespeople. The Internet also allows customers to go directly to The Home Depot suppliers as the logical source for product information and research. Once they access a supplier website, customers may be directed to a competitor, or they may bypass retailers altogether and purchase direct from the manufacturer.

Suppliers selling online in competition with retailers can be particularly disruptive when price points are undercut. The Home Depot recognized the potential dangers of disintermediation and attempted to stop channel conflict early on by issuing a well-publicized letter to its thousands of suppliers. That letter stated, in part:

> *Dear Vendor . . . It is important for you to be aware of Home Depot's current position on [its] vendors competing with the company via e-commerce direct to consumer distribution. We think it is shortsighted for vendors to ignore the added value that our retail stores contribute to the sales of their products . . . We recognize that a vendor has the right to sell through whatever distribution channels it desires. However, we too have the right to be selective in regard to the vendors we select and we trust that you can understand that a company may be hesitant to do business with its competitors.*[6]

Anecdotal evidence indicates that The Home Depot had some success with this early approach. Rubbermaid, for one, later referenced The Home Depot letter when questioned about its decision to halt its foray into the e-commerce arena. "We had been selling online, but then a year and a half ago Home Depot sent a letter to most of its suppliers," said the manager in charge of Rubbermaid's website. "That's when we decided not to sell online. It jeopardized our relationship with the brick-and-mortars that are our customers."[7]

Under the Frequently Asked Questions section of Rubbermaid's website is the question: "Why don't you offer direct order over the Internet?" Rubbermaid's response states simply:

> *Retail stores are currently the best way to distribute our products and serve consumers. Rubbermaid ships their product by the truckload direct to the retail store's distribution warehouses. They in turn ship to the individual store locations close to your home. We suggest that you check with local retailers for items illustrated on this site.*

Maytag Corporation has elected not to compete with distributors—at least for the time being. "[G]oing direct would mean competing with our existing customers," says Arthur Learmonth, director of manufacturing, engineering, and logistics at Maytag, "and that's not something we want to do."[8] Instead, Maytag generates leads on its site and sends them to the retail partners that are closest to the consumer—giving the retailer the benefit of presales without even asking.[9]

Wal-Mart's approach to channel conflict is another reason suppliers like Maytag fear the wrath of the large retailers. They have taken a heavy-handed approach, akin to The Home Depot's, to managing suppliers. "Once our suppliers sell online, they become our competitors," says Melissa Berryhill, Wal-Mart public relations officer. "And we have to reevaluate their having access to our retail system. We're not telling our suppliers how to run their business, only how we're going to run ours."[10]

Few retailers have as much leverage as Wal-Mart and The Home Depot, however, and even when suppliers don't sell their products online, other supplier issues can be just as damaging. For example, retailers need to take note of the manner in which suppliers use the brand, or how they direct prospective customers for further research and possible purchase. When suppliers engender trust and increase site traffic by using a well-known brand like The Home Depot, and then actively direct purchasers to a "Where to Buy" or dealer list that fails to include that brand, it takes a direct bite out of revenue.

How common is supplier noncompliance? Cyveillance reviewed thousands of the suppliers of one large retailer, examining broken links, competitive content, sales in direct competition, and other site activity that constituted noncompliance according to the retailer's policies. The study found that only 5 percent of suppliers actually followed the guidelines. Of the 95 percent of suppliers that were not in compliance, 15 percent were selling products in direct competition or actively directing buyers to competitive retail channels.[11]

The implications of noncompliance are significant. Most people use the Internet either to make purchases or research their offline purchases. Furthermore, among those individuals who make online purchases, online research heavily influences their offline purchases as well. Merchants need to realize that a significant share of sales are now being generated from online research, regardless of where the transaction takes place.

Distributors

By their very nature, distribution networks are customer-facing and therefore play an important role in the presentation of a supplier brand to the end-consumer. While a well-managed distribution network can drive revenue and reinforce branding, there are many potential pitfalls. If storefronts, agents, or dealers are not complying with guidelines, they can undermine brand equity. Examples of damaging activities that are common within online distribution networks include:

➤ Unauthorized or misleading promotions

➤ False or missing product information

➤ Inconsistent pricing schemes

➤ Invalid warranties and guarantees

➤ Undesirable product placement

➤ Inconsistent company branding

Figures 4-3, 4-4, and 4-5 are further examples of the ways distributors may engage in damaging online activities, by either featuring competitive products, misusing a brand within a domain name, or directly linking to a competitor's website.

Companies can manage branding risks through the creation and implementation of guidelines. Appendix C provides examples of some monitoring and enforcement guidelines that hotel chains have established for individual hotels and franchise owners. The guidelines address the aforementioned points as well as other issues such as site linking, privacy, and operational requirements.

While some of these distributor offenses may not seem very threatening,

Figure 4-3. *IBMnotebook.com and IBMlaptop.com feature competitor products.*

distributor and dealer noncompliance is more than just an annoyance. Loss of control of distribution can have a serious impact on an organization's bottom line, resulting in significant brand tarnishing, revenue leakage, extensive customer service and warrantee costs, and even legal liability.

For example, customers unknowingly buying from unauthorized dealers will still expect standard warranties and customer satisfaction guarantees from the parent company. Outdated or bogus promotions and incorrect pricing can cost time and money by creating a flood of calls to customer service departments. Positioning a high-end watch on the same site as a $10 plastic watch can devalue the product and brand prestige in a customer's mind.

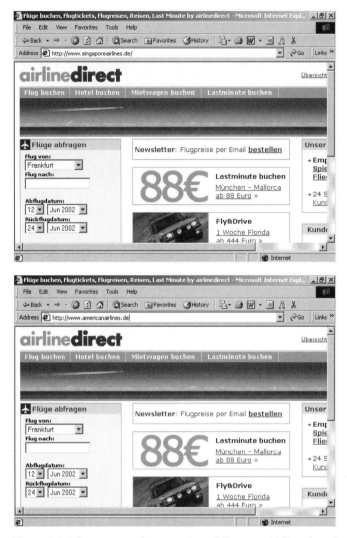

Figure 4-4. *The same travel agent registered SingaporeAirlines.de and AmericanAirlines.de.*

While manufacturers need to be concerned about distributor activities, they must also strike a careful balance depending on whether they are acting from a position of strength. Remember that distributors fear that the Internet will allow manufacturers to disrupt their own branded customer experience and divert revenue away from them. An overly aggressive approach by the manufacturer without the leverage to back it up can backfire and damage distributor relationships. As a manufacturer, your situation is most precarious and potential consequences most dire when a few distributors are responsible for a large percentage of your sales.

Suppliers with larger distribution networks have their own set of concerns

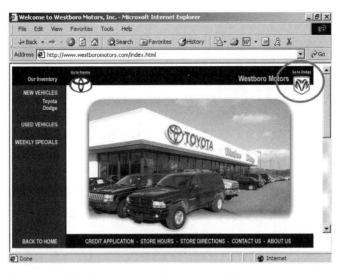

Figure 4-5. *This Toyota dealership includes a link to the Dodge website.*

and complications. One of the most formidable challenges is getting consistency in branding and customer experience across large agent or dealer networks that may be engaging in sales activity both online and offline. Trying to gain control over thousands of representatives can seem akin to herding cats. Yet managing the network is a necessary evil because the combined reach of your agents and dealers is such that their influence on brand image can sometimes eclipse that of the brand owner.

Despite the challenges, some manufacturers have had great success in their efforts to avoid channel conflict and retain control of their brand while still capturing the benefits of conducting business online. In the insurance industry, companies like SAFECO and Allstate assign a traditional agent to each online buyer and give them a cut even if the transaction is completed online. Other companies such as Polaris and Mary Kay have gone even further.

MARY KAY

Instead of selling in competition with its 800,000 beauty consultants, Mary Kay, Inc. decided to help them by providing online tools and individual sites, making it easier for the consultants to manage their businesses. Mary Kay's corporate website (see Figure 4-6) directs customers to the personalized site of their local consultant, where they can shop, place online orders, or find a number to call for phone support.

In addition to avoiding any channel conflict, this innovative approach

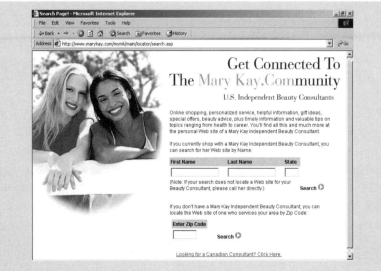

Figure 4-6. *MaryKay.com connects shoppers with their local beauty consultant.*

has allowed the Texas-based cosmetics company to gain operational efficiencies, exert control over the customer experience, and maintain branding consistency. Beauty consultants are more productive while customers have a convenient way to shop whenever they want.

"The Internet has freed up my time and allowed me to keep in touch with my customers," stated one beauty consultant who has 500 customers on her e-mail address list. "My service is better and my business has tripled in three years. What's most important is that my customers can reach me anytime."

While the initiative required a substantial investment, it is reaping great rewards. The convenience of shopping online is now an integral aspect of the branded Mary Kay customer experience. Internet orders account for more than 70 percent of Mary Kay's revenue and have boosted profitability by contributing to efficiency gains. The cost of online order processing, for example, is about one-third that of offline orders. "Supporting the beauty consultant is the core of our business," says Kregg Jodie, executive vice president and CIO. "The key to our success was developing technology that reinforces our business model."[12]

POLARIS

When snowmobile maker Polaris Industries, Inc. launched Purepolaris.com, it made sure its carefully crafted website would attract new customers and build the brand while simultaneously fostering goodwill among its 1,500 dealers. Polaris decided having an e-commerce site was imperative, though "not so much for sales but for service."[13]

To limit cannibalization of dealer sales, Polaris doesn't sell snowmobiles online. Instead, it leverages the power of its brand by promoting a wide range of high-margin items, such as Polaris-brand apparel, accessories, and collectibles—products that dealers are less likely to stock in their brick-and-mortar stores because of inventory cost and physical space constraints. To extend the brand and drive more customers to the site, Polaris also invited retailers to join an exclusive program that pays a premium commission rate to dealers that promote and link their sites to Purepolaris.com (see Figure 4-7). Its strategy has proved beneficial to the channel. If the buyer arrives via

Figure 4-7. *Polaris dealers promote Purepolaris.com on their sites.*

a dealer site, the dealer gets a larger percentage of the consumer's online purchase. Dealers that don't participate still get a commission, but at a lower rate. "Frankly, we needed an e-commerce solution that could help us generate revenue without upsetting our channel," said Scott Swenson, general manager of Pure Polaris.[14]

To further engender amity with distributors, Polaris also deployed software on its website to direct customers to the nearest dealer's location and provide information such as the dealer's hours and types of services. Since Pure Polaris went live, more than 900 of Polaris's 1,500 U.S.-based dealers have created direct links from their own websites to Purepolaris.com. The overall initiative has successfully boosted sales and brought the manufacturer closer to its customers—giving the company valuable insights into customer demographics and merchandising trends.

Third Parties

It's not enough to be concerned about the web activities of your legitimate, authorized partners. Customers are also likely to encounter your brands, products, or services on other sites operated by parties that are *not* your partners. Unaffiliated third-party sites that appear to have a relationship with your company or brand can affect the customer experience in a positive way, provided the branding and product information are consistent and accurate. Fan sites, for example, are third-party sites that can sometimes add value by reinforcing the brand.

But third-party sites can negatively affect the customer experience when they misrepresent your brand, position your products poorly, or sell gray market goods. Unaffiliated sites (such as the example shown in Figure 4-8) often leverage brands to attract additional visitors that might otherwise have navigated to the brand owner's official site or to the website of one of its legitimate partners. What's worse, whenever your brand is used, your customers may not be able to distinguish whether the relationship is legitimate or not.

Customers are likely to land on unauthorized sites that are selling your products or those that explicitly claim a relationship with you. Some sites may post an "official" statement falsely maintaining that they are authorized partners of yours. In other instances, the relationship may be more implicit, such as an unaffiliated site displaying your logo or link. Although these sites may not have a formal relationship with you, it is doubtful the customer will understand the distinction. Author Don Tapscott noted, "For ongoing relationships

Figure 4-8. *Flycathaypacific.com is not sponsored by Cathay Pacific Airways.*

with customers to be strong, companies must view the world through their customers' eyes."[15] Any experience a customer has on a website claiming or implying a relationship with you is likely to affect customer perceptions of your brand.

THE RED CROSS

The American Red Cross (Red Cross) experienced firsthand how unscrupulous third-party sites can be. In the wake of the September 11, 2001 terrorist attacks, a wave of fraudulent e-mails, online postings, and websites appeared leveraging the Red Cross brand to prey upon the public's desire to help the victims. According to some reports, fraudulent spam e-mails began appearing within one hour of the disaster.[16] The e-mails and websites solicited donations and falsely claimed to be sponsored, affiliated, or "official" sites of the Red Cross.

"People are looking to use this [event] as an opportunity to profit," said Phil Zepeda, spokesperson for the Red Cross. "It's almost beyond comprehension. It's a further tragedy beyond what has already happened."[17]

Beyond sites committing outright fraud, hundreds of online merchants used the Red Cross brand to promote themselves or drive commerce by stating they would donate a portion of their proceeds to the Red Cross (see the example in Figure 4-9). Many did not even disclose the terms or what portion would be donated. While the intentions of some of the merchants may have been good, this practice is in direct violation of Red Cross policy, which prohibits using its brand in this fashion.

To ensure that all donations make their way to the organization and are properly acknowledged, the Red Cross established five official partner agreements to facilitate online donations. Any other merchants claiming to be collecting on behalf of the Red Cross were out of compliance with the official guidelines, and there is no real way to determine whether the funds ultimately made their way back to the Red Cross. In fact, if the unauthorized merchants collected funds directly, they may have violated the law, which states:

Whoever wears or displays the sign of the Red Cross or any insignia colored in imitation thereof for the fraudulent purpose of inducing the belief that he is a member of or an agent for the American National Red Cross . . . [s]hall be fined . . . or imprisoned. (United States Code, Section 706)

Whoever, within the United States, falsely or fraudulently holds himself out as or represents or pretends himself to be a member of or an agent for the American National Red Cross for the purpose of soliciting, col-

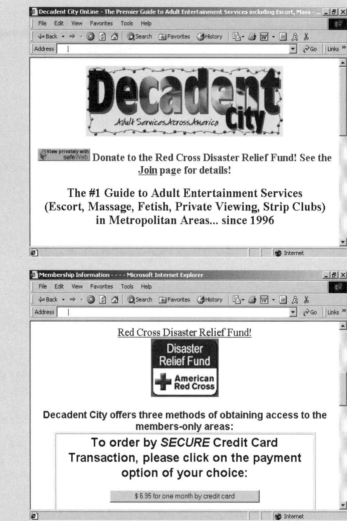

Figure 4-9. *Adult site used Red Cross brand without authorization.*

lecting, or receiving money or material, shall be fined . . . or imprisoned not more than five years. (United States Code, Section 917)

While the Red Cross brand was the primary target of this Internet abuse, the organization was not alone. Consumer advocacy groups and government agencies such as the U.S. Department of Justice and Britain's National Criminal Intelligence Service (NCIS) attempted to get the word out to the public. A spokesperson for NCIS told Reuters: "We were very quickly made aware of a number of scams after the attacks and were not surprised. These fraudsters typically exploit human misery. . . . They are without scruples because this is how they make money. It is very grubby money."[18]

The Red Cross and the Better Business Bureau both embarked on campaigns of public education. Within three days of the attack, both organizations issued press releases aimed at deterring criminals and educating prospective donors. They also spoke with reporters and posted warnings online.

The Red Cross went even further, launching an aggressive marketing campaign in an attempt to proactively curb further abuse by reaching donors directly. The advertisements successfully drove donors to the correct channels, assuring that the funds did not fall into the wrong hands.

More than $1 billion in donations were made in the six weeks following the September 11 terrorist acts, and an estimated 15 percent to 25 percent of these donations were made online.[19] The Red Cross experience highlights the fact that brand owners need to be especially vigilant when there is money on the line. The anthrax scare further illustrated the potential for Internet fraud when various parties used Bayer Corporation's Cipro brand to prey on public fears and perpetrate another round of online scams.

Monitoring Partners

Evaluation of your partner sites is an essential component in understanding the overall online experience of your customers in association with your brand. Even if you don't maintain an online presence, your customers are probably going online and being exposed to your brand in some fashion. Oftentimes customers have significant interaction with your partners. Here is a step-by-step process for addressing the potential for brand abuse in online partner networks.

Step 1: Prioritization

Depending on the level of resources you have to dedicate to monitoring online networks, the first step will be to prioritize your efforts. Getting the best return on your monitoring efforts means spending time where you'll have the greatest impact.

If your business maintains a website, a good first step is to examine the server logs to see where most of your traffic originates from. If you use an affiliate program, for example, it is common for a relatively small percentage of affiliates to generate the bulk of your site traffic, so you'll want to focus your efforts on these partners. Here are other ideas to help you prioritize your time:

> ➤ Prioritize your largest partners, since these are often the relationships where you have the most to lose.

➤ Give higher priority to partners that have high-profile brands of their own. They have more incentive to engage in practices to leverage the value of their brand at your expense.

➤ For supplier and affiliate networks, monitor how conversion rates vary from different referral sources. High traffic and low conversion rates, for example, may indicate that visitors are being lured in an unauthorized fashion.

➤ Monitor referrals over time. Fluctuations up or down are worth investigating and may uncover both violations and best practices.

➤ Prioritize partners that you know are shared with your competitors. The websites of these partners are most likely to be the "battleground" where market share is won and lost because customers will use these sites to make decisions leading to an ultimate purchase.

➤ Periodically attempt to search for your brand name using search engines. It would be worthwhile to review the practices of any partners that show up frequently in the search returns, to evaluate the extent to which they are using your brand.

➤ Look for inconsistencies with what's happening offline. For example, if your largest supplier for your brick-and-mortar outlets isn't referring you traffic online, it may be a good idea to investigate why.

➤ Pay close attention to "problem" partners. If you've had compliance issues in the past—either online or offline—these partners are more likely to be repeat offenders.

Step 2: Brand Management

Once you have assessed the nature and scope of any partner issues, you must proactively manage your brand presence on partner sites. This means going beyond monitoring your partners' sites for compliance with your guidelines and policies; it means developing an offensive strategy to prepare for future competitive assaults and take advantage of competitor lack of attention or weakness.

One of the first steps is to carefully craft and communicate partner policies and guidelines. It's also advisable to proactively fill the demand for brand-related content and functionality—provide partners with regular updates of approved content, logos, colors, links, etc. to make sure they support the desired customer experience.

Guidelines are necessary and should be established and maintained in a living document. Lessons learned while monitoring partner networks should be incorporated into guidelines for the future. Just as important as the guidelines are how effectively they are communicated and supported. For example, requiring your partners to use a specific-format logo is much easier if a communication channel is already established and tools are available for the partners to easily download the newest version.

Step 3: Enforcement

Finally, guidelines don't do much if they are not monitored and enforced. Ultimately, partner decisions are driven by practical evaluation of costs and benefits. The incentive for compliance (or the cost of noncompliance) needs to outweigh the benefits a partner gets through other options. For example, if you know that a partner stands to generate more revenue by failing to accurately disclose the terms of a promotion, it is important that the partner realize that any noncompliance is likely to be detected, and that the penalty for the offense is severe.

THE BUSINESS CASE

Well-managed partner networks can serve as ambassadors of the brand and may be an effective way to extend brand reach. Partner networks may be the only exposure customers have to a brand, or they may be leveraged for discrete elements of the online customer experience, such as the upfront research or processing the purchase transaction. In either case, when customers encounter your brand as depicted by others, there is an implicit association. Even when your partners' websites comprise just a part of the overall customer experience, they can play a significant role in influencing brand image and the customer decision-making process, which can work to your favor or detriment.

When considering the impact partner noncompliance with corporate guidelines can have on your company's revenue, there are a multitude of factors to examine. They include the popularity of the brand, the size of the network, the strength of the partner's own brands, the degree to which the products or services are researched online, and numerous other factors, depending on the specific situation.

Example One

An auto manufacturer has discovered that 50 percent of its 1,500 online dealerships are not complying with the guidelines and policies it has established.

The most common noncompliance problems include displaying competitive content, engaging in customer diversion tactics such as cybersquatting, and failing to fix broken links to the manufacturer's site. Some of the dealers are actually leveraging the auto manufacturer's brands to attract site traffic and then selling advertising to competitors.

Studies show that most new car buyers research their purchases online. While each noncompliance issue can disrupt the customer experience and hurt revenue, the following calculation illustrates how one factor in particular, competitive content, can contribute to lost sales.

Step	Assumption
1	Number of dealers displaying competitive content: 50
2	Average number of monthly competitive impressions per site: 20,000
3	Percentage of customers who click through to competitive site: 1%
4	Conversion rate of customers who click through: 0.5%
5	Total number of customers lost = (1) x (2) x 12 x (3) x (4) = 600
6	Average value of a customer: $20,000
7	Total annual cost = (5) x (6) = $12,000,000

Example Two

Retailer A has 10,000 partners in its affiliate program. Affiliates get commissions for all the customers who visit the affiliate site first, then click through to the retailer's site and conduct a transaction. Retailer B, a head-to-head competitor, offers a similar program and shares many of the same affiliates, but it launched a plan to take market share by paying out higher commissions.

A number of popular affiliates decide to take advantage of their status as partners to boost their commissions from Retailer B. These affiliates prominently display Retailer A's brand to draw more traffic. Then they alter many of the logos and links to Retailer A on their site so they actually lead users to Retailer B. In this manner, the affiliates leverage the brand equity of Retailer A to divert customers and increase their referral fees from Retailer B. To calculate what this practice may cost Retailer A in lost customer sales over the course of a year, you can apply the following assumptions:

Step	Assumption
1	Number of affiliates abusing brand: 100
2	Average number of monthly unique visitors to affiliate site: 50,000
3	Total potential customer exposures per year = (1) × (2) × 12 = 60,000,000

4   Percentage of buyers diverted to competitor = 2%
5   Conversion rate at competitor site = 2%
6   Total number of customers lost = (3) × (4) × (5) = 24,000
7   Average lifetime value of a customer: $400
8   Total annual cost = (6) x (7) = $9,600,000

As with most customer diversion tactics, this deceptive approach would never be tolerated offline. It could be considered the equivalent of a corner hardware store hanging a sign outside that says THE HOME DEPOT. Once inside, however, the customer realizes it's not actually The Home Depot you are thinking of—it's a competitor.

THE BOARD ROOM SUMMARY

Partner roles are changing online. Partner networks offer opportunities to extend brand reach and acquire new customers. Left unmanaged, however, online partner networks can sometimes undermine the customer experience and destroy brand equity. Be aware of the following:

➤ The online environment has added another layer of complexity to the dynamics of partner relationships.

➤ Channel conflict and new revenue models have resulted in extremely high levels of noncompliance among partner networks.

➤ Because there is a strong incentive for third parties to claim affiliation with a powerful brand, partner issues can extend beyond companies with official relationships.

➤ Brand abuse and partner noncompliance issues can cost a company millions of dollars each year, even for companies that don't do business online.

➤ Carefully managed, partner networks offer the opportunity to strengthen a brand, improve the customer experience, and gain market share.

Chapter 5

Counterfeits and Gray Markets

W hile the Internet has opened up valuable new distribution opportunities for many companies, in some cases it has resulted in a loss of
control. The same characteristics of the Internet that make it appealing—global
reach and accessibility—have given rise to "gray markets" and the sale of counterfeits. Gray markets exist when branded products are diverted from normal
or authorized distribution channels. Conventional distribution channels are
challenging enough to protect; since online gray markets and counterfeit issues
are less understood, they can be even more difficult for companies to wrap
their arms around.

An organization's online distributors (like its physical stores) are likely to
comprise the bulk of the customer experience. How a brand is represented and
its products or services distributed online will have an increasingly significant
influence on margins, market share, and brand image. When branded products
are counterfeit or sold illegally, the customer's experience and company revenues are undermined.

Counterfeit and gray market goods are widely distributed online and include everything from cigars and golf balls to auto parts and cosmetics. Various
factors—antiquated regulatory and enforcement systems, the impact of global-
ization, and a lack of corporate vigilance—have resulted in an online environment where counterfeiting crimes go largely unpunished, all but ensuring that
the Internet will comprise a disproportionately large share of industry's losses.

Not only are there branding problems and financial implications of such sales, but customer safety can be put in danger as well. A leading helmet manufacturer, for example, came to the realization that it had a severe gray market problem—hundreds of vendors were selling its products online, a practice that the manufacturer strictly prohibits for safety reasons. The ensuing concern centered not on revenue leakage, but rather the protection of its customers. In this instance, the helmet manufacturer's safety guarantee cannot be upheld unless approved dealers properly fit the helmet for each individual consumer. In addition to endangering lives, these unauthorized online sales violate the terms of distribution agreements, cannibalize sales of dealers who follow the rules, and expose the manufacturer to potential liability issues.

Gray Markets

When products are delivered through approved distribution channels, companies are able to protect their brands by ensuring the appropriate levels of quality, service, and support. Unfortunately, products sometimes make their way to the consumer through unauthorized means, often referred to as gray markets.

Nortel Networks' website defines gray marketing as "new . . . products being sold by unauthorized resellers and/or authorized business partners in violation of their distribution agreements, i.e., selling to unauthorized resellers or selling outside their authorized territories."[1]

Product diversion or gray marketing can happen within the country of product origin or across international borders, and the expansive reach of digital networks has exacerbated the problem. It can also involve the distribution of products through unintended channels, such as the sale of institutional products to the consumer market.

In cases where the unauthorized sales activity is done for tax evasion or is illegal in nature, it is referred to as the "black market." Gray and black marketing costs brand holders and product manufacturers billions of dollars every year in lost sales, unauthorized returns, and lost control of product distribution.[2] Almost always, gray and black market products are sold at a lower price than is offered by an authorized dealer (see Figures 5-1 and 5-2).

An example of a popular target for gray and black marketers is infant formula—which further demonstrates that online criminals will target any conceivable market where there is money to be made. The FBI says that the theft of powdered formula is a multimillion-dollar business for international crime organizations, which repackage the powder.[3] New labels are affixed to the product to make the formula appear to be a more expensive variety or to change the expiration date, putting babies at risk.

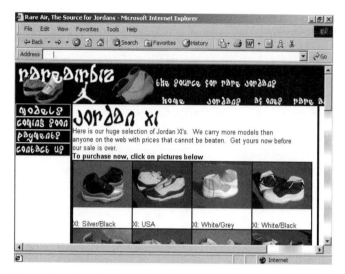

Figure 5-1. *Unauthorized site uses Nike logos and sells low-price "factory variants."*

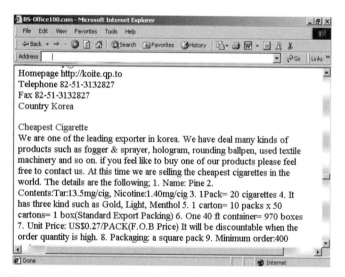

Figure 5-2. *Korean exporter offers to ship miscellaneous products abroad, including cigarettes for $0.27 per pack.*

In one instance, law enforcement officials seized more than 60,000 cans of stolen infant formula in Texas. Some of the expiration dates had been replaced, then the formula was repackaged in counterfeit cases and shipped to large northern cities for distribution.[4] Often such gray and black market infant formula ends up being sold over the Internet by merchants and on auction sites.

Baby formula manufacturers must also combat the online sale of institutional product to consumers. Diversion of lower-price institutional products to the consumer channel undermines price points and can result in millions of dollars in lost revenue.

Combating Gray Market Activity

The Anti-Gray Market Alliance (AGMA), an industry group formed to help address the unauthorized distribution problem, suggests that companies take several actions to combat gray markets:[5]

> Put internal controls in place to protect against products leaking to the gray market

> Educate sales force personnel to look for red flags when making initial sales

> Educate services and warranty personnel on what to look for in substandard product

> Educate distribution channels about the corrosive impact of gray market practices

HEWLETT-PACKARD COMPANY

High-profile brands that are victims of gray market abuse, such as Compaq Computer (now Hewlett-Packard Company), have taken their fight against gray markets even further by promoting their efforts on their websites to discourage criminals. In addition to working closely with industry organizations such as AGMA and the Information Technology Association of America, Compaq launched a number of proactive, internal initiatives. For example, it set up a "Cross Border Office" within its worldwide sales and marketing division in an effort to improve customer relationships. The office is dedicated specifically to stopping Compaq's products from being resold on the gray market.

Compaq also established a Gray Market Code of Conduct for all of its employees, and it educates employees worldwide of the risks associated with gray marketing. Internal sales policies and practices are designed to minimize flow of gray market product, while a Partner Awareness Program aims to raise awareness among Compaq's business partners regarding the risks and implications associated with participation in gray marketing.

Part of any effective effort to curb gray market activity is to make sure there are adequate deterrents in place. Compaq disciplines or terminates employees who have been a party to gray market deals. The computer maker also threatens to de-authorize resellers found to be illicitly brokering products, and to pursue legal action in cases where contracts or laws are violated.

"Compaq is committed to maintaining the integrity of its products and the high levels of product quality and service that our customers have come to expect," said Compaq senior vice president and general counsel Thomas C. Siekman in the wake of a search-and-seizure operation conducted in cooperation with U.S. Marshals. "Companies or individuals who would attempt to counterfeit Compaq products—or illegally divert Compaq products through gray market activities—will be held accountable. We will continue to protect our customers, our authorized sales channel partners, and the Compaq brand. . . ."[6] Criminals beware.

Counterfeiting

While the issues created by gray markets can be problematic, the distribution of counterfeits can be even more damaging to a brand. Reconnaissance International, a publishing/consulting firm, estimates that counterfeiting worldwide is a $500 billion problem, and the proceeds from counterfeiting have been shown to fund criminal organizations and underwrite terrorism.[7]

"What you can see in brand damage is just the tip of the iceberg," says a spokesperson for New Balance Athletic Shoe Inc., which has taken action to stop product counterfeiting. "The longer a marketer lets it run, the more the damage accelerates."[8]

Beyond the near-term revenue and profit losses are the longer-term consequences of lost brand loyalty among both customers and authorized dealers. Customers are exposed to the low quality of fake products. Resellers not only have to compete with illegal products, but they are also called upon by the customers to correct problems caused by the counterfeits.

Tommy Hilfiger Corp., Polo Ralph Lauren Corp., and Nike, Inc. all struggle with an ongoing battle against counterfeiting of their brand apparel. The three manufacturers joined forces in a lawsuit filed against Visionary Content Management, which allegedly sold counterfeit Tommy Hilfiger, Polo Ralph Lauren, and Nike brand products on its DesignersDirect.com website. In addition to seeking monetary damages, the manufacturers asked the court to permanently ban Visionary Content Management from the unauthorized use of their trademarks.

"Tommy Hilfiger, Polo Ralph Lauren, and Nike continue to be very vigilant in their efforts to protect the integrity of their brands, particularly on the Internet, where a number of unauthorized sellers who do not buy 'direct' from these 'designers' continue to offer counterfeit merchandise to unsuspecting consumers" said Steven Gursky, counsel for the plaintiffs.[9]

Copier Supplies

Meanwhile, companies like Xerox Corporation and Lexmark International wage a battle against the online distribution of counterfeit copier supplies. A survey done by the Imaging Supplies Coalition, a trade association for manufacturers of imaging equipment and supplies, estimated the impact of counterfeit toner, inks, cartridges, and other copier supplies to be more than $1 billion annually worldwide.[10]

In May 2000, Lexmark filed suit against EFAM Enterprises in New York seeking a permanent injunction and damages of $6 million. U.S. Customs seized more than 2,000 counterfeit toner cartridges imported by EFAM that were labeled with unauthorized reproductions of Lexmark's trademarks. "We will aggressively pursue those who attempt to sell counterfeit Lexmark products," said Paul Curlander, Lexmark's chairman and CEO. "This activity misleads our customers and damages the equity we have built in our brand."[11]

Lexmark competitor Xerox has faced the same challenges. "Counterfeiting damages our reputation and brand in our customers' eyes," said Kamalakar Shenai, vice president of Xerox's imaging supplies business. "We do everything we can to protect customer satisfaction and Xerox brand equity." In its efforts to address the issue, Xerox audits the Internet to uncover imposter sites and eliminate illegal use of Xerox brand supplies.[12]

"Stepping up our online surveillance complements Xerox's overall strategy to aggressively protect its brand, wherever it appears. More important, this further helps us protect Xerox customers who expect that when they purchase Xerox-branded products and supplies, they also purchase genuine Xerox quality," said Donna Del Monte, manager, consumables strategy, Xerox Supplies Group.[13]

For its aggressive approach to online monitoring and other management initiatives to combat distribution of counterfeit toner and consumable products, Xerox received an award in 2002 for "outstanding achievement by a company" from *Authentication News*, an industry publication, and the Global Anti-Counterfeiting Group.

Pharmaceuticals

The pharmaceutical industry offers another good example of how the online distribution of counterfeits can affect business in the twenty-first century. Consumers are increasingly replacing a trip to the pharmacy with a more convenient click on the Internet, where they find websites offering impressive variety and availability, competitive prices, and a positive customer experience.

In today's highly competitive environment, online pharmacies are attracting new customers by offering convenience and a sense of privacy that's difficult to achieve at a local drugstore. Unfortunately, the Internet is also a burgeoning channel for the distribution of counterfeit drugs. The World Health Organization estimates that 10 percent of the world's medicines are forgeries, resulting in revenue losses to the pharmaceutical industry of tens of billions of dollars annually.[14]

> *"With the introduction of Internet sites selling prescription drugs with almost no regulatory framework, the environment and the incentive for using fake drugs, making fake drugs, and selling them directly to consumers is obvious."*
>
> —Rep. John Dingell, U.S. House of Representatives[15]

With the number of consumers purchasing prescription and nonprescription drugs online rapidly increasing, the cost of genuine pharmaceuticals rising, and the sophistication of counterfeit production and distribution growing, the availability of counterfeit pharmaceuticals online is poised to skyrocket beyond the already-alarming rates. Government agencies and global organizations such as the International Chamber of Commerce (ICC) have recognized the scale and urgency of the dangers associated with the online distribution of counterfeit pharmaceuticals.

Online Monitoring

To successfully combat gray markets and counterfeiting in the new millennium, a company must develop and maintain a comprehensive, multidimensional strategy that includes the Internet as a core component. With so many pages of content on the Internet, it can be a daunting task to identify, analyze, and prioritize online distributors.

Depending on the nature of the product, there can be thousands of potential outlets. Suspect transactions are routinely made through commercial websites, personal web pages, auction sites, Usenet newsgroups, Internet Relay Chat (IRC) channels, and e-mail.

Given the breadth and complicated nature of the problem, the challenge then becomes identifying the distributors and prioritizing efforts to achieve the greatest impact with limited resources. Although manual searching can be inefficient, when coupled with other strategies, it can sometimes be the best approach for small companies. For major, consumer-facing drug brands where there is more at stake, a more expensive but thorough Internet monitoring solution may make sense. Proprietary data mining and analysis technologies are commercially available that can be programmed specifically to monitor for suspect distributors.

To indicate how broad the scope of the issue can be, the U.S. Food and Drug Administration (FDA) devoted more than 10,000 staff-hours per month to investigate Internet sites for online distribution of counterfeit pharmaceuticals.[16] Once suspected perpetrators are identified, there remains the considerable task of confirming that the site is engaged in distributing gray market or counterfeit products.

The effort can be complicated by the fact that sites engaged in improper distribution activities are more apt to employ tactics similar to those used in the porn industry that cast an even broader net and hinder enforcement efforts. For example, single sites may lie at the hub of dozens of other redirect sites, or they may be one of many "mirror" (duplicate) sites. Such networks may be erected specifically to elude authorities or to fool search engines and divert customers.

Criteria That May Signal a Suspect Distributor

The good news is that the use of these questionable tactics and the presence of certain content can provide an indication that a site is engaged in suspicious activity. Searching for specific clues that indicate a site is more likely to engage in suspect activity is an effective way to prioritize follow-on investigative efforts. With limited resources, it is wise to target enforcement activities on the most suspicious sites. Here are some criteria that may signal that an online distributor is suspect:

➤ Product is offered below cost or at unreasonably low prices.

➤ Inadequate, misleading, or false product descriptions are given.

➤ There is no return policy or warranty information.

➤ The website is not a registered domain but part of a larger community, such as personal pages hosted by an Internet service provider.

➤ The site uses jargon and vernacular only people "inside" the industry will understand.

➤ The site uses overly aggressive capture tactics more common to the porn industry, such as redirecting, seeding, typo-piracy, "mirror sites," mouse-trapping, or spawning (see Figure 5-3).

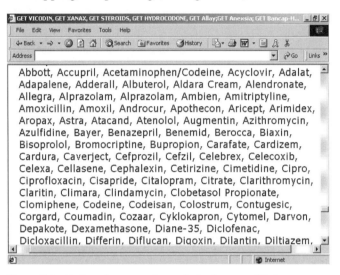

Figure 5-3. *Online pharmacy site seeds the bottom of its home page with brand names to attract customers.*

➤ The site doesn't offer a secure transaction capability or doesn't have a stated privacy policy.

➤ The site advertises miraculous or "amazing" results.

➤ The site is based outside of the country whose customers are targeted by the site.

➤ Misspellings or derivatives of the proper brand name are evident.

➤ The site does not provide a domestic address and phone number for customer service, or contact information does not match the site registration information.

PHARMACY INTERNATIONAL, INC.

An online pharmacy called Pharmacy International, Inc. spammed Usenet newsgroups with messages in an attempt to drive traffic to the site. The messages promoted instant purchases with "no prescription required" and attempted to prey on public fear by promoting the availability of drugs to treat anthrax (see Figure 5-4). In addition to using questionable customer acquisition tactics, there were other warning signs. Among them:

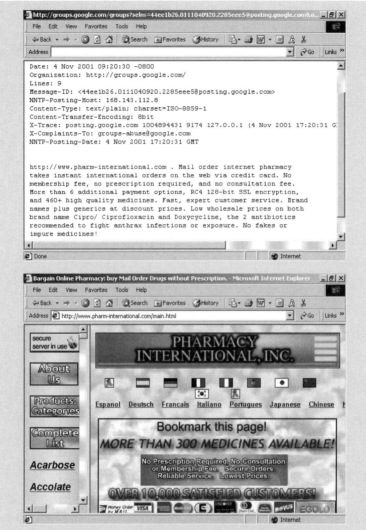

Figure 5-4. *Online pharmacy exhibits traits that make it suspect, such as use of spam and claiming "no prescription required."*

➤ No contact information other than e-mail

➤ Absence of a stated privacy policy

➤ Low prices

➤ Claim that "no prescription required"

➤ Targeting consumers outside of the site's base operation in Kuala Lumpur

Review and prioritization of suspect distributors based on these and other industry-specific criteria is the most efficient and effective way to get the best return on your investment in enforcement. Enhancing your efforts with technology can further help to flag suspicious sites for investigative action (see Chapter 9).

Hint: Companies may be able to find examples of unauthorized distribution by using free online shopping search tools such as Froogle.com, whose advanced search features include the ability to confine results to a user-defined price range.

Testing Authenticity

Once the suspect online distributor is identified, analyzed, and prioritized, the remaining steps are to acquire, test, and validate the product's authenticity. In cases where an agency, association, or company is ordering from a suspect online distributor, it is to the investigator's advantage to use a post office box or other disguised address to reduce the chance the online perpetrator may recognize the investigator.

After a sample of the suspect product is obtained, the authenticity must be tested. Overt protection devices such as holograms and tamper seals are one measure of authenticity. Best practices for managing the counterfeit problem also include forensic fingerprinting—or embedding hidden "markers" within the product. Depending on your needs, these kinds of anticounterfeiting solutions can be outsourced to companies that have the resident expertise and experience necessary to effectively manage covert marking and product authentication.

Even as enforcement becomes more aggressive, thwarting online distribution abuses is difficult at best. Unlike street vendors, who tend to congregate in certain areas, Internet-based distributors are scattered around cyberspace and range from organized, sophisticated merchants to shady manufacturers to school kids operating out of a basement. Further complicating efforts is the possibility that when a site is shut down, it might soon reappear somewhere else.

Identifying, analyzing, and prioritizing online gray market and counterfeit distributors is a substantial undertaking, as evidenced by the number of agencies and level of effort currently engaged in this pursuit. Yet there is a reason leading companies are attacking the problem. There is too much at stake, in terms of lost sales or lost brand equity, to ignore the problem. Companies that have devoted resources to confronting the issues are generally well rewarded for their efforts.

••••••••••••▶
THE BUSINESS CASE
••••••••••••▶

The risk to public well-being is clearly the greatest cost associated with the distribution of counterfeits online, as suspect websites circumvent established procedures meant to protect consumers. But even in cases where counterfeit sales do not pose safety threats, companies can incur significant costs as a result of lost sales and brand dilution. Media coverage of contaminated or counterfeit products can substantially undermine public trust and brand image, alienating customers and weakening revenues for years to come.

The sale of counterfeits also dilutes the revenue of other businesses in the value chain and threatens to undermine relationships with legitimate distributors. There is an expectation that manufacturers will proactively maintain the integrity of their distribution channels. If companies do not exercise reasonable precaution against counterfeiting, they may also expose themselves to liability or even run afoul of the law.

"Increasingly, manufacturers will be required by law enforcement agencies to exercise due diligence in protecting their products from being copied," predicts Peter Lowe, assistant director of the ICC's Counterfeiting Intelligence Bureau. In advising brand owners to be on the constant lookout for ways to protect their products, he states "manufacturers cannot afford to sit back and expect to avoid becoming victims of counterfeiting."[17]

Example

A golf ball manufacturer has discovered that large volumes of counterfeit balls are being sold online. The golf balls are wrapped in imitation packaging and marked with the manufacturer's brand. The premium balls typically retail for about $40 a dozen, though the counterfeits are being sold for $24. The counterfeiters are distributing high volumes of golf balls through a wide range of online channels, including auctions and e-commerce sites. Most of the sites are operated out of developing countries and the products are shipped abroad. We can estimate how much revenue the manufacturer is losing by using the following step-by-step assumptions and calculation:

Step	Assumption
1	Number of sites where balls are sold: 50
2	Average quantity of boxes sold daily on each site: 15

3   Total boxes sold on e-commerce sites per year $= (1) \times (2) \times 365$ $\cong 274,000$

4   Annual lost revenue to online counterfeits $= (3) \times \$40 \cong \$11$ million

---

THE BOARD ROOM SUMMARY

Unauthorized online distribution, including gray market activity and counterfeiting, can undermine profits, destroy brand equity, and even endanger the well-being of customers. The key points that brand owners must remember are these:

➤ Maintaining the integrity of your distribution channels allows you to ensure the appropriate levels of quality, service, and support.

➤ Counterfeiting and gray marketing undermine your authorized dealer relationships by forcing them to compete with bogus products and to service customers who purchased the diverted or bogus products.

➤ To combat gray markets and counterfeiting, a company must develop and maintain a comprehensive, multidimensional strategy that includes the Internet as a core component.

➤ Best practices exist to help companies prioritize their online monitoring and enforcement efforts.

➤ The benefits associated with defending a brand against counterfeiting and gray markets usually outweigh the costs.

Chapter 6

Defending Against Digital Piracy

Digital technology and the Internet have increased the ease with which high-quality graphics, text, audio, video, and software can be copied and widely distributed. As a result, vast repositories of branded digital content are now only a click away—books, movies, music, stock quotes, and computer games—all free for the taking. What does this mean? If your value proposition centers around digital assets, copyright issues pose an unprecedented business threat. Piracy has the potential to completely undermine the integrity of your distribution channels.

"The explosive growth of Internet users has spawned an equally explosive growth of Internet abusers," said Brent Renouf, Canadian counterfeit investigator at Microsoft Canada. "Cybersavvy criminals increasingly use the speed and anonymity of the Internet to sell and distribute counterfeit software, music, and videos worldwide. The potential revenue losses to legitimate businesses are enormous."[1]

Piracy has long been a problem for those in the content business, but the scope of the current situation is unparalleled in history. A few simple queries on a leading peer-to-peer (P2P) file-sharing network should effectively put to rest any doubts about the magnitude of the situation. P2P networks place everything from *Seinfeld* episodes to your favorite Beatles soundtracks at your fingertips. Anybody who wants to can easily download, usually for free, digital print and audio versions of best-selling books, music, or your choice of the newest movies—often before they hit the theaters!

The convenience is unprecedented, as is the quality, speed, and nearly unlimited prospects for dissemination. Consumer adoption rates reflect the added value and convenience—studies show that more than half of all Internet users have downloaded music, for example.[2] Over half of Americans use streaming media, too, according to the Cable and Telecommunications Association for Marketing. There is no easy solution in sight as ever-improving technologies (e.g., compression techniques, broadband networks, file-sharing services) and demographic trends further exacerbate digital piracy issues and hinder enforcement efforts.

The problem is complex and poses a daunting challenge for intellectual property owners. Beyond the World Wide Web, there are numerous online environments where piracy occurs, including e-mail groups, chat rooms, instant messaging sessions, auctions, file-sharing networks, binary newsgroups, and file transfer protocol (FTP) sites. There is also a multitude of enabling technologies and practices, including the "framing" of web content, in-lining, and password sharing, that make it easy to duplicate and distribute digital content.

Companies are struggling to manage piracy with varying degrees of success. Depending on the specific situation, it is sometimes possible to proactively prevent revenue leakage by identifying unauthorized use and distribution of digital assets. When pirated content is distributed via websites, for example, some companies and industry associations have not only recouped "lost" revenues, but they've even added incremental revenue streams by turning these content distributors into licensees.

Music

The music industry has the dubious distinction of being the digital piracy guinea pig. It is one of the first industries to come face-to-face with the Internet's ability to undermine the integrity of more conventional distribution channels. The preponderance of downloadable music available online from services such as KaZaa, BearShare, and Morpheus (see Figure 6-1), among others, has given rise to vehement controversy over copyright issues and resulted in a seemingly never-ending series of highly publicized legal battles.

There is clearly a lot at stake as music piracy continues to proliferate online, though financial estimates vary widely. In the courts, the Recording Industry Association of America (RIAA) claimed $150,000 per copyrighted work in damages from MP3.com for allowing users to download copyright-protected

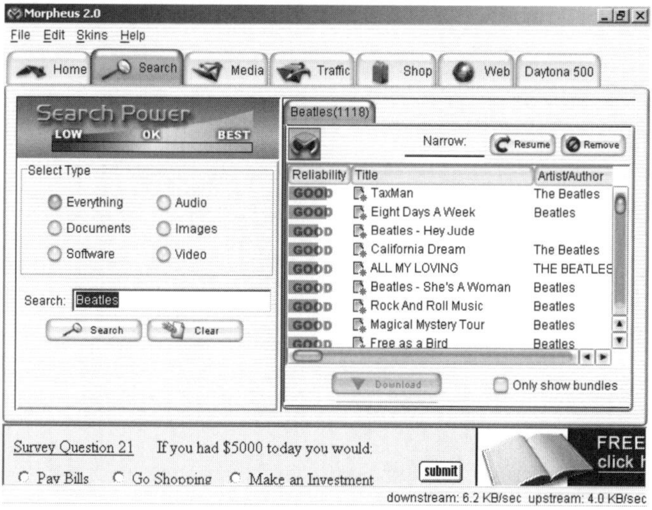

Figure 6-1. *A Morpheus search for the Beatles yields more than 1,100 results.*

songs.[3] In another highly publicized legal battle, heavy-metal band Metallica sued Napster for damages of more than $10 million, placing the value at $100,000 for each pirated song.[4]

RIAA cited online piracy as a major factor when total annual U.S. shipments from record companies dropped more than 10 percent in 2001, representing a dollar value decrease of about $600 million. "When 23 percent of surveyed music consumers say they are not buying more music because they are downloading or copying their music for free, we cannot ignore the impact on the marketplace," said Hilary Rosen, CEO of the RIAA, in reference to a study conducted by Peter Hart Research Associates.[5]

During the same time period, music sales fell five percent on a global level to $33.7 billion. Though the economy was at least partially to blame, the International Federation of the Phonographic Industry (IFPI) attributed much of the drop-off to the proliferation of free music on the Internet. "The industry's problems reflect no fall in popularity of recorded music. Rather, they reflect the fact that the commercial value of music is being widely devalued by mass copying and piracy," said Jay Berman, IFPI chairman and CEO.[6]

On the opposite end of the spectrum, some people claim the net effects are positive, arguing that the increased accessibility of music files is a convenience people will be willing to pay for, which will help drive growth in music sales, both offline and online. Sales of portable digital music players (see Figure 6-2) are one indicator of the growing consumer demand for digital music downloads, which could bode well for the future revenue potential of online music subscriptions. "Digital music subscriptions have the potential to revive the

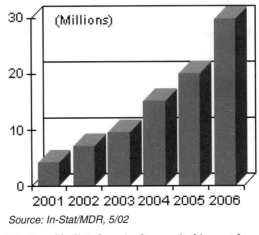

Source: In-Stat/MDR, 5/02

Figure 6-2. *Portable digital music player unit shipment forecast.*
Includes solid state and revolving media products.

flagging music industry," said Aram Sinnreich, Jupiter Research senior analyst.[7]

While such optimistic forecasts may eventually prove true, most people are
still not paying for the music they download, and organizations with the most
at stake have decided not to leave things to chance. Coalitions within the music
industry have approached the piracy situation by attempting to control the
unauthorized downloading of artists' works while at the same time partnering
with new online distribution channels.

Some industry leaders have resorted to legal action to eliminate providers
that facilitate free music distribution, as seen in the legal suits that arose against
Napster and MP3.com by the major record labels. This may be the only recourse for some intellectual property owners to combat free distribution on
peer-to-peer (P2P) file-sharing networks.

Sales Leads

Web and FTP sites distributing pirated music have offered other possibilities.
Music industry associations such as the American Society of Composers, Authors, and Publishers (ASCAP) and Broadcast Music, Inc. (BMI) have capital-
ized on the opportunities afforded by the transfer of music online by
aggressively licensing sites on the Internet that offer the music of their members. In so doing, these associations have taken the first steps in positioning
themselves to capture a share of the billions of dollars in projected online
music revenues.

This proactive licensing approach is similar to how intellectual property owners of market data and text take the offensive online to generate revenue. Historically, the best return on this investment in converting offenders into licensing sales is achieved by focusing on the most highly qualified leads, enabling the association to take action quickly on websites that are the most likely to help them recapture licensing revenues. Any site unwilling to be licensed, and any sites that may be undesirable licensees, should be dealt with through legal action to protect copyrights and safeguard legitimate distribution channels (Chapter 10 outlines the steps for launching an aggressive plan of attack).

One way of evaluating whether websites engaged in piracy may be suitable licensees is to estimate how many licensable music files are present and whether music files are sound clips, full-length songs, program files, or streaming files. Site traffic levels can also be valuable in approximating the potential scale of distribution and, in the case of sites that engage in advertising or commerce, how much revenue they might be generating as a result of music distribution.

A site's ability to pay licensing fees can vary widely and should be considered when applying limited sales resources to pursue large volumes of leads. In addition to assessing a website's traffic levels, other ways to make a rough evaluation of the site's potential include checking for the presence of advertising or commercial activities and noting the level of professionalism evident in the site design.

Larger businesses are better sales targets, so the presence of investor information and other company details can be an indicator of size. Whether the site owns its own domain (as opposed to using personal pages whose root domain is part of a larger community such as AOL or Yahoo!) is another indicator of the commercial potential of the website.

ASCAP

Prioritization of licensing opportunities is the approach that the American Society of Composers, Authors, and Publishers has used to pursue online leads and generate incremental revenues. Since ASCAP represents more than 120,000 artists, the organization engaged a vendor to support its online monitoring efforts. Harnessing proprietary technology tools allowed ASCAP to successfully "pursue music performance licenses from top-tier Internet sites that are offering our members' work on their sites," said Chris Amenita, an ASCAP spokesperson. "This has allowed us to license over 1,700 sites, more than any other rights organization in the world, and take full advantage of revenue opportunities while protecting our members' rights on the Internet."[8]

Unfortunately, while the music and recording industry is coming to grips with web distribution issues, it faces an ongoing battle tackling other environments. Billions of music files are now swapped every month using popular P2P file-trading networks that enable the exchange and download of copyrighted music for free. P2P networks provide a forum for individuals to openly and anonymously share digital files, and it's proving to be a difficult nut to crack.

Decentralized P2P networks such as Gnutella and FastTrack have gained popularity, effectively turning members' home computers into network servers. Since these networks have no central point at which the system can be shut down, they pose a more complicated puzzle for rights associations than centralized networks like Napster, whose servers stored an index of available songs. Appendix D provides additional background on the different frameworks for P2P networks.

Video

Online video piracy has lagged behind music primarily because the large size of digital video files results in longer download times. This is not to say that the issue is new. As far back as 1999, for example, Lucasfilm Ltd. worked with outside counsel to help defend the movie *Star Wars: Episode I—The Phantom Menace* against online piracy during the weeks immediately preceding and following the public opening. They succeeded in shutting down more than 300 Internet sites offering pirated copies of the movie. Many of the sites were distributing copies even before the film opened in theaters. In addition to those that were shut down, hundreds of other individuals who were making the film available for download withdrew their copies voluntarily after receiving a warning.[9] The same phenomenon repeated itself in May 2002, when illegal copies of *Star Wars: Episode II—Attack of the Clones* appeared online a week before the scheduled release (see Figure 6-3).

On the positive side, the Lucasfilm marketing team took full advantage of the online demand for content and made promotional video trailers available for fans to download from the Star Wars website. Perhaps providing a glimpse of the future, more than 35 million copies of the *Phantom Menace* movie trailers were downloaded before the movie debuted. It is now cited on the Lucas-

Figure 6-3. *Copies of* Attack of the Clones *were available on Gnutella a week before the scheduled movie release.*

film website as one of the biggest Internet downloads in history. "The number of trailer downloads may have driven more people to the theater," said Jim Ward, Lucasfilm vice president of marketing. "But frankly, our primary goal is to keep as many people as possible engaged with the Star Wars brand for as long as possible."[10]

Despite the success of Lucasfilm's promotion, which was made possible by the small size of the clips, video downloads still faced technological constraints. More recently, though, advances in compression technology and access to higher-speed Internet connections through digital subscriber line (DSL) and cable modem services have dramatically accelerated movie trading. The forum for video piracy has also shifted to P2P and Internet Relay Chat (IRC) channels, or "chat rooms" (see Figure 6-4). Though still in its infancy, some estimates already peg daily feature film downloads at 600,000 per day.[11]

Video piracy runs the gamut from television shows and cartoons to music videos, but it's the multibillion-dollar movie industry that seems most concerned. While a downloaded movie may not be able to seriously compete with a customer's theater experience, this is not the biggest fear. Four-fifths of a typical film's revenue comes from sales after the release at the theater.[12] This includes video sales, rentals, and cable television revenues, all of which could be jeopardized by rampant online piracy.

With the knowledge of how things have unfolded in the music industry, movie studios are hedging their bets and attacking the issue on multiple fronts. In addition to taking selective legal action, the copyright owners have stepped

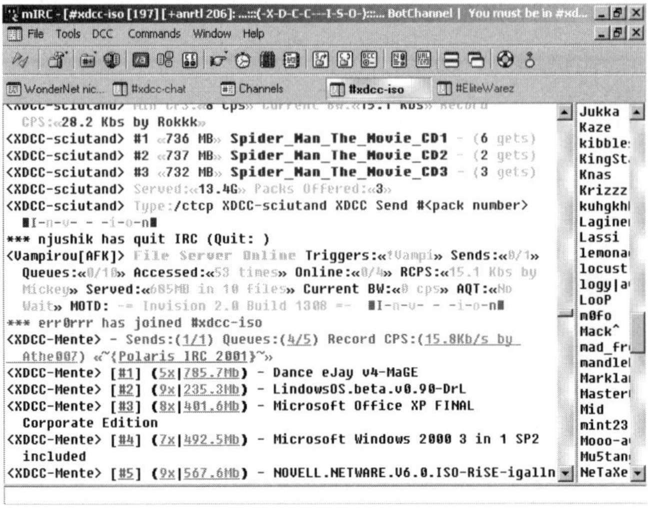

Figure 6-4. *Movies and other digital assets being shared on IRC.*

up lobbying efforts and are experimenting with encryption technologies and online distribution channels that generate revenue through licensing and/or subscription fees.

Cease and Desist

The approach to digital copyright infringements such as video piracy varies widely depending on the scope of the issue that the organization is attempting to manage. Rights organizations or industry associations, for example, may be dealing with millions of incidents of piracy over the course of a year on behalf of their members.

To keep the level of effort from spiraling out of control, these organizations often rely on proprietary technology for monitoring, prioritization, and work-flow management. The Motion Picture Association of America (MPAA), for example, contracts with a vendor that monitors for offenses and delivers incident reports using a tool that facilitates follow-up by automatically merging Internet service provider (ISP) contact information into letter templates. Some organizations process these communications in batches, though they are al-most always given a cursory review before being sent.

Organizations typically take action to have the incident remedied with the assistance of the offender's ISP under the provisions of the Digital Millennium Copyright Act or other regional legislation. As a result, the offender will often lose Internet access for a period of time. According to a 2003 court ruling, ISPs must abide by copyright holder requests to track down computer users who illegally download copyrighted material. The case arose from RIAA efforts to track down a Verizon customer who was sharing music files.[13]

Customer Convenience

Part of the reason that online file-sharing networks have attracted so many users is that they offer a higher level of value and convenience to users relative to conventional distribution methods. Customers have a tendency to adopt the practice that involves the least amount of effort on their part and generates the best results.

While online video downloads offer tremendous potential for customer convenience and flexibility, current file-sharing networks have a number of disadvantages. Historically, one of these has been the time to download. Movielink.com's website notes that depending on the size of the movie file and the user's connection speed, downloads can take 40 minutes or longer. Even with high-speed Internet connections, time to download remains an inconvenience today, albeit one that is diminishing. Customers tend to prefer instant fulfillment.

"Right now it's more difficult to download movies than music," notes David Kessler, director of France's National Cinematography Center. "In the future it will be just as easy."[14]

A second inconvenience is that users really have no sure way to tell what they are downloading until the download is complete—which may be hours later. And even when it's the correct movie, the freely distributed files are sometimes of substandard quality—copies made by someone in the theater filming the screen using a handheld video camera.

Finally, there may be technological deterrents in place that complicate the process. Rights owners have begun to examine ways to frustrate pirates using various techniques, such as launching mini "denial of service" attacks that lock up the servers offering the files for illegal download. Other rights owners endorse "spoofing," or flooding P2P networks with "decoys" of popular files that don't work.

In one of the first publicized cases of spoofing in the music industry, the band Barenaked Ladies released a number of tracks online in 2000 that appeared to be legitimate versions but contained a short sample of the song and a message from a band member stating, "Although you thought you were downloading our new single, what you actually were downloading is an advertisement for our new album."

Cary Sherman, president of RIAA, calls spoofing "an appropriate response to the problem of peer-to-peer piracy" and "a self-help measure that is completely lawful. . . . I think it would be crazy if record labels or motion picture studios or any other owners of content didn't take advantage of those kinds of measures."[15]

Many other intellectual property owners have experimented with digital watermarking or encryption. Copy protection technologies and digital rights management plans are one of the approaches pursued by the movie industry to help control the piracy problem.

Copy Protection and Digital Rights Management

Instead of going after online pirates, some have decided to protect their content by implementing copy protection technologies such as the incorporation of digital "watermarks." Others believe that the solution can be addressed by modifying interactive hardware such as computers and video recorders to render them incapable of replicating copyrighted material.

Jack Valenti, head of the Motion Picture Association of America, has stated that before legal copies of films will be available for anyone with fast connections to download online, strong copy protection technology will be necessary. "Once valuable works can be protected, broadband and the Internet will take off," said Valenti, but for now, "movies cannot flourish on the Internet because of thievery."[16]

Most people agree that copy protection and digital rights management plans may serve as a deterrent, but ways around them will always be found. No form of encryption is impenetrable. By the time a copy protection solution is rolled out, there is usually some kind of utility circulating online that allows pirates to crack it.

In a keynote address to attendees at the National Association of Broadcasters convention, Netscape cofounder Marc Andreessen said that efforts to copy-protect music, movies, or television shows are destined to fail. "If a computer can see it, display it, and play it—it can copy it," said Andreessen. He cited the software industry's expensive, failed attempts at encryption to support his argument that copy protection is ineffective.[17]

> "No one in history has succeeded in stopping technology. The transformation to digital media will happen with or without Hollywood's embrace."
> ——ANDY GROVE, CHAIRMAN OF INTEL CORP.[18]

But this doesn't mean the industry shouldn't take steps to protect content, be it movies or any other digital asset. What companies or rights organizations need to evaluate is whether the investment in rolling out copy protection systems will create a substantial enough deterrent for people to seek content from legitimate sources. In other words, does the system cause enough of an inconvenience that customers prefer to seek the content through legal distribution channels?

It is even more important to recognize that there are two sides to this equation. "Piracy is often a symptom of inconvenience and lack of appropriate pricing," said Peter Chernin, president of NewsCorp.[19] Effective, sustainable solutions focus not only on deterrents but also on legal alternatives. The likelihood of any plan being successful is directly related to both the consequences of piracy and the convenience associated with other options available to the customer.

> *"Either content companies will find ways to embrace the Internet to offer customers greater value or their epitaph will read: 'They were morally right as the market turned left.'"*
>
> —ROB FIXMER, *Interactive Week*[20]

In a move to counter file-swapping services, five major movie studios—Sony Pictures, Paramount Pictures, Universal Studios, Warner Brothers, and Metro-Goldwyn-Mayer Studios—formed a joint venture called Movielink to provide video-on-demand services over the Internet encoded with digital rights management technology.

Predicted Valenti: "If you give people a legitimate alternative to stealing, they'll take that legitimate alternative." Valenti believes that the potential in online movie delivery is great enough to further fuel the move to high-speed Internet connections by creating a spike in consumer spending on broadband.[21]

Software

Though estimates vary widely, nobody can argue that software piracy is not big business—and it has been for years. The Internet has only exacerbated the problem. The growth in technology both online and offline has fueled a strong demand for software and created a thriving market for pirated wares, creating a global multibillion-dollar industry for criminals.

"Piracy is a huge issue—it is much bigger than people believe," said Julia Phillpot, antipiracy and licensing compliance manager at Microsoft."Official figures from the Business Software Alliance [of which Microsoft is a founder member] claim a quarter of software installations are from a copy, but it is more like 70 or 80 percent."[22]

The Internet makes distribution of pirated software more convenient than ever—users can now easily locate and purchase black market and gray market software products online. They can also download pirated versions of anything from popular video games to workplace utilities, all for free through P2P networks, FTP sites, and other online forums (see Figure 6-5). As a result, the software industry is confronted with the challenge of attacking piracy issues not unlike those in the film, music, and book industries.

Anne Kelley, a Microsoft corporate attorney, confirms that online distribution issues are substantial. In order to prioritize offenders, her department focuses primarily on filing cases against resellers. "The large resellers . . . the brick-and-mortar ones, we don't really have problems with. It's the online auction sites," she said. "When we do our test purchasing we find 90 percent of the product we obtain on the Internet is counterfeit."[23]

The Business Software Alliance (BSA) agrees with this assessment and characterizes mail-order piracy on the Internet as a serious threat to the software industry, accounting for an increasing portion of the estimated $11 billion in lost sales that software publishers suffer annually.

"As consumers increasingly shop for software online, the proliferation of vendors offering pirated products is of major concern to the industry," said Bob Kruger, vice president of enforcement for the Business Software Alliance. "BSA is working to stem this tide by bringing enforcement actions, educating consumers, and enlisting the assistance of auction site operators and Internet service providers."[24]

Taking action is complicated by the fact that offenders are located throughout the globe. Microsoft's campaign against Internet piracy and criminal counterfeiting has involved legal actions in numerous countries including Argentina, Brazil, Canada, Colombia, Germany, Hong Kong, Hungary, Macau, Malaysia, Peru, the Philippines, the People's Republic of China, Poland, Romania, Singapore, Taiwan, Thailand, Venezuela, the United Kingdom, and the United States.

The problem is particularly acute in Asia and Eastern Europe. Software publisher Adobe Systems has experienced so many problems in Asia that the company has announced that it may be necessary to stop producing Chinese and other Asian-language versions of Adobe products. While Adobe executives recognize the tremendous market potential in the region, the piracy rate in China is estimated to be more than 90 percent. In Vietnam, it's more than 95 percent. With only 5–10 percent of its software going to paying customers, it is hard for Adobe to get a good return on their investment.[25]

As software companies attack the problem individually, there are also broader efforts made by industry associations to provide tactical support as central coordinators between business, government, law enforcement, and the public. Examples include the BSA, the Software & Information Industry Asso-

Figure 6-5. *Adobe software programs being shared on a P2P network (LimeWire) and the Web.*

ciation (SIIA), and The Interactive Digital Software Association (IDSA), which is an industry association representing companies that publish video and computer games. Trade associations also provide education and training and lobby in support of policy and legislation that will help to deter piracy.

> *"Microsoft has put significant resources behind its global anticounterfeiting efforts. We're also working cooperatively with law enforcement agencies, industry partners, and business organizations to help protect consumers and bring counterfeiters to justice."*
>
> —MICROSOFT CORP. ANTIPIRACY STATEMENT[26]

AGFA MONOTYPE
CORPORATION

Agfa Monotype is the leading developer of fonts and type technologies. It has more than 3,000 fonts in its typeface collection, including some of the world's most recognizable fonts such as Arial and Times New Roman. The company markets its font software directly to consumers via the fonts.com website. It also licenses the fonts to computer software and hardware developers such as Adobe, Lexmark, and Microsoft.

Because font software can easily be duplicated and distributed, piracy poses a serious risk to Agfa Monotype. Left unmanaged, trademark and copyright infringements threaten to undermine the company's business model and dilute its trademarks.

Recognizing the critical need to protect its intellectual property, Agfa Monotype has taken an aggressive approach to online monitoring and the defense of its digital assets. "Agfa Monotype has a significant investment in its font collection," says Bill Davis, vice president, marketing. "We vigilantly protect our intellectual property."

At a high level, Agfa Monotype takes two approaches to defending its digital assets:

1. Monitoring online and offline environments for software and hardware products that use Agfa Monotype's fonts. These incidents represent licensing opportunities.

2. Monitoring the Internet for the unlicensed distribution of fonts. Agfa Monotype typically sends these offenders cease-and-desist letters.

Agfa Monotype works closely with Stack & Filpi, its Chicago-based law firm, to identify and stop all infringements of its copyrights and trademarks. The lawyers monitor the Internet for both font trademark names and font file names. In addition, Agfa Monotype's employees are on the constant lookout for products that may include its fonts without a proper license. Over the past decade, this approach has resulted in the discovery of, and remedies for, many infringements, both online and offline.

Agfa Monotype has identified hundreds of websites that were improperly redistributing the company's fonts. Many of these websites have free or shareware fonts and unknowingly posted the company's commercial fonts. These offenders are sent firm cease-and-desist letters requiring that the fonts be removed. When Agfa Monotype finds a company selling its fonts without a proper license, it typically takes a more aggressive stance and may threaten further legal action if the situation is not immediately remedied to its satisfaction.

Text and Images

Movies, music, and software aren't the only content up for grabs online. The Internet has opened new channels for the distribution of images and text-based content such as e-books and news and wire services. Through the use of the online channel, media and traditional news services have successfully increased the size of their customer bases, which allows them to leverage their content and capture new revenue streams. Unfortunately, the Internet has also made it easier for criminals to copy proprietary content and use it for their own profit.

Content is now more susceptible than ever to unauthorized use and broad distribution. News articles or a photograph, for example, can be replicated by simply copying and pasting. Basic coding can frame another site or in-line an image, serving it up from someone else's server and thereby consuming the content owner's bandwidth in addition to stealing its intellectual property.

E-Books

While electronic books are not as widely downloaded as music or videos, it is easy to find a pirated version of almost any popular book online. Publishers that take the threat seriously are monitoring the issue to gauge the severity of the problem.

Pirated books appear online in several different formats. Some are hacked versions of copy-protected e-books released by legitimate publishers and downloadable at booksellers like Amazon.com. Most are scanned versions of traditional paper books that have been converted into text or digital format. When in text format, e-books can then show up in standard HTML—usually on the Web or in newsgroups (i.e., Internet discussion groups that operate like a public e-mail in-box.)

The distribution of full versions of popular books in text format, however, is not prolific. What is much more common is for books to be distributed online as digital audio files, similar to music or video files. While the availability and location of the files is often discussed in e-mail groups or chat rooms, the files are readily found in similar environments as music or videos—P2P, IRC, and FTP (see Figure 6-6).

The environments where digital files are exchanged make the $7.1 billion college textbook market particularly vulnerable.[27] College students tend to be savvy Internet users and heavy users of P2P networks. With the average price of a textbook at nearly $70, purchasing textbooks for a typical semester's course load can be a costly proposition.[28] If students can get the content online for free on P2P networks, the "discount" can outweigh other considerations.

Figure 6-6. *Grisham novels on the P2P Morpheus network in various formats, including MP3 audio files of books-on-tape.*

The Stephen King Experiment. Stephen King has been at the forefront of e-book online distribution models, publishing the novel *Riding the Bullet* exclusively on the Web through his publisher, Simon & Schuster. In a free promotion, websites offering the book delivered some 400,000 downloads in the first day.[29]

"Paving the way for the little guy," King later bypassed his publisher altogether and offered his book *The Plant* directly to consumers for a nominal fee. Readers downloaded the book in installments directly from his website. More recently, King has ventured into wireless distribution by making a collection of short stories available for transmission to personal digital assistants (PDAs).

Stephen King's very well publicized forays into the digital age also tested the threat of e-book piracy. While hackers did crack an encrypted version of *Riding the Bullet,* the experiment was widely acknowledged as a success. King's experience offered powerful evidence of consumer demand for books in digital formats.

From the publishers' view, however, the glass was half-empty. The fact that the encryption was hacked exacerbated fears of e-book piracy and uncontrolled online distribution. Taking a cautious approach, publishers are now erring on the side of heavy-duty copy protection and digital rights management (DRM) solutions to safeguard against piracy. This puts digital content at a disadvantage to traditional paper books, which can be freely reread and shared with friends. Because these technological limitations make the customer experience more cumbersome, the demand for books in digital format is likely to be met through piracy until more sustainable solutions are implemented that balance user-friendliness with the need to protect copyrights.

News Services

While text and image piracy can affect anyone who generates proprietary content, it is particularly damaging for services such as The Associated Press (AP), Reuters, and United Press International that rely on licensing fees as their primary source of revenue. Sites that pirate news service content create revenue leakage and devalue the content, undermining broader licensing strategies. In addition, when a site redistributes content without paying requisite fees, it can undermine a news service's overall strategy and set a precedent for free content—in effect making it a commodity by creating multiple sources.

Apart from the ease with which news content can be copied, pirates also target news because consumer demand is rising. Premium news content can help attract customers and drive revenues through advertising, merchandising, and referral fees. But only the best content can generate revenue; the customer experience is undermined when content is stale or disorganized, and then visitors are not likely to return. Customers set high standards. They expect pictures and stories that are nothing less than timely, entertaining, informative, and insightful.

The key to attacking news piracy is to take the offensive and turn the consumer demand into revenue. The legitimate providers of high-quality information and news content must defend themselves while proactively leveraging the value of their products and services to sign licensing deals. In other words, apply a combination of the carrot and the stick.

Typically, the websites that are pirating news content are often the best targets for licensing revenue as well (as is the case with online music, as discussed previously). Copyright owners should keep this in mind when determining what course of action to take.

While it is sometimes necessary to aggressively take action or even shut down these sites, content owners are often better off signing them up—particularly if the site is professional and appears to meet many of the criteria of a good licensee. Each case should be evaluated, prioritized, and dealt with appropriately.

One way to prioritize enforcement efforts is to note which sites are using news content to generate revenue as opposed to simply posting copy. The former offense presents a more significant threat and provides a stronger basis for further action should it be necessary. At the same time, revenue generation on the site can also be indicative of that site's potential ability to pay the requisite licensing fees.

Criteria for Identifying Licensing Revenue Opportunities. One approach that has been successful for some intellectual property owners is to group offenders according to a set of custom-defined criteria. This process can be helpful in prioritizing the infringements and determining which follow-up action is most appropriate. Examples of criteria that have been found to be useful to news organizations include:

➤ *Degree of Theft.* Is it a one-time event or does theft happen on a recurring basis? Is the pirated content a core element of the site?

➤ *Revenue Generation.* Is there commerce or advertising present on the website? Is the site leveraging your content for financial gain?

➤ *Context.* What other content is present, and is it offensive or inconsistent with brand image? How professional is the site design? Is it well maintained?

➤ *Number of Sites Pirating Content.* Is this one site in isolation or is there an organized network of sites pirating your news content?

➤ *Existing Relationship.* Is the offender violating the terms of an existing licensing agreement, has its agreement expired, or is there no preexisting relationship whatsoever?

➤ *Visibility.* How popular is the website? How many unique visitors does the site get every month?

THE ASSOCIATED PRESS

AP has been very successful in defending its brand by managing online distribution issues. The Associated Press diligently monitors the Internet to proactively identify unauthorized use of its content, not only to boost revenues, but also to protect AP and its members, including more than 15,000 newspaper, radio, and television subscribers worldwide.

"Gathering news and information for our members is the heart and soul of our business," said James R. Williams III, vice president and director of AP's broadcast division. By cracking down on pirates and making sure all online content is licensed, AP ensures "that our content is used properly and that the integrity of our products is preserved for the exclusive use of our customers."[30]

Market Data

The migration of customers online within the financial services sector has out-paced most other industries. Today there are tens of millions of online accounts as well as many more offline accounts where financial transactions are influenced by online research. A study by Harris Interactive estimated that 44 percent of banking customers and 74 percent of brokerage customers use the Internet as a source for gathering financial information.[31] The audience of investors who rely on this market information online is expanding as financial markets and Internet use become more global.

One of the results of this evolution has been a change in customer expectations. In particular, online investors now expect instant access to information and research at little or no cost to aid them in their decision making. While many sectors struggle to identify sustainable revenue streams online, the providers of financial market data—including exchanges, market indexes, data vendors, and hosts—simultaneously face a unique and tremendous opportunity. But to reap the rewards of the online channel, proactive strategies must be developed and implemented. Otherwise, piracy of market data will dilute brand equity and completely undermine the integrity of market data distribution channels.

As online brokers and financial news, investment, and advisory sites compete to attract and retain customers, market index and equity data has become indispensable to their success. Regardless of the brand awareness or quality of a financial website, the inclusion of stock quotes and market indexes, or even the association with well-known brand indexes such as the Dow, Nasdaq, Russell 2000, or FTSE brand names, lends credibility or legitimacy to a site.

The high demand and value associated with well-recognized brand indexes and exchanges place the owners and distributors of equity and index data in a position of power in the value chain. In essence, every site on the Internet that currently displays stock quotes, market data, or proprietary index methodologies represents a potential licensing opportunity.

If the revenue opportunities are ignored, piracy will decimate the value associated with premium brand market index or equity information, especially real-time quotes. Sites that choose to display data but do not pay the associated licensing fees are revenue leaks. This loss equates not only to the lost revenue opportunity, but also to the ability to license other sites—nobody wants to pay for something that others get for free.

In addition, diligent oversight of this content is necessary to limit the proliferation of unlicensed use. For instance, adept website designers can literally copy or "scrape" index and equity data from unknowing sites to their own site. While it is difficult to totally prevent these practices from occurring, locating sites that pilfer this information and taking action against them is practicable and can help curb piracy. Rui Moura, director of corporate marketing and communications for Frank Russell Company, observes that "with the massive distribution capability of the Internet, even a single misuse can be lethal in terms of lost revenue to the company."

Moura's sentiment is shared by John L. Jacobs, senior vice president of the Nasdaq Stock Market. "The Nasdaq name brings with it credibility and legitimacy among the investing public, which is extremely important for us to maintain," said Jacobs. "The Nasdaq indexes are indispensable benchmarks in the financial community. Maintaining control over our brand and indexes on the vast, unstructured Internet ensures that the name we have so carefully built will not be eroded by others seeking to capitalize on this established credibility."[32]

The central challenge for any strategy that combs the Internet for licensing opportunities is intelligence collection. Owners or distributors of equity and index data must first identify which sites to target as "sales" leads. Given the huge number of financial and business-related sites and the ever-increasing size of the Internet, this number can sometimes be large, especially for leading market indexes or exchanges.

Depending on the volume of sites identified, a method for prioritization must then be considered to target resources most efficiently. It helps to develop a profile of those sites that most likely or more easily can be converted into licensees. For instance, online broker or institutional investor sites may hold a greater likelihood of quickly entering licensing agreements than news sites, financial portals, or personal websites. Numerous characteristics, ranging from audience traffic to the total size of assets managed, can be used for prioritization criteria.

Leveraging the Internet as a profitable sales generator can be challenging. In addition to collecting and prioritizing these sales leads, a strategy should be developed that addresses pricing strategies, licensing terms, and management processes. Compliance, legal, licensing, and sales divisions must develop and coordinate procedures to take the appropriate actions.

Organizations with limited resources have the option to outsource the sales and contracting processes, as well as the audit functions. Additionally, the availability of workflow process tools enable exchanges, indexes, and data vendors and hosts to integrate sales leads generated from the Internet into the existing organization.

Organizations that actively leverage the sales leads that the Internet offers can gain additional, significant, and sustainable revenue streams. While taking action on these opportunities often requires additional resources and processes, experience has shown that the return on investment meets even the most demanding hurdle.

For those who do nothing, on the other hand, the consequences can be dire. Equity or index data providers that ignore the issue not only face lost revenue, they also risk undermining the value of their brand.

THE BUSINESS CASE

While the Internet as a distribution channel creates numerous opportunities and efficiencies for legitimate business, illegitimate operations are also capitalizing on the very same capabilities of the Internet. Content can now easily be copied and redistributed. The estimated amount of proprietary content that is pirated each year is staggering.

Example

An association that protects the rights of content creators identified nearly 5,000 unauthorized sites distributing its intellectual property. Of these 5,000, the association licensed 2,000. The average fee for receiving a license to distribute the association's proprietary content over the Internet depends on factors such as the amount of content that can be downloaded, the revenue generated, and the amount of traffic visiting the site. The potential for new revenue can be approximated by using the following assumptions and a two-part calculation:

Part A

Step	Assumption
1	Number of sites licensed: 2,000
2	Average annual licensing fee: $1,000
3	Total annual licensing fees generated = (1) $\times$ (2) = $2,000,000

Sites that did not pay or were deemed unsuitable as licensees were issued cease-and-desist letters, thereby shutting them down and forcing their customers to legitimate channels, which also raises the revenue potential as follows:

Part B

Step	Assumption
4	Sites ordered to cease and desist: 3,000
5	Average annual traffic to sites that are shut down: 100,000 unique users

6   Percentage of site visitors who will now purchase through author-
        ized channels: 1%
7   Average annual purchases: $40
8   Annual revenue gain = (4) × (5) × (6) × (7) = $120,000,000

**THE
BOARD
ROOM
SUMMARY**

Digital content such as books, music, videos, and software is copied and widely distributed online, creating
both threats and opportunities for brands and copyright
owners. Bear in mind these key points:

> ➤ There are many factors hindering enforcement efforts
>   and contributing to the growth of online piracy.

➤ The piracy problem is complex and extends beyond the World Wide
Web to Internet Relay Chat, P2P networks, instant messaging, online
auctions, e-mail, Usenet newsgroups, and FTP sites.

➤ Some organizations are able to proactively prevent revenue leakage and
add incremental revenue streams by identifying unauthorized use and
licensing the distribution of digital assets.

➤ Others defend their intellectual property through deterrents such as
copy protection technology or legal action.

➤ The most sustainable solutions include the creation of favorable alternatives to piracy by making legitimate distribution channels more convenient.

➤ The potential revenue implications of piracy can be enormous for companies whose digital assets are core to their business.

Section 3

Trust

"I think we in the technology industry have fallen in love with technology. And in the end it is not about the technology. . . . Privacy and security, or trust, are vital to consumers, and that is what we should focus on."
CARLY FIORINA, CEO OF HEWLETT-PACKARD COMPANY, ADDRESSING THE PROGRESS & FREEDOM FOUNDATION'S ASPEN SUMMIT (AUGUST 19, 2001)

Chapter 7

The Costs of Compromised Privacy and Security

Privacy and security are among the most contentious and volatile issues a company faces in the twenty-first century. One survey by Harris Interactive actually found that more Americans are concerned about loss of personal privacy than they are about health care, crime, or taxes.[1] As a result, failure to meet customer expectations in this regard can undermine brand loyalty and damage corporate image, hurting a company's bottom line.

In the book *Firebrands: Building Brand Loyalty in the Internet Age*, author Michael Moon defines branding as "the systematic and consistent application of product or service design, storytelling, media, and technology to the buying and using experiences of customers throughout a satisfaction life cycle."[2]

Technology is the enabler that lets companies create differentiated buying and using experiences for each customer based on the customer's personal habits and preferences. How that customer information is collected, protected, and used is then an integral part of a branded customer experience. But the collection of data invokes the notion of privacy and trust. Unfortunately, privacy protection is not a straightforward issue—there are trade-offs to be considered.

Many of the information collection and tracking technologies that are the subjects of hot debate are the same tools that allow a company to provide customers with the most personalized and convenient online experience—from book recommendations to airfare sale alerts. People generally want the personalization, but without the privacy trade-off. And when they are willing to share information with a company, they expect it to stay between the individual and the company—a view that is not always consistent with that of privacy and security experts.

As online partner networks grow, however, companies are easily associated with controversial privacy issues on the basis of their partners' behavior and policies. What's worse, when affiliates, suppliers, distributors, agents, etc. represent themselves as approved partners, there is an implied association that can set an expectation in the consumer's mind regarding the trustworthiness of the company. So when a partner violates consumer trust, it can damage your brand image as well (see Chapter 4).

The negative implications of being associated with partner privacy snafus are exacerbated by the fact that privacy concerns are at the top of consumers' minds. There is a lot at stake. Substantial brand equity can be eroded should privacy violations occur or information security be compromised. In today's networked world, privacy and security concerns, or trust, must be carefully considered in crafting any customer experience or branding strategy.

> *"Brands are not just taglines; they're the essence of how customers feel about your company. Once upon a time, these feelings were based solely on human contacts. But today, it's technology—not just people—that's building relationships with the customer."*
>
> —JEFF SMITH, DIRECTOR OF CONSULTING FIRM PROPHET[3]

Information Collection Technologies

To better manage the trade-offs and risk to a brand, you first need a basic understanding of the online privacy issues and practices that can have an impact on brand image. These include the disclosure of how information is collected and used, as well as the manner in which information is protected. While information may be collected through open disclosure, the use of technologies such as cookies and web beacons can facilitate the collection of information in a more covert manner.

According to *Computerworld,* "The wave of the future is an integrated data-snapshot of a customer that includes clickstream data; previous purchases, if any, not only from the website but from other channels; the consumer's customer service history; and demographic data."[4] But companies must strike a delicate balance between using data analysis to improve the customer experience and protecting customer privacy.

Cookies

Cookies are files that a website puts on your computer to store pieces of information about you. When you revisit the site, the site can look for those cookies to "remember" those pieces of information. As a result, cookies make it possible to improve the customer experience through personalization and features catered to that individual.

For example, as an online shopper selects items for purchase, the site may send a cookie to the shopper's hard drive indicating what items are in his virtual shopping cart. Should the shopper leave the site and come back later, the cookie can help the site to recognize him and allow the shopper to resume where he left off on his last visit. The same shopping site may use cookies to store all of the shopper's information and preferences, such as credit card number and mailing address, so that customers don't have to complete lengthy forms for every purchase.

Cookies have been the source of great controversy for several reasons. First, they can store a wide range of information—from mundane zip codes to highly sensitive medical information or bank account numbers and passwords. Second, cookies are usually used without customers knowing about it.

Cookies gained further infamy when people began to realize that online advertising companies use the technology across a very large network of sites. While cookies are designed to be read only by the same entity that places them on the visitor's machine, if the same network is hosting advertisements on thousands of pages online, the information collected can be extensive.

Every time a visitor views a banner ad, for example, a cookie can be used to track her online viewing habits. This application of cookies can allow an advertising company to develop a detailed profile of individuals based on their preferences and where they go online. The prospect of a large company gathering this amount of data can be daunting for consumers. Concerns about "Big Brother" are further heightened by the idea that the information might be married with personal data collected from offline sources.

Web Beacons

While awareness has risen regarding the use of cookies, web beacons remain a lesser-known data collection technology, so they are not as well understood. Web beacons are graphics inserted in a web page for the purpose of collecting information about visitors without being detected. A server records user information whenever the image is loaded from a web page. While often innocuous, web beacons are sometimes perceived to be malicious since they are specifically designed to go unnoticed.

Usually invisible, a web beacon is sometimes also referred to as a "web bug," a "clear GIF," or a "1x1 GIF," in reference to the fact that a web beacon most often has a width and height of only one pixel. In addition to the distinct size parameters in the image tag, a graphic can also be identified as a web beacon by examining the code to determine whether the image is loaded from a different web server than the rest of the page.

What makes people nervous about web beacons is the extent of information that they can collect without being noticed. This information includes:

➤ The user's IP address

➤ The URL of the page where the web beacon is located

➤ The location of the web beacon itself

➤ The time and date it was served

➤ The type of browser used to retrieve the web beacon

➤ Previously set cookie values

The cookie values are of greatest concern to consumers since cookies store information that can be used in combination with web beacons to facilitate in-depth personal and transactional profiling. Web developers take advantage of the ability to collect this information to customize and streamline a user's experience. Others use web beacons for even less obtrusive reasons, such as to provide an independent accounting of how many people visit a site, or to gather statistics on browser usage.

The degree to which such practices might be of ethical concern is an issue of debate. As the debate receives more media attention, however, brand owners are well advised to maintain high levels of cross-departmental communication and cooperation. In this manner, managers can remain cognizant of information collection practices that may generate privacy concerns for their customers and ultimately tarnish a brand.

Whether or not the intent is benign, a company may want to avoid association with the inappropriate use of web beacons, cookies, and other similar technologies because of the risk they pose to established brands. In some circumstances, the collection of visitor information through technology, while potentially beneficial in terms of customization, could be perceived as a violation of privacy policies. Such an accusation can expose a company to unwanted repercussions in terms of corporate and brand image.

TOYS ''R'' US

When Coremetrics offered to help Toys "R" Us, Inc. collect and analyze customer data, it must have sounded like a good outsourcing opportunity. Using JavaScript-enabled tools that included cookies and web beacons, the Toysrus.com website would collect data on visitors and forward it to Coremetrics. The analytics firm would then dissect the data and generate reports, providing Toys "R" Us with valuable insights into customer demographics by helping to identify which pages and promotions were most popular.

Unfortunately, bedlam ensued when a scathing press release was issued by Interhack Corporation, a security firm based in Ohio that discovered what Coremetrics was doing while conducting an Internet privacy project. The press release announced that use of the Coremetrics service by Toys "R" Us threatened to "place unsuspecting web surfers—including children—at risk of becoming victims of real-world crimes, including stalking and identity theft." The release went on to point out that the use of this system was in violation of the Toys "R" Us privacy policy, which stated that the company does not share information about users with third parties.

In fact, while the Toys "R" Us privacy policy didn't specifically mention its relationship with Coremetrics, it did state that Toysrus.com may "utilize a service provider to assist us in aggregating guest information."[5] But the devil is in the details where privacy statements are concerned, and the story was picked up by major media outlets such as CBS and CNN.

Toys "R" Us spokesperson Tuesday Yhland denied the allegations. "We do not sell, rent, or trade visitor information to other parties," she said. The company hired Coremetrics to analyze its customers' data "to enhance the customer shopping experience."[6] But the explanations and denials from Toys "R" Us and Coremetrics only seemed to fuel the fire as privacy advocates and trust programs took advantage of the opportunity to raise public awareness, labeling the practice an "unforgivable breach" of confidentiality.[7]

In the days following the initial press release, the first of twelve class-action lawsuits was filed alleging that Toys "R" Us allowed third-party access to customer data in violation of its own privacy policy. The suit called the practice a "gross abuse of the trust parents and their children have placed in Toys 'R' Us" and sought damages for customers who made purchases from the site.

Toys "R" Us soon posted a revised privacy policy on its website and parted ways with Coremetrics after an engagement that Toys "R" Us characterized as a "very short-term trial-based relationship." Records from Toys "R" Us were subpoenaed as part of an investigation of its privacy policies and according to a company spokesperson, they turned over "thousands of documents related to our privacy policies."

When the first settlement was announced, Mark Herr, director of the New Jersey Division of Consumer Affairs, focused on the toy retailer's use of cookies. Herr characterized the use of cookies without consumer's consent as "an unconscionable business practice" that violates New Jersey's Consumer Fraud Act. Toys "R" Us agreed to pay a $50,000 fine and provide "a complete and accurate summary" regarding disclosure of personal information.[8]

Unfortunately for Toys "R" Us, a much steeper price had already been paid in the form of negative publicity and lost brand equity. The consequences were heightened by public fears. In fact, this was confirmed when a related Harris Interactive survey was released around the same time the settlement was disclosed. The survey found that online privacy remains a top concern among consumers, with three-quarters of respondents saying one of their major concerns regarding privacy is that companies they patronize will provide their information to third parties without their permission.[9]

Information Security

Safeguarding personal information is also important so that both you and your customers don't become the victims of identity theft or credit card fraud. Online fraud is extremely difficult to measure and estimates vary widely. Visa International says that fraud accounts for 25–28 cents of every $100 spent online, about four times worse than the "real world" rate of 7 cents per $100. But IT research firm Gartner, Inc., for example, estimates online fraud to be about nineteen times worse than the offline rate. The Gartner study found that one in every fifty consumers has been the victim of identity theft.[10]

No matter which estimate is correct, the increase in e-commerce activity means that the overall cost of fraud is on the rise. Visa confirms that while the online fraud rate has been stable in recent years, the overall cost has grown, as e-commerce now represents about 4 percent of Visa card purchases. According to James McCarthy, a senior vice president at Visa's eVisa business unit, "If we don't get to the root causes . . . the losses will continue to grow."[11]

Online fraud undermines consumer confidence, both in individual brands as well as in online commerce as a whole. According to a Harris Interactive survey, 70 percent of surveyed consumers said they are concerned that their transactions might not be secure, while nearly the same percentage were worried that hackers could steal their personal data.[12] A comprehensive survey conducted by Ipsos-Reid reported that potential online credit card fraud is a major concern for 46 percent of adults around the world and a moderate concern for 26 percent.[13] Numerous other reports have shown similar levels of distrust in Internet security given that stolen credit card information is routinely posted in online chat rooms, for example (see Figure 7-1). For companies that conduct business online, protecting customers from fraud is critical for protecting brand integrity.

Customer Information Collection

One way that online merchants can assuage consumer fears is by using the industry standard security protocol, Secure Sockets Layer (SSL), to encrypt sensitive information that is transmitted over the Internet during e-commerce

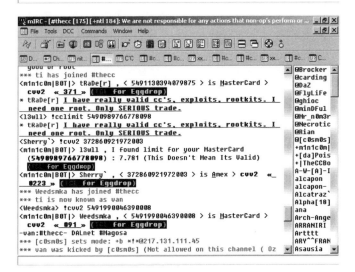

Figure 7-1. *Stolen credit card information posted in chat rooms.*

transactions. The use of SSL encryption for online transactions has been widely adopted, and most card associations have policies requiring merchants who accept their card to use SSL. It should be noted, however, that encryption only protects card information as it is transported from the shopper's computer to the merchant's server. Security experts are quick to point out there is little evidence to indicate whether the lack of SSL on many sites is a vulnerability that is widely exploited.

From the perspective of the merchant, other than providing some reassurance to the more knowledgeable, security-conscious customer, encryption of e-commerce transactions offers very little direct benefit. A nonencrypted transaction still generates revenue for the merchant, and since encryption cannot provide evidence that the customer is the legitimate cardholder, encryption does not directly reduce the merchant's fraud rate. In the event that the nonencrypted credit card information is stolen, it is not apt to be detected, and the cost would likely be borne primarily by other merchants later on.

Information security expert Mark Fischer puts the transmission of nonencrypted data in perspective. "No one knows if hackers are intercepting unencrypted credit card information off the Internet . . . it does not interrupt the data flow and would be invisible to the e-commerce merchant," says Fischer. "But the biggest obstacle is being in the right place to capture the credit card data. Only a very small percentage of the traffic on the Internet includes someone's credit card information. Imagine how many hours you would have to listen in on people's cell phone conversations to hear them giving their credit card to a catalog merchant."

Fischer's further assessment of the situation is less reassuring for consumers. "In most cases, it would be far easier to find an e-commerce site with poor host security and grab the database of information from the server than to collect and sift through all of the traffic going into an e-commerce site and extract the credit card numbers," he adds.

Customer Information Storage

The pace of emerging technologies, inherent openness of digital networks, and unparalleled levels of mobility and anonymity have left everyone susceptible to the risk of being hacked. Hackers have little fear of recrimination since Internet attacks are generally quick and easy—in fact, not only is it difficult to catch intruders, but most go entirely undetected.

Part of the challenge is that by its inherent nature, e-business poses a challenge to security professionals. While the general goal of network security is to keep strangers out, the whole point of e-business is to share controlled information with the rest of the world. As a result, it can be a complicated challenge to make sure websites are designed, configured, and maintained in a way that fully supports the desired customer experience—including the security necessary to ensure the ongoing protection of personal information.

To a network administrator, a web server represents a potential window to your local network, and while most visitors may be content to peer through, you can be sure a few will try to access proprietary information that is not meant for public consumption.

Despite these facts, many companies remain unaware of the risks associated with their online presence. The results can range from defacement of your site's home page to the theft of your entire database of customer information. Loss of confidentiality can be devastating to a business and corporate image, particularly if the data is related to finances or medical records, where security breaches may result in substantial loss of consumer confidence.

Though it can be ruinous to have sensitive information stolen, it can be almost as bad when hackers change or erase information, resulting in the loss of integrity and availability. Availability is particularly important in a service-oriented business that depends on information such as airline schedules or stock quotes.

The risk is real. Hackers have compromised the sites of some of the world's leading brands including Nike, McDonald's, and Microsoft. Even more disturbing from a branding perspective are hacking incidents perpetrated against brands in the financial industry such as Western Union, where perpetrators gained access to the credit and debit card information of 15,700 customers. While no incidents of fraud were reported, Western Union and its customers were still faced with the inconvenience of canceling cards and changing passwords. But the true damage was the blow to brand image and customer trust. "Sounds like a big (mistake) on someone's part at a site you'd expect to be locked down tight," said one of the Western Union customers affected by the security breach.[14]

The seriousness of the potential consequences is part of the reason that so many instances of hacking go unreported to authorities. Depending on the situation, the outcome can range from a minor loss of time and productivity in recovering from the problem, to a significant loss of money or brand equity. In the case of companies that manage crucial infrastructure systems (e.g., transportation, telecommunications, power grid, and financial systems), security breaches could even threaten public safety.

"When you go online and expose yourself to the world as you do in e-business, the downside of a security breach is huge," says Chris Parsons, senior vice president of strategy and business planning for BellSouth. "In fact, you may never recover."[15]

PLAYBOY

Playboy Enterprises is an example of a company whose customers value discreetness. It must have been particularly disturbing when customers received e-mail (see Figure 7-2) directly from a person who hacked the Playboy website. The hacker used a Playboy.com return address to send the messages, making it appear that it had been sent from Hugh Hefner's mail account.

Not only did each e-mail contain the recipients' name and credit card numbers, it also claimed that "a shady hacker group" had maintained full access to the Playboy corporate network since 1998. The e-mail further warned that "your details are currently circulating the underworld of anarchists and credit card fraudsters, so we highly recommend that you contact your bank."[16]

"We are confident that not all of Playboy.com customers were affected," stated Playboy spokesperson Laura Sigman.[17] Playboy.com quickly sent a letter advising all online customers for the past five years to contact their credit card companies to be sure that no unauthorized charges had been made. In addition to notifying customers about the problem, the letter also described the steps being taken to make sure it wouldn't happen again. "We recognize the value that you place on your privacy and security and want to assure you that we are doing everything possible to rectify the situation," said the letter from Playboy.com's president.

Some observers lauded Playboy's rapid reaction to the incident, believing it would mitigate damage to customer confidence. But others weren't so sure since this kind of incident preys on "the greatest fear of many online shoppers—that their personal information will be stolen and used by thieves."[18]

Corporate Identity Theft

Brands are increasingly being abused to perpetrate corporate identity theft and defraud consumers. Of the total number of fraud complaints being received by the government, 70 percent occur on the Internet.[19] The scams take many forms, ranging from simple to complex. One common approach is to lure unsuspecting customers to what appears to be a "trusted" website where they are tricked into sharing personal information such as credit card numbers, bank account numbers, or other data that can be used by criminals (see Figure 7-3).

Often the customer will first be contacted by a spam e-mail that includes a link to a website that might not be discoverable by any other means. The

To:
From: Hugh Hefner <hef@playboy.com>
Subject: ingreslock 1524 security announcement

dear user,

since the summer of 1998, a shady hacker group known as 'ingreslock 1524' have maintained full access to the playboy enterprises inc. (pei) corporate network. even when the pei websites were defaced by BoW/H4G1S and were 'secured', we retained our full access (no, installing ssh doesn't make you secure).

we did have some very big plans to use the hundreds of thousands of customer details (names, addresses, order history & credit card information) harvested to automatically purchase hundreds of different products from different online companies (amazon, barnesandnoble, qvc, yahoo, even playboy) to be sent to each playboy customer, thus resulting in over 10 million dollars worth of fraud claims being made to credit card and in turn, insurance companies globally.

incase you think this is some kind of hoax, we have included your personal details below -

Name -
[DELETED]
Credit Card Number & Expiry -
[DELETED]

your details are currently circulating the underworld of anarchists and credit card fraudsters, so we highly recommend that you contact your bank before much fraud is committed. we have also distributed over a million e-mail addresses to marketing and 'spam' organisations, so you will certainly havea lot of fun deleting unwanted e-mail into the future!

online companies can learn many lessons from this compromise -
1. do not use the same root or administrative (oracle, webserv, etc.) user passwords across different hosts on the same network.
2. never assume that by installing the latest security patches and installing ssh, that you are secure.
3. do not use insecure authentication methods, including nis, nis+ or .rhosts.
4. do not protect your passwords with des in your shadow files, use md5.

end users can learn an important lesson from this compromise -
1. do not trust companies with your details online.

its been emotional. we'd like to thank the playboy systems team for providing us with an interesting and challenging target. i'm sure that a big security company will make easy money auditing their systems and hopefully deploying a more secure network - although we'll be back to test it again.

- m4rty

martyn luther ping
minister of information
ingreslock 1524

Figure 7-2. *The e-mail sent out to Playboy subscribers by a group calling itself "ingreslock 1524."*

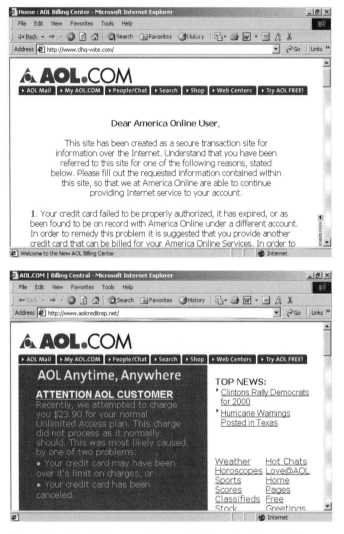

Figure 7-3. *Fraud sites created to steal information from AOL customers.*

e-mail and website might be disguised as a place to update customer billing information, or the messages may promote a very attractive offer that sounds too good to be true. The unauthorized inclusion of a reputable brand is a favorite way to get the victims to overcome their skepticism. Often the fraudulent e-mails and websites are designed with the "look and feel" of a legitimate site, including logos, slogans, recognizable color schemes and fonts, etc. Another favorite trick is to construct the spam so that it looks like it originated from a legitimate company or even a famous person.

While spam filters have become more sophisticated, they can't help you manage fraudulent e-mails being distributed to your customers outside your firewall. Improved technologies and approaches are in the nascent stages with regard to protecting your customers from this kind of abuse. Chapters 9 and 10 provide some insights into how to monitor for spam abuse and take action against it. Educating customers and heightening awareness are additional approaches that can help manage the risk of customer loss resulting from corporate identity theft and spammers abusing your brand.

SYMANTEC

When Symantec Corp. discovered that spammers were targeting its customers, the company, which makes security software, decided to set up a Spam Watch Response Center (see Figure 7-4) on its website. The center helps to

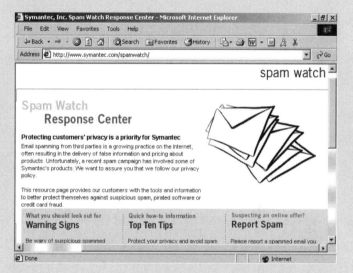

Figure 7-4. *Symantec set up Spam Watch in response to brand abuse.*

educate customers and provides a convenient means for customers to report spam abuse of the Symantec brands. Symantec also arms customers with clues on how to identify suspicious promotions not affiliated with Symantec (see Figure 7-5); it gives specific warning signs and even some real screen shot examples.

Managing Privacy and Security

At a minimum, companies need to remain cognizant of privacy and security practices within their own domain. Once their domain is assessed, brand managers and privacy officers should be aware of how their company's intellectual property is being represented by their online partners, who are often perceived

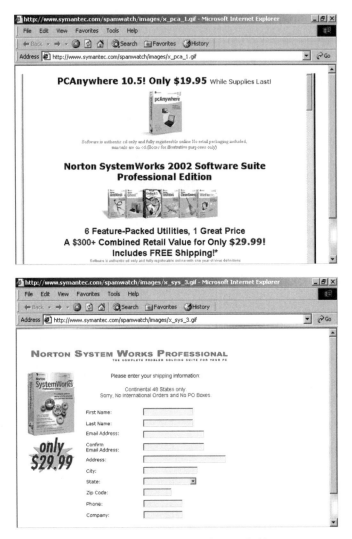

Figure 7-5. *Examples of suspicious e-mails provided by Symantec to help protect customers.*

as an extension of the brand itself. This representation includes how a customer's privacy is safeguarded. Partner compliance guidelines should be expanded to include privacy provisions, and partner adherence to these guidelines should be monitored on an ongoing basis.

> *"The growth of the digital economy will be intimately linked to how effective organizations can be in dispelling consumers' privacy fears and establishing a level of trust and consumer confidence that is mutually beneficial to both sides."*
> —ANN CAVOUKIAN AND TYLER HAMILTON, AUTHORS OF *The Privacy Payoff*[20]

As public awareness of online privacy and security issues begins to rise, the fact that websites are collecting information from visitors without permission is likely to generate more controversy. Those companies that move proactively to carefully balance the need for customer information with their right to privacy will be better positioned to weather the storm.

THE BUSINESS CASE

How can a company quantify the corporate risks associated with hackers, fraud, and the potential loss of consumer trust? The best answer is that there is no across-the-board answer. For the majority of companies, the risks identified may never materialize on a significant scale. By the same token, a breach of customer privacy may be devastating to a company's bottom line, in terms of the costs of recovery and downtime, decreased market valuation, and lost brand equity.

Maryfran Johnson, editor-in-chief of *Computerworld*, sums it up well. "Privacy protection is like airline security. Nobody jokes about it anymore. That's because there's so much money at stake," she says. "Companies that prove they can keep client data to themselves will simply make more money by attracting trusting customers. Those that fail to protect private information will pay through the nose in lawsuits."[21]

Peter Cullen, chief privacy officer of Royal Bank of Canada, concurs with this assessment. Privacy "is one of the key drivers of a customer's level of commitment and has a significant contribution to overall demand." Cullen states that privacy "plays a measurable part in how customers decide [to] purchase products and services from us. It brings us more share of the customer's wallet."[22]

The following example illustrates how protecting privacy and security might translate into a competitive advantage.

Example

A major long-distance carrier has its website hacked. Customer billing information is stolen from an internal database and posted anonymously to a website. The incident receives press attention and undermines customer loyalty. A major competitor takes advantage of the opportunity to launch an aggressive marketing campaign to recruit these customers. While not specifically mentioning the incident, the competitor decides to focus the ads on trust. The ads highlight a long history of world-class privacy and security policies and programs.

As a result of the incident and competitor's response, the carrier loses an estimated one-tenth of one percent of the $100 billion long-distance market, costing the carrier about $100 million in annual revenues.

THE
BOARD
ROOM
SUMMARY

Privacy and security are a high priority for shoppers and key elements of the online customer experience. Any perceived breach of consumer trust can severely undermine brand loyalty and damage corporate image. Brand owners should remember these key points:

➤ Companies must strike a delicate balance between using data to improve the customer experience and protecting customer privacy.

➤ Merchants can engender consumer trust and mitigate risk by properly securing the transmission and storage of sensitive information.

➤ When an online partner violates consumer trust, it can sometimes be just as damaging to your brand image as when the infringement occurs within your own company.

➤ Apart from loss of brand equity and consumer trust, there are other ways a breach of customer privacy can hurt your company. It could potentially result in a drop in the company's stock price, or it could have a bottom-line impact in terms of the costs of recovery and downtime, and the cost of litigation.

Section 4

Competitive Intelligence

"It is from the character of our adversary's position that we can draw conclusions as to his designs and will therefore act accordingly."
CARL VON CLAUSEWITZ, PRUSSIAN GENERAL, *On War*, 1832

Chapter 8

Using Online Competitive Intelligence to Outmaneuver Competitor Brands

S ignificant intelligence regarding a company's overall sales and marketing strategies can be extracted by analyzing a brand's online presence. The opportunity to garner this information can work to your advantage or disadvantage, depending on whether you are the one gaining the insights. It's important to know what information can be gleaned through online competitive intelligence, and what information others can infer from your own brand presence. Armed with this knowledge, you are better positioned to move from the defensive to the offensive—gathering competitive intelligence and using your brand to influence the competition's decision making.

While the Internet is already widely embraced as a data source for traditional competitive intelligence, few companies have exploited its full potential for providing insights into competitive branding issues. Some of the more prescient companies have moved beyond discrete online information sources to monitor a competitor's brand.

Basically, any intelligence you can gather from monitoring and analyzing your own brand online can also be collected for your competitors' brands. As a result, online competitive intelligence can offer a direct window on the implementation of competitor strategies, allowing you to employ countertactics or leverage the knowledge for your own benefit. Although it can be challenging to hone in on the relevant information necessary to glean these insights, the rewards can be substantial for those who are successful.

Publicly accessible intelligence can sometimes answer broader sales and marketing questions, such as:

➤ Where, and in what context, do our competitors have a brand presence online? What does their brand reach reveal about their target customer and marketing strategies?

➤ What are our competitors' partnership strategies, and who are their top online partners? How are our competitors leveraging the value of their partnerships to drive sales and gain market share?

➤ What kind of brand commentary is available online about our competitors? What can it tell us about consumer perceptions and product direction?

"The Internet is invaluable to our business. It's still only one part of our collection process, but it's an important part."
—JIM WALSH, DIRECTOR OF SPECIAL MARKETS WHO HANDLES COMPETITIVE INTELLIGENCE FOR SBC COMMUNICATIONS, INC.[1]

The Internet as a Competitive Intelligence Source

The Internet is recognized as a valuable data source among competitive intelligence professionals. Most experts have a list of discrete sources they rely on, including subscription-based portals, job boards, patent databases, and their competitors' own websites. While most competitive intelligence professionals have adopted the Internet as a resource, there are still a surprising number of major corporations that have not taken advantage of the Internet for this purpose.

"Established companies will be most successful when they deploy Internet technology to reconfigure traditional activities or when they find new combinations of Internet and traditional approaches," concluded Michael Porter in his March 2001 *Harvard Business Review* article "Strategy and the Internet." Those competitive intelligence professionals who have embraced the Internet to supplement their conventional activities have an advantage over those who have not.

The rewards for gathering online competitive intelligence are particularly great given the unbelievable wealth of publicly accessible information that exists online. Even among those who are already using the Internet for competitive intelligence, few have done more than scratch the surface of its potential as a data source. Part of the reason is that the sheer amount of online data can make it challenging to collect and filter the findings, particularly for major brands. But it is this same breadth of data that increases the likelihood of uncovering valuable information that, when analyzed, will support data gathered from other sources of intelligence and result in smarter business decisions.

Brand Presence

A competitor's online brand presence can take many forms, including text versions of brands and slogans, logos, links, etc. While the size and explosive growth of the Net make it difficult to quantify overall brand presence, it is possible to get a general understanding of the extent of a competitor's presence relative to your own. One way to quantify brand presence is to enter competitor brands on a search engine such as Google and check the number of returns. If you can filter out "false positives" (see Chapter 9), estimating the number of results can serve as a good proxy for a competitor's online brand presence.

Another approach to quantifying brand presence is to confine the search to a limited area, such as relevant industry, consumer opinion, financial, or other relevant message boards. Such metrics can be tracked over time and sometimes cross-correlated with sales metrics to discern the impact of online and offline events, such as advertising campaigns and public relations issues.

The next step in analyzing brand presence is to characterize the *context* in which the brand appears. The easiest way to get a contextual feel for brand presence is to categorize occurrences by the nature of the site where the brand is present. Depending on your objectives, brand presence can be broken into either generic categories, such as commercial sites and personal pages, or more specific categories such as "e-commerce sites offering athletic apparel" or "environmental activism hate sites."

Compiling a comprehensive list of specific, online brand locations is not usually feasible for major brands—at least not without access to proprietary technology. When a brand is far-reaching, a rough way to characterize the context of brand presence is to dissect a representative sampling of URLs from search engine results. These results can then be used as a model, as shown in Figure 8-1.

Beyond relative breadth and context, the challenge of analyzing a premier brand's Internet presence can be met by focusing on the particular aspects of the presence that are most likely to yield competitive intelligence. Three categories of information can be extracted from your competitors' brand presence and analyzed—brand reach, partner identification, and online commentary.

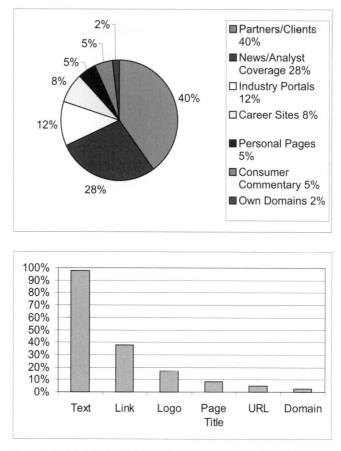

Figure 8-1. *Model of online brand presence for a professional services company, based on search engine results.*

Brand reach reveals who is viewing your competitors' brands online, while partner and commentary analyses focus on discrete segments of a competitor's presence that can uncover information that, when analyzed, provides useful competitive intelligence. Together, brand reach, partner identification, and online commentary can yield powerful insights into a competitor's online sales and marketing strategies—insights critical to gaining a competitive advantage.

Brand Reach

Brand reach is, simply put, the online audience the brand is reaching. There are two basic approaches to determine the audience. The first is to infer brand reach from the context in which the brand is seen. Site content often provides clues regarding the target demographics of the viewer. For example, the language, contact information, geographic focus, or apparent ethnicity of the site can be good indicators of who is likely to visit the site. If a competitor's consumer product brand appears on a large number of Spanish language sites that offer recipes for Mexican and Cuban food dishes, you can probably make some valid conclusions about the primary demographic sectors the brand is reaching through those sites.

The ability to draw competitive insights is certainly not limited to the culinary world. Almost every site, from one selling auto parts to one dispensing advice on medical conditions, offers substantial clues that allow you to determine the target audience. The competitive intelligence to be gleaned can range from the discovery of new product applications to forays into new demographic or geographic markets.

As an example, through brand reach analysis, a leading insurance company determined that a head-to-head competitor was actively pursuing a targeted, profitable market segment for people engaged in a specific lifestyle. Internet intelligence further revealed that the competitor was offering special promotions to penetrate that market. The insurance company used this intelligence to rapidly deploy a counterstrategy to protect market share. In this case, the counterstrategy included a targeted advertising campaign and proactive extension of "loyalty discounts" to select, profitable customers the company deemed to be at risk of switching insurers.

To obtain more specific information than you can glean from context clues, a competitor's brand presence can be combined with audience data, such as traffic and demographic information (see Figure 8-2), to assess brand reach. Though typically there is a fee associated with gaining access to this type of information, it can provide more accurate results. Detailed traffic and demo-

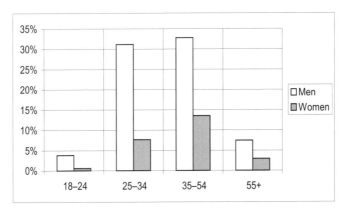

Figure 8-2. *Example of online brand reach (age and sex) for a professional services company, based on a model developed from 1,000 search engine results.*

graphic data is available through audience measurement companies such as comScore Networks or NetRatings, Inc.

The logic employed to analyze brand reach is the same as that used in the analysis of Internet advertising, but brand reach is a more powerful metric because it goes beyond tracking paid advertising placements. Whereas Internet ads are typically limited to a targeted online campaign, brand reach reflects the appearance of a brand as a result of third-party actions or offline marketing activities, for example. This kind of enhanced modeling of online brand presence can further help you understand a competitor's strategy.

This is not to say that you shouldn't also track advertising—such competitive intelligence can give you even more clues about competitive strategy. Intelligence on your competitors' "ad buys" or "media buys" are available through online ad measurement services such as AdRelevance, which is owned by NetRatings, Inc. AdRelevance lures customers with the promise to "discover every detail of your competitor's advertising strategy." The primary difference between advertising and brand reach is that, depending on the care with which your competitors' ads are placed, they can sometimes provide you with intelligence into where the competition wants to be, as opposed to where they actually are.

Competitor Brand Abuse

The effort behind online branding can be just as deliberate as offline campaigns, though many companies continue to neglect their presence on the Web. The flip side of a competitor's purposeful, controlled branding strategy is brand abuse, such as a third party's unauthorized claims of affiliation with your company, or having your brand somehow associated with objectionable content. Noting whether a competitor is experiencing this type of unintentional brand reach can reveal what communities the brand is reaching; it is also an indication of the strength or weakness of a company's overall attention to online branding.

Knowing whether your competitors are attentive to their brands online can help you gauge what kind of response you can expect if you launch some type of online competitive assault. It can also expose a vulnerability that you may choose to exploit.

Competitor Absence

As valuable as it is to identify your competitors' target customers from their brand presence, it can be equally important to note where your competitors are absent. A lack of brand presence on a particular site, or category of sites, where you would expect to see your competitors might indicate a lack of focus. It could also telegraph a change in target market. In either scenario, the intelligence will be useful in helping you to plan your online strategy.

Linking Relationships

Online shoppers and researchers traverse the Web via hyperlinks, making linking relationships as critical to determining a competitor's marketing strategy as any other aspect of brand reach. The public nature of the Web makes it possible to monitor who is linking to whom and to obtain a more comprehensive understanding of brand placement and proliferation.

Hint: Some search engines offer the ability to find who is linking to your competitor's home page or domain through an advanced search feature called a "reverse lookup."

Links are key because they are a primary tool used by consumers and researchers to traverse the Web. Analyzing links is one way to understand the consumer experience offered by a competitor, as well as the competitor's customer acquisition strategies. A link analysis can also be of value in helping to identify a competitor's online partner relationships, bundling and coupling strategies, and more.

Partnerships

Broadly speaking, online partnerships can be detected when your competitor has a brand presence on another site and the business relationship is stated or implied. Competitor partner relationships that can often be found online include affiliates, suppliers, distributors, agents or dealers, service partners, vendors, and even clients or customers.

Partner sites frequently compose a significant percentage of a brand's online presence and are more likely to be sites on which your competitor's presence is sanctioned. Although partner sites are a subset of the greater universe of sites that represent a competitor's brand reach, they deserve perhaps the most attention of any type of site within the context of evaluating the competitor's sales and marketing strategies.

At a high level, an analysis of online partners can reveal competitors' business models and how, if at all, they are leveraging the value of their partnerships on the Internet. Competitive business models on the Internet do not always mirror offline models. For example, manufacturers that distribute through retailers offline may choose to sell direct to customers on the Internet. Retailers that take control of the customer experience in their stores may allow their suppliers to play a more integral role online (see Chapter 4).

Monitoring how your competitors are leveraging their online partners has a twofold purpose: to help you understand your competitor's strategies and to present you with an opportunity to craft counterstrategies. For example, if your competitor prohibits its suppliers from selling online, there may be an opportunity for you to approach select suppliers with an agreement that allows them to sell online in exchange for your exclusive rights to distribute their products offline.

Relationships with partners online are also important because of the degree of influence they have over the consumer. As discussed in Chapter 4, partners are often perceived as extensions of a company in the eyes of its customers, and these partners can play a large role in shaping a company's brand image. For example, a retailer found that the online brand image of a competitor with a large affiliate network was shaped almost entirely by partners. Armed with this information, the retailer was able to establish preferred relationships with select competitor affiliates and issue guidelines that influenced the way the competitor's brand was represented.

Recruiting Competitor Partners

Competitive intelligence can also be used to identify new online partners. Best practices are to prioritize your competitor's partners according to defined criteria so that you are investing resources in pursuing only the top prospects. Criteria for prioritization might include factors such as the relevance of the partner's site content and audience focus, the apparent professionalism of the site, and the site's popularity.

Other criteria specific to the nature of your business should be considered when evaluating competitive partners. For example, distributors that are generating revenue are more likely to be capable of paying for content. Therefore, when using competitive intelligence to identify new partners for licensing content, it may also be advisable to prioritize them by criteria indicative of revenue generation, such as the presence of e-commerce activity or advertising.

In some instances, the Internet can also prove valuable by identifying a competitor's customers. For example, some e-commerce software or web products are identifiable by viewing the page source code, which often includes hints regarding the kinds of technology used. Customers in certain types of businesses are more readily obvious to the visitor. United Parcel Service (UPS), for example, can use the Internet to find retailers that only offer shipping through FedEx. In fact, given that 75 percent of FedEx's volume gets booked online[2], such an approach would allow UPS to dissect the FedEx customer base and, if tracked over time, take note of trends.

A credit card company could do the same thing—Discover Financial Services might pinpoint the merchants that accept Visa, MasterCard, and American Express. To make the effort more manageable, the intelligence collection efforts could be prioritized by focusing exclusively on the top-trafficked sites that account for a large percentage of the transactions. Likewise, content providers can find out to whom a competitor syndicates content, with the goal of improving its own licensing efforts.

If your competitor drives customers to its site through an affiliate model, competitive intelligence on these partners can be a gold mine. As discussed in Chapter 4, affiliates are sites that link to a company and deliver new customers in exchange for some kind of referral fee or commission. Within the affiliate business, it is not uncommon for 3 percent of the affiliates to generate 97 percent of the business. Finding those 3 percent that are driving almost all your competitors' online business, while difficult, can be extremely valuable—particularly if you can successfully recruit them away!

Hint: Audience measurement companies can generate reports that allow your business to determine the sources and magnitude of a competitor's referral traffic.

The more that partner intelligence suggests that a competitor has a focused online marketing strategy, the more value there is to be gained by analyzing its partner relationships. A focused strategy that includes a well-managed partner network is generally the result of a well-thought-out plan of attack and substantial investment of time and resources.

The intelligence resulting from analysis of a direct competitor can be used to create or enhance your own network of partners. In addition to learning from best practices, you will be in a position to leverage your competitors' investments in a partner network to your own advantage. However, if your competitor closely monitors its partners, it could be more challenging to establish a relationship of your own.

In summary, identifying partner relationships offers the potential for various opportunities. Benefits may include, but are not limited to, pursuing agreements with competitors' partners, approaching a competitor's top partners with attractive offers of exclusivity, or exploiting the gaps in a competitor's network by preemptively entering into agreements with sites on which your competitor does not currently have a presence.

AMAZON.COM

Amazon.com knows better than most how valuable online intelligence is, and nothing demonstrates conviction more than money. In the summer of 1999, Amazon quietly acquired a small audience measurement firm in San Francisco called Alexa Internet. The deal was valued at $250 million. Amazon recognized the value of online intelligence, and Alexa Internet generates it en masse—according to Alexa's website, the company gathers "in excess of 250 gigabytes of information per day" and houses an index of the Internet that is the largest in the world.

If information is power, then Amazon carries a very big stick. Billing itself as "The Web Information Company," Alexa Internet tracks the online habits of more than 10 million people around the globe as they navigate the Web. The intelligence captured includes how shoppers are reaching Amazon's competitors—vital information when you are aggressively battling your way to the top of the online retail space. With strategic analysis derived from Alexa's clickstreams, Amazon could easily and accurately pinpoint its competitors' top affiliates—giving Amazon the ability to initiate laser-focused recruiting efforts to bolster its own formidable affiliate network while simultaneously dealing a harsh blow to the competition.

Online Commentary

The Internet is widely used by competitive intelligence professionals to learn about competitor activities. Common sources for tactical information include competitors' sites, Securities and Exchange Commission (SEC) and other government filings, financial message boards, patent filings, résumés, job listings, and news articles. In addition, competitive online commentary can sometimes prove more useful in analyzing sales and marketing strategies.

Usenet newsgroups and message boards, for example, are rife with consumer opinion. As discussed in Chapter 2, what once required facilitated focus groups can now be achieved, in many cases, through observation of unsolicited opinions on public display in various online forums for customer feedback. The challenge becomes aggregating and analyzing the valuable comments.

The customer commentary found online about a competitor and its products is unfiltered (with the exception of some messages that may be blocked for abusive language or profanity), direct, and straight from the people who use the competitor's products. Competitive customer feedback can take many forms, and it's possible to glean competitive sales and marketing strategies from this raw data. Examples include:

➤ Customer comments, both positive and negative, related to product quality, service, and features

➤ Customer comments, both positive and negative, about promotions and the pricing of competitor offerings

➤ Feedback and descriptions of customer experiences

➤ Detailed comparisons of competitor products and services relative to other available alternatives

This competitive intelligence can be found primarily on the Web, including user communities, message boards, consumer review sites, blogs, and personal pages. In some instances, valuable intelligence can still be gathered from Usenet newsgroups and chat rooms, though feedback collected from these environments is sometimes skewed toward the more technology-inclined market segment than the broader Internet audience.

The process of aggregating online commentary is useful not only for gaining the consumer's views on the strengths and weaknesses of competitive offerings, it can also help identify consumer reaction to specific promotional activities. As discussed in Chapter 2, online commentary can provide a better understanding of the consumer decision-making process, allowing a clearer vision of competitive product and service differentiation from the perspective of the customer. This kind of intelligence can be leveraged both for near-term improvements and long-term product planning. As patterns surface in competitive commentary, they can often be exploited for competitive advantage. Best practices can be adopted and "worst" practices can be exploited.

Here are four real examples that provide an indication of the types of insights that can be gleaned by monitoring your competitor on the Internet:

1. A major tobacco company analyzed the online activities of three competitors and discovered that one of them was developing a "healthier" cigarette. Online documents revealed that the competitor didn't intend to sell this new cigarette but planned instead to patent and license the processes and technology.

2. A major tire manufacturer monitored competitor sites and industry-related online destinations. Internet intelligence revealed that the most trafficked sites focused on side-by-side tire comparisons, and that customers were

using the Internet to conduct research before buying at brick-and-mortar stores. As a result of these findings, the tire manufacturer abandoned plans to launch an e-commerce site and instead focused on a site that would complement offline channels.

3. A *Fortune* 50 insurance company found online documents revealing that its top competitor was planning to roll out a fully functional online banking service throughout the United States in the coming year. Analyzing the competitor's partner sites further revealed that the company was aggressively targeting a new market segment.

4. A leading multibrand hotel chain examined the online strategies of a competitor. The analysis revealed that the competitor was courting foreign customers traveling to the United States, but that only 1 percent of that company's U.S. hotel sites had foreign language capabilities.

Collecting the Data

The first step in deciphering your competitors' strategies is the collection of the dataset to be used for the generation of information. This information will then serve as the basis for intelligence. Free search engines are a good start for data collection and can provide a satisfactory high-level overview, though more robust solutions should be considered if competitor brands are pervasive. Proprietary data mining and analysis technologies, programmed specifically for such tasks, are invaluable for filtering out the "noise" (see Chapter 9).

Since the quality of the output will depend on the input, it is important to cast a broad net when gathering intelligence. At the same time, it's also advisable to keep the dataset manageable by screening out content that is less likely to be relevant. Depending on your goals, this may mean prioritizing more recently posted content or zeroing in on the most credible sources.

In the end, it's wise to treat all intelligence with some level of skepticism, regardless of whether it is based on the analysis of online or offline data. The benefit of gathering and analyzing data from many different sources is that the intelligence generated can help to corroborate a source and provide the most informed decision making.

Counterintelligence

"The good news is your competition's kimono is more open than ever," says Larry Chase, publisher of *Web Digest for Marketers*. "The bad news is, so is yours."[3] Just as the Internet facilitates competitive insights, it has made protecting company secrets all the more challenging. As one competitive intelligence professional notes: "Every firm has competitors as interested in knowing your plans as you are in knowing theirs, maybe even more so."[4] Recognizing that corporate websites have become a rich source of competitive intelligence information, some companies are beginning to limit what they post. The value of incremental branding needs to be carefully weighed against the potential value of the intelligence your brand presence may give to the competition.

But not all aspects of your brand presence are within your immediate control. The fact remains that the bulk of a company's presence online is outside of its own domain. The Internet's propensity for rapid propagation of information has made it far more difficult for companies to protect sensitive information. Even seemingly nonsensitive information can be of great value to your competitors. For example, if you win a major new customer, do you really want to put out a press release or see a news article that quotes the customer's decision makers? The customer contact will immediately be added to your competitor's target account list, if they weren't there already.

Hint: Some companies screen for site visitors from competitor IP addresses and route them to a version of their website that discloses less information, or they may block them altogether.

The value of competitive intelligence has elevated the importance of selective disclosure in order to control the outflow of information. In this practice, monitoring your own presence on the Internet can be as important as monitoring your competitor's. Knowing and consciously managing what intelligence is available to a competitor can help limit your risk; it's also a way to influence your competitor's decision making. "Selective disclosure of information about itself is a crucial resource the firm has in making competitive moves," noted Michael Porter. "The disclosure of any information should only be made as an integral part of competitive strategy."[5]

Actionable Information

Information gleaned from Internet sources cannot really be considered intelligence unless it is actually used for decision making. Regardless of the source of the information, the ultimate test of an organization's competitor analysis efforts is the extent to which its output becomes intelligence.

"Learning about competitors must never be allowed to become an end in itself," states Liam Fahey. "The purpose of competitor analysis is not to learn about competitors; it is to use that learning to make the right decisions and to make them faster and better than rivals."[6]

To maximize the chance that intelligence will be used within the organization, it is beneficial to implement formal processes for information collection, analysis, and communication. Having a system in place will increase efficiency, improve knowledge management, and significantly raise the overall chances of realizing the value of competitive intelligence.

Whatever the level of system sophistication, the importance of communication cannot be stressed enough. Gathering data is a waste of time unless it is used in formulating strategy, and creative ways must be devised to put the analyses in concise and usable form before it is delivered to top management. To extract full value from the intelligence, it is also important to communicate tactical intelligence in a timely fashion to field-level staff and others who have been trained to use the information in a professional and effective manner.

John Hovis, director of investor relations at Avnet, Inc., which distributes electronics components, discussed the importance of actionable information during his keynote address at the Society of Competitive Intelligence Professionals' Fifteenth Annual International Conference. "What is intelligence? It's actionable information," said Hovis. "In other words, it's giving your decision makers inside your company the opportunity to look at a body of information and take action. But you'll never get them to take action unless you tell them what it means. Because they don't have time to sit down and figure it out."

> *THE*
> *BUSINESS*
> *CASE*

Here are two examples of how online competitive intelligence can be turned into market share gains or another competitive advantage for a business.

Example One

A media company that syndicates science and nature-related content uses competitive intelligence to determine whom its competitors have syndication deals with. The media company regularly monitors the Internet for the presence of competitive content. Once its competitors' partners are identified, they are ranked according to criteria to determine which ones are the most attractive. The factors weighed include the traffic levels on the potential partners' sites, the level of professionalism, and how closely the content fits with the media company's own objectives.

In an attempt to gain market share, the media company approaches the best competitor partners and offers them extremely enticing syndication deals. Exceptional deals are tendered for sites willing to terminate their relationship with a competitor and enter long-term exclusive syndication relationships. Using the following assumptions and calculation, the media company estimates how much revenue it can potentially earn from syndication fees as a result of its new strategy:

Step	Assumption
1	Number of sites approached: 200
2	Syndication deals: 100
3	Average annual syndication fees per site: $5,000
4	Total annual fees generated = (2) × (3) = $500,000

Example Two

A specialty retailer was able to determine that a competitor was routinely criticized for poor customer service—specifically, customers were upset that the company did not accept the return of web purchases in offline stores. Based on this intelligence, the specialty retailer decided to aggressively promote a cross-channel, hassle-free return policy, thereby taking advantage of a competitive weakness to win market share.

THE BOARD ROOM SUMMARY

The Internet is a window into competitive branding tactics and strategies through unmatched access to information and direct observation of competitor activity. Brand owners should remember these key points:

➤ Although the sheer volume of online data makes collection and analysis more challenging, it can be a valuable source of sales and marketing intelligence on your competitors, providing insights into everything from target demographics to business models and product plans.

➤ Both your company's strategies and those of your competitor can be telegraphed by online content and activity.

➤ Some of the specific mechanisms that can be used to determine a competitor's strategy include the analysis of its brand reach (i.e., who is viewing the competitor's brands online), partners, and online commentary.

➤ Each of these approaches can yield information that, when analyzed, can provide your business with valuable competitive insights.

➤ Armed with online intelligence, a company is well positioned to protect itself, win market share, increase profitability, and outmaneuver the competition.

Section 5

Taking Action

"If you can't protect what you own, you don't own anything."
JACK VALENTI, PRESIDENT AND CEO OF THE
MOTION PICTURE ASSOCIATION OF AMERICA

Chapter 9

How to Use Online Monitoring to Control Your Brand and Capture Revenue

Companies operating without intelligence are flying blind—missing opportunities and flirting with potential disaster. Simply stated, if you don't monitor how your brand is being used online, you are exposed. Others will be free to leverage the value of your brand and profit at your expense. Your brand integrity may be compromised, the customer experience will suffer, and customer loyalty undermined. Implementation of an effective online monitoring program is the first step to gain control of your brand and capture revenue.

At a high level, there are two ways to monitor how a brand is being used online: Wait to see if stakeholders such as customers or employees report incidents, or scour the Internet to collect intelligence on a proactive basis. Though relying on stakeholders for unsolicited reports of abuse may seem like less work in the short term, it's not the most effective approach to intelligence gathering. In many ways, combating brand abuse is like containing the outbreak of a disease—early detection is crucial! This is because of the speed with which abuse can proliferate and the broad exposure a single incident can get in a short amount of time. Traffic levels online are far higher than most people realize. By the time an employee, for example, randomly discovers an incident of abuse, it's likely to have affected thousands or even millions of other people. It may also have spread to other locations.

Smart companies go beyond informal reporting mechanisms and implement a process for aggressively monitoring online activity. Combined with preemptive measures, such as establishing and communicating partner compliance guidelines, online monitoring maximizes the chance of nipping abuse in the bud. It is also necessary for managing online risk. Organizations that are informed and aware of relevant online activity can react to situations in real-time and can take advantage of a window of opportunity to address problems before they escalate.

But even the best online monitoring plans are not foolproof. The digital landscape has grown so enormous that there is too much ground to cover—and that's okay. The costs associated with 100 percent comprehensive searching are very likely to outweigh the benefits, particularly if done without the aid of advanced search and filtering technologies. Best practice in defending the brand involves managing risk, not eliminating it. This provides the most attractive return on your monitoring investment. To effectively manage risk and defend the brand, companies need to implement a process for collecting and prioritizing intelligence.

Once you understand who is leveraging your brand, where your customers are going, and in what context they are experiencing your brand, you will be armed with the intelligence necessary to take action. Companies that implement an effective monitoring program have taken the first step toward gaining a competitive advantage, improving customer loyalty, and driving incremental revenue.

The What-Where-How Approach

Since there is too much at stake to ignore what's happening online, the first logical question is where and how to start. Considering the vast size and rapid growth of the Internet, gathering the intelligence necessary to defend a brand can seem overwhelming—particularly if the brand in question has a significant online presence.

In many ways, your level of success will be directly proportional to both the level of effort you put in and how you allocate resources. Prioritizing your monitoring efforts is critical, particularly when manual work is involved. Companies should prioritize what they are monitoring, where they monitor (i.e., in which online environments), and how they monitor. Once intelligence is gathered, it should then be categorized and further prioritized to construct a plan of attack (see Chapter 10).

What to Search For

The first step is to scope the potential issues and investigate where to focus your online monitoring efforts. Companies should use a good amount of common sense to consider their brands and digital assets in the context of their business model to determine what types of activity are most likely to affect them. Companies that own digital assets, for example, are likely to be susceptible to piracy, while popular brands are likely to be the subjects of online commentary and the targets of customer diversion tactics.

While you may rely somewhat on gut instinct, it is a good idea to conduct some test searches to confirm whether your assumptions are correct regarding which brands are abused and the nature of the abuse. Without substantial experience monitoring online brand issues, it's easy to be wrong. For example, almost no entity believes its brand is being associated with objectionable content, even though almost all recognized brands are affected. Also, by gathering intelligence, each organization will discover issues specific to its industry and business model, some of which have not previously been considered.

Once identified, the brand abuse issues facing a company should be clearly prioritized and protection efforts apportioned accordingly. The more dire the circumstances and the more resources available, the broader and deeper the efforts can go. Some companies start with cybersquatting, for example, then work their way through other customer diversion issues (see Chapter 3). Other companies mobilize all possible resources to combat counterfeiting (see Chapter 5), focusing primarily on distribution outlets such as auction and e-commerce sites, allowing other brand issues to wait. It all depends on the specific situation and business issues.

As the owner of a well-known brand, Dow Corning Corp. elected to focus on online commentary and brand abuses such as misrepresentation of its brand or logo, false relationship claims, and association with objectionable content. The company also prioritized sites diverting customers from Dow Corning's website. "We have spent fifty-seven years building Dow Corning and servicing our customers. As the Internet becomes a critical channel for business, we must ensure that we continue to meet the needs of our customers on and offline," said Joe Plevyak, Dow Corning director of e-business.[1]

Where to Search

To target your online monitoring efforts, it is helpful to remember that each threat to a brand has specific online environments where it is more likely to be found. The Internet is much larger than the World Wide Web. Though many of the more traditional, well-publicized forms of brand abuse, such as cybersquatting and metatagging, occur on the Web, there may be other online environments that should take precedence, depending on the nature of the brand.

Alternative online environments continue to emerge for a variety of reasons. The first is that the Web has limitations. As a whole, the Web has an abundance of outdated content and is not particularly well suited for the transfer of large documents. Piracy, for example, is more likely to occur over peer-to-peer (P2P) networks or using Internet Relay Chat (IRC) and file transfer protocol (FTP), all of which are designed specifically to improve the convenience and privacy with which individuals can transfer large files.

Examples of Internet environments where some of the more common brand abuse incidents are likely to occur are listed in Figure 9-1.

Some brand abuse issues are much easier to identify than others. Preliminary monitoring efforts should be focused on those parties with the most potential to do you harm. As such, it's important to remain aware of which of your partners and competitors have an online presence and monitor their sites regularly. When there are too many partners for this practice to be feasible, efforts should be focused on the highest-priority partners, using the criteria outlined in Chapter 4. If possible, it is also a good idea to subscribe to your partners' or competitors' e-mail newsletters, which may contain information not otherwise disclosed online.

One way to find out who is associating with your brand online is to do a "reverse lookup." This is an advanced feature that some of the leading search engines offer that provides you with a list of everyone who links to your home-

	World Wide Web	Message Boards	Auctions	FTP	e-Mail	Usenet Newsgroups	P2P Networks	IRC
Objectionable Associations	x				x			
Commentary		x			x	x		x
Cyber-Squatting	x							
Typo-Piracy	x							
Search Engine Manipulation	x							
Mislabeled Links	x							
Unsolicited Messages					x			
Spawning	x				x			
Mouse-Trapping	x							
Partner Non-Compliance	x				x			
Counterfeiting and Gray Markets	x		x		x	x		x
Piracy	x		x	x	x	x	x	x

Figure 9-1. *Internet environments where brand abuses are most likely to occur.*

page or domain. Doing a reverse lookup is useful for finding out which part-ners are linking to you (and which are not). It can also allow you to identify unaffiliated entities that are claiming or implying a relationship with you.

Another way to determine who is linking to you is to monitor your server log files, which can tell you the origin of the visitors to your site. The most significant sources of site traffic should be monitored closely so that you under-stand the context by which your customers arrive at your website.

How to Search

While partners and known competitors are often easy to find, it can be more challenging to find those unaffiliated offenders that are scattered throughout cyberspace. The brand can show up in many different forms and in many different online environments. Fortunately, a plethora of free online search services are available to help companies that elect to defend their brand with in-house resources.

Some online environments are more difficult to search than others, and new environments continue to evolve while others fade away. Most online environments have utilities that provide their own query capabilities or are searchable through free, third-party services designed to help users navigate cyberspace. For example, each P2P network, message board community, or auction site has its own integrated search utility.

Web and FTP sites, on the other hand, have thousands of online search engines vying to help visitors find what they are looking for. Many of these same search engines offer image searches, which can be used to supplement your efforts by identifying the presence of logos. There are also metasearch engines, such as Dogpile.com, that allow you to query multiple search engines through a single portal.

The following are a few examples of publicly available search services that can be used to identify incidents of online brand abuse:

Search Environment	Search Services
Web content	Google, AlltheWeb
Domain names	Netcraft, DomainSurfer
P2P networks	KaZaa, BearShare, WinMX
Usenet newsgroups	Google Groups
Message Boards	BoardReader
FTP	AlltheWeb, FileSearching

Stakeholders. Online monitoring efforts can be enhanced by involving stake-holders such as employees, partners, and even customers. Each stakeholder who spends time online is another pair of eyes that can report incidents. But relying on stakeholders to help defend the brand won't be effective if they are approached in a haphazard manner. You need to put processes in place to educate stakeholders, collect reports, and take action against offenders.

Employees can, for instance, help monitor more challenging environments such as spam. If employees understand how important it is to defend the brand, they can monitor the spam they receive in their personal e-mail boxes and be on the lookout for abuses. The company can make it easy to report offenses by allowing employees to forward suspect spam to a corporate e-mail box set up specifically for the task. By raising awareness and putting such processes in place, companies can significantly improve their online monitoring efforts across all Internet environments.

To encourage participation, it's always a good idea to proselytize the need to defend the brand. Engaging employees in the fight to preserve brand integrity can also foster a stronger team environment, strengthen allegiance to the company, and cultivate respect for the internal champions of brand protection.

Hint: Offer employees an incentive if they report an online brand abuse. For example, a gift certificate might be awarded to the employee who reports the most egregious incident, or you might enter everyone who reports an abuse in a monthly prize drawing.

INTERCONTINENTAL HOTELS GROUP PLC

The Internet has made it extremely difficult for hotel chains to maintain control over their distribution channels. One of the biggest challenges has been trying to stop franchisees from making rooms available through discount travel sites at lower rates than those available on the chain's own websites. When franchisees put inventory on discount sites, it puts pressure on room rates and undermines profitability.

InterContinental Hotels Group PLC, which also owns the Holiday Inn, Staybridge, and Crowne Plaza brands, has been at the forefront of Internet monitoring and realizes how challenging it can be to keep more than 3,300 owned, leased, managed, and franchised hotels in compliance. This is particularly true when attempting to combat an issue like price erosion, where monitoring needs to include third-party discount travel sites.

Faced with this dilemma, InterContinental identified an opportunity to engage their enormous customer base to help them identify pricing violations. The hotel chain launched an Internet rate guarantee program that encourages guests to let them know if they discover a cheaper room rate on third-party sites. When a lower price is reported, InterContinental offers the guest the lower rate, plus another 10 percent off that. InterContinental then charges the guilty franchisee a $75 penalty for the policy violation. This clever approach has effectively harnessed the company's entire customer base to help support online monitoring efforts, improve profit margins, and drive incremental revenue.[2, 3]

Customer Eyes. A brand manager can establish a process to routinely check for the emergence of online abuse. Using customer diversion as an example, one approach would be to enter variations of the brand name, including common misspellings and typos, plus images and slogans as search terms into the top search services and review the returns. Similar variations may be used to check for cybersquatters and typo-pirates.

For this approach to be effective, it's very important to consider the diverse vehicles by which your customers navigate the digital landscape, which are not necessarily the same ways *you* navigate the Internet. To determine whether a brand is being used for customer diversion or is being associated with objectionable content, too many brand managers make the mistake of conducting a few test searches through a top portal. When they don't find any abuse, they conclude that their brand is not abused. When in doubt, always look at things through your customer's eyes. For example, while Google and Yahoo! may be very popular, there are thousands of search portals online, some of which you've never heard of but still get hundreds of thousands of visitors every month. Some cater to specific interests, industries, or demographics; others use aggressive marketing tactics to help offset inferior search results.

Search leaders such as Google use the most sophisticated technology and do a relatively good job in their ongoing battle against manipulation, while the lesser-known search portals are more easily duped. These second-tier search engines may also sell paid placements more indiscriminately, allowing competitors and others to purchase top placement in the returns when a customer enters your brand or slogan (see Chapter 3).

By employing aggressive customer acquisition tactics, some of these seemingly obscure search portals attract surprisingly high numbers of people, despite substandard search and screening capabilities. This is important to keep in mind if you suspect your brand may be used to divert customers.

At the same time, there are far too many search vehicles to review each one manually. An effective in-house monitoring solution will seek out off-the-beaten-path search engines and rotate through them periodically to scan for activity of interest. They will also look for portals that cater specifically to their target markets.

False Positives. Another trick for getting the most out of your monitoring efforts is to minimize the number of potential false positives. If the brand in question is also a common word, such as *Monday, universal,* or *enterprise,* it will be more difficult to estimate true brand presence, as well as to find and take action on some types of brand abuse. If the brand is a unique word such as *Compaq* or *Zippo,* there is really no question that it is actually the trademark.

As an example, examining the top 100 returns for the word *enterprise* may reveal that ninety of them relate to terms such as Enterprise Resource Planning or Starship Enterprise, or are generic uses of the word *enterprise,* such as in reference to a business venture. If, however, these results were generated while attempting to gather brand intelligence for Enterprise Rent-A-Car, there are some options:

> ➤ Advanced search options are offered by most search engines and can be selected to exclude results with certain words, such as *starship* or *ERP* (the common acronym for enterprise resource planning).

> ➤ The search can be redone using the complete brand name as an exact string match. This is usually done by adding quotation marks: "Enterprise Rent-A-Car"

Detecting Objectionable Associations. While a comprehensive search may require the support of proprietary search technologies, there are a number of ways to investigate whether your brand is being widely associated with objectionable content:

1. *Popular Search Engines.* Just as the most advanced search engines do a pretty good job of filtering abuse, they can also aid in identifying examples of abuse, when prompted accordingly. The key is to make sure your search reflects that you are, in fact, looking for the brand in an abusive context. If you want the right information to rise to the top of your search results, you can enter the brand in the search accompanied by explicit words that would appear only in an objectionable context. If you would like to see if Brand A is associated with pornography or gambling, for example, you might enter "Brand A casino," "Brand A sex," "Brand A XXX," or other more explicit combinations.

2. *Obscure Search Engines.* You may not even have to craft specially worded search terms to assist some second-tier search engines in order to view the

abuse (see Figure 9-2). Since search engines come and go practically by the day, you can peruse search engine directories and randomly pick candidates to use for checking abuse. The broader you cast the net, the more likely you are to uncover abuse. Depending on your target market, it may be a good idea to include foreign search engines and engines that offer paid placement in their listings.

3. *Domain Name Searches.* The most abused brands show up not only in the content of the site, but sometimes also in the domain name. There are a number of free domain name search engines online where you can enter your brand and see who is cybersquatting your brand names (see Figure

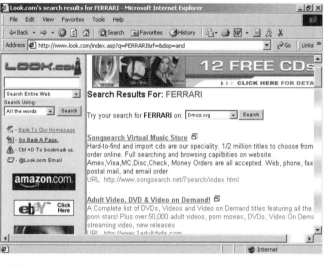

Figure 9-2. *Top returns for "Ferrari" on two search engines include a site selling adult videos and a virtual casino.*

9-3). Many times it's immediately obvious from the domain name that a site contains objectionable content. For example, the owner of Brand A may find a site named www.branda-xxx.com or www.branda-casino.com. Figure 9-4 is another example.

Note that when doing domain searches, it is important to use an engine that automatically allows for "wild cards." This means that the search engine will return any domain that contains the brand, even if there are characters

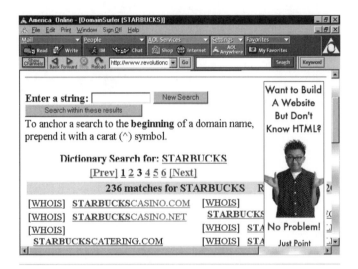

Figure 9-3. *A domain name search reveals potential abuse of the Starbucks brand by online casinos.*

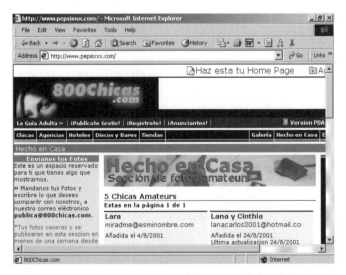

Figure 9-4. *Pepsixxx.com is a Spanish language adult website.*

before and/or after the brand. Otherwise you'll have to speculate on the exact spelling of the offending domain.

It is also important to search for registered domains that contain common typos and misspellings of the brand name (see Chapter 3 for the discussion on typo-piracy), which is a favorite customer diversion trick. Look for inverted characters, extra letters at the beginning or end of the brand name, and the absence of a "dot" after www or before com. Oftentimes the people who register these domains operate sites that contain objectionable content.

Allocation of Resources

After the initial assessment of the problem, a company needs to put processes in place and dedicate the resources necessary to collect intelligence and monitor the Internet on an ongoing basis, and to follow up on resolutions to the problems. Allocation of resources is important not just from a practical standpoint; it also demonstrates commitment. Without commitment, any efforts are likely to be halfhearted and destined to failure. (Chapter 11 covers how to mobilize your forces for a sustained campaign against brand abuse.)

At the same time, resources should not be disproportionate to the situation. For example, if a company does not have a well-known brand, and preliminary searches indicate a negligible online brand presence, defending the brand may be a part-time responsibility. But for a larger enterprise, there may be millions of dollars at stake, so it is in the company's best interest to respond accordingly.

At a tactical level, there are a variety of ways to approach the allocation of resources for online monitoring. While some businesses like The Coca-Cola Company hire full-time people dedicated to the task, others attack the issues with a team made up of current staff members who have other responsibilities. Such a team would typically extend well beyond the boundaries of a marketing organization to include legal, business development, and distribution, etc.

Regardless of what departments are involved, it is most effective to have a single person spearhead the effort. No matter who is designated as the point person, dedication and careful prioritization of online monitoring efforts remain central to getting the best possible return on investment.

Should abuse remain elusive because brand presence is overwhelming, false positives are too difficult to sort through, or time and staff remain in short supply, it may be time to consider outsourcing. Depending on the scope of the potential problem and the level of comprehensiveness desired, it can sometimes be advantageous to outsource all or part of the job to professionals—many of whom have access to proprietary technology and bring relevant experience to bear.

When to Outsource

There are a number of indicators that can signal that a company should evaluate outsourcing its online monitoring effort. Factors depend on the nature of the brand or digital asset; they also vary according to the type of abuse. Considerations include the magnitude of the brand or digital asset presence online, the popularity of the brand as a search term, the popularity of a brand in domain names, the number of sites linking to the domain, the size of partner networks, and the general status of partner relationships. All of these factors can be easily estimated and will provide an indication of both the potential for abuse and the likelihood that the brand may be too prolific to monitor in-house.

The attractiveness of a brand is often a moving target, so good planning also looks to the future. For example, consider whether the launch of a new brand or a major advertising campaign might change the status quo. If so, it is best to have the resources in place to proactively monitor and contain abuse before it gains momentum and spirals out of control.

Monitoring your brand online is a challenging prospect to begin with. But as a brand's presence and level of abuse rise, it becomes increasingly difficult and inefficient to monitor and take action without the benefit of advanced technologies and automation. At some point, it can become impractical to monitor popular brands online manually.

Factors That Can Make Online Monitoring a Challenge

➤ *Duplication of Effort.* When sorting through results from multiple search engines, it can be complicated to determine what information has already been reviewed and what has not.

➤ *Limited Access to Results.* Most search engines will not allow you to view all the returns to your query. Even though the hits may be in the millions, search engines generally do not allow users to access more than the top one or two thousand results.

➤ *Unlimited Search Combinations.* While searching on a brand name may seem straightforward, it is difficult to predict all the variations and word combinations that customers may use. For example, a customer hoping to reserve a Hertz rental car may enter Hertz, Hertz rental, Hertz rental car, Hertz discount, Hertz New York, Hertz Atlanta, etc. The combinations are practically limitless, and each query is likely to yield different results even when using the same search engine.

➤ *Incomplete and Delayed Results.* Search results are based on content that's collected whenever the pages were last indexed. Your customers, on the other hand, are viewing pages in real time. Search engines either don't index many of these pages, or the pages may not have been indexed recently.

➤ *Limited Content Accessibility.* Not all online content is stored. Activity on some online environments, such as P2P networks and chat rooms, is not recorded anywhere and must therefore be monitored in real-time.

➤ *Hidden Brand Abuse.* On the Web, some abuses may only be evident by reviewing the source code of the page, which can be very time-consuming to do manually.

➤ *Limited International Coverage.* Few search engines provide adequate global coverage, requiring you to use a combination of regional search engines. Even Google, for example, returns a different set of results depending on which of their country-specific websites you use to conduct the search. If you are experiencing brand abuse on an international scale, it is often more challenging to identify incidents.

When internal resources fall short of what's necessary to monitor a brand, online activity goes unmonitored. The level of risk rises in direct proportion to the level of unmonitored online activity. A company must therefore determine what level of risk it can tolerate. As the risk or cost of abuse approaches intolerable levels, it is time to either allocate more internal resources or to contract the work out.

Outsourcing was the route chosen by Unilever, whose stable of brands includes Lipton, Breyers, Snuggle, and Dove. "For decades, Unilever has maintained an unwavering commitment to its consumers," said Katrina Burchell, trademark counsel for Unilever. "A large part of keeping our brand promise to the people who use our products means partnering with those companies [that] can help us maintain that brand value."[4]

Citing the growth of its online brand presence, Frank Russell Company also opted to outsource its online monitoring and brand protection effort. "With the burgeoning use of our indexes as standard economic barometers of the U.S. equity market, we find it increasingly difficult to track their online use," noted Rui Moura, director of corporate marketing and communications.[5]

How to Outsource

If you decide to investigate your options for outsourcing, it is wise to do so with care. Online monitoring and brand protection are relatively new services, so the market landscape is constantly changing.

Research also shows that there are many niches in the brand and digital asset protection space. Companies with "brand protection" in their taglines or list of services may specialize in anything from domain name administration to forensic fingerprinting, which sometimes makes it difficult to compare apples to apples.

If you don't have firsthand knowledge and experience working with a service provider, it is worthwhile to carefully evaluate your options and do some research. As with any procurement process, a rigorous evaluation process will help ensure the best brand defense and best return on your monitoring investment. Factors you'll want to consider when evaluating candidates for online monitoring services include the service provider's background, its security provisions, its range of services, its partner network, its client list, and the experience and qualifications of its staff. Figure 9-5 is a useful checklist you can use when evaluating an outsource vendor.

The scope of services you require is also a consideration. Smaller companies purchasing lower-end services may not need to do as much due diligence.

Company Background

Given the potential implications of intelligence gaps, it is good to go with a stable company that you can work with over the long-term in a partnership to help you manage risk and defend the brand. Consider the vendor's experience and the reputability of both the company and its corporate officers. If the company is publicly traded, you can evaluate its overall financial stability through SEC filings. If it is a private company, you can look at other information sources such as:

➤ The company's investors and reported funding situation.

➤ Corporate accountants or bank officers.

➤ Supplier references.

➤ Company profiles available from business information companies such as D&B (Dun & Bradstreet).

Company Background:
- ☐ Established company
- ☐ Reputable corporate officers
- ☐ Financially stable
- ☐ Adequate technology infrastructure
- ☐ Toured facilities (optional)

Security:
- ☐ Adequate physical and cyber security
- ☐ Emergency backup systems and processes in place
- ☐ Sufficient redundancy

Services:
- ☐ Acceptable source coverage (breadth, depth, frequency)
- ☐ Acceptable incident coverage (types of abuse or intelligence)
- ☐ Acceptable approach to automation and relevancy
- ☐ Delivery format and incident details evaluated
- ☐ Prioritization included with service
- ☐ Workflow management utilities included (optional)

Partnerships:
- ☐ Reputable partners
- ☐ Partner services relevant
- ☐ Good partner references (optional)

Experience and Qualifications:
- ☐ Impressive client list
- ☐ Relevant experience
- ☐ Qualified staff
- ☐ Good client references
- ☐ Interviewed delivery manager (optional)

Figure 9-5. *Vendor evaluation checklist.*

Once you have assessed stability and integrity, it is worthwhile to take a close look at what the vendor brings to the table in terms of the resources that it can deploy on your behalf. Remember the reasons you are considering outsourcing in the first place and make absolutely certain the vendor addresses these concerns to your satisfaction. Consider not only the specific services that the vendor offers, but also the technology and infrastructure that the vendor brings to bear. These are the foundation of the online monitoring system. To establish vendor qualifications in this area, you can inquire about security, hardware, storage capacity, bandwidth, and the technology employed.

Security

Security measures and backup and emergency provisions are important considerations. Any system downtime or situation where the vendor's systems are compromised translates to lost time and money for you, not to mention potential PR headaches if sensitive data is stolen. Security is important because the information stored can sometimes be sensitive or may include information you are making efforts to contain.

Scope of Services

It is advisable to understand exactly what you will receive as part of your service, including both the breadth of coverage and the specifics of the output. These are things that can play a role in determining the value of the service and return on investment. Questions you may want to ask include:

> ➤ What specific Internet environments are included in the proposed solution?

> ➤ Are the entire environments covered or select portions? If the coverage is not complete, what specifically is covered and what is not?

> ➤ How often is each environment monitored?

> ➤ Is source code reviewed, or is the search limited to visible elements?

> ➤ Does the vendor own technology that will offer an advantage over doing it yourself with search engines?

> ➤ How exactly does the vendor determine if something is relevant or not?

As for the output from the monitoring efforts, you will want to understand what is delivered beyond a URL or copy of the incident itself. For example:

> ➤ Will traffic information be included to help prioritize incidents?

> ➤ Will incidents be prioritized at all and, if so, based on what criteria?

> ➤ Will a copy of the original incident be archived in case there is a legal action?

> ➤ To what extent can the output be customized or configured to meet your requirements?

> ➤ What is the delivery format (i.e., e-mail, web-based, hard copy, etc.)?

> ➤ Is contact information provided to aid in follow-up?

> ➤ Are workflow management utilities included to help reduce the level of effort required when contacting offenders?

A sample scope of work for a request for proposal (RFP) is included for your reference as Appendix E. This scope of work is a mock-up document that combines miscellaneous elements from actual RFPs issued for online monitoring services. Each organization that puts out an RFP will have company-specific issues and should develop its own custom version. The sample is included for illustrative purposes only.

Partnerships

When dealing with an unknown entity, it is sometimes possible to gain insights into the service provider's reputability based on the quality of its partnerships. In addition, it is good to know what resources a vendor may be able to deploy on your behalf through partnerships should the scope of service stray into peripheral areas where you may require additional support. Note that asking for partner references can help to assess the robustness of the relationship and allow you to determine the extent to which the two companies have worked together in the past. Nobody wants to be a guinea pig, at least not unknowingly or at full price!

Experience and Qualifications

You can tell a lot from a list of current clients and service descriptions. It is safe to say that companies aren't tossing around money freely—blue-chip clients are hard to come by and usually demand the best from their vendors. Ask for a list of clients that have been customers for at least a year. While it is still necessary to make your own decision based on your own needs, having a client list to evaluate allows you to benefit from the decisions that other companies have made before you.

Reviewing a client list may not be enough by itself, however. It is important to put this information in some context. For example, half the clients may be participating in a free trial, and may be dissatisfied with their service to boot! Or they may be receiving a service unrelated to what you are seeking. Once you have narrowed down your list of vendor candidates, ask for (and follow up on) references because it will help you to answer these questions and others.

Staff qualifications are also worth digging into. After all, these are the individuals you will entrust to help you monitor online activity for your brand defense effort. They are also the people you will interact with on an ongoing basis and entrust with sensitive information.

➤ ➤ ➤

Outsourcing requires a certain level of trust. Armed with this information, you'll be able to gain a clearer understanding of the options available to you and make a decision you're comfortable with. The knowledge will also help ensure that if you elect to outsource, you get what you pay for.

THE BUSINESS CASE

To protect its brand and identify sales leads for licensing content, a market data provider decides to monitor online activity. Their highest priority is to find incidents where the market data is being used to provide real-time quotes without authorization, and then approach the offending party with a licensing agreement.

As a result of a program designed to encourage employees to report incidents of brand abuse, the licensing manager knows that most of the offenders are financial websites. So to get the best return on her monitoring investment, the manager decides to focus on the Web. By consulting SearchEngineWatch .com, she is able to get a list of leading Web search engines, as well as some focused specifically on financial services. Instead of just entering the brand name into the search engine, she further targets her search results by adding phrases such as "free real-time quotes" to her queries.

To identify licensees that are most likely capable of paying licensing fees, the manager filters out sites that are personal pages or lack any visible source of revenue such as advertising or commerce. These offenders are forwarded to the legal department for further action. She also disregards the websites of existing licensees, unless they are using the market data outside the scope of their current agreement.

The market data provider's average licensing customer generates about $15,000 per year in revenue. By establishing a well thought out process and spending a few hours each week monitoring the Internet, the licensing manager is able to uncover 60 solid sales leads over the course of a year, and successfully convert 40 percent of the leads into signed licensing agreements. By prioritizing online monitoring, the company is able to generate an incremental revenue stream of $360,000 in the first twelve months.

THE BOARD ROOM SUMMARY

To defend the brand, you need to monitor online activity. This intelligence gathering can be done in-house or it can be outsourced to a vendor. Brand owners need to remember these key points:

➤ Aggressively monitoring online activity is the first step toward managing online risk.

➤ Prioritizing which online environments and types of brand abuses you want to monitor will provide the best return on your monitoring investment.

➤ Online monitoring efforts can be enhanced by involving stakeholders, such as employees, partners, and even customers.

➤ As the online brand presence and level of abuse rise, it becomes increasingly difficult to monitor without technologies to automate the process.

➤ If the risk associated with unmonitored brand use reaches intolerable levels, it is time to either dedicate more internal resources or consider outsourcing.

➤ When outsourcing, a rigorous evaluation process will help ensure that you procure the right services from the right vendor.

Chapter 10

Constructing Your Plan of Attack

The two major elements of defending the brand are gathering intelligence and taking action. Once you are monitoring the online environment, how do you launch an aggressive campaign against abuse? Fortunately, many companies have already had to solve this problem. From their experiences, insights can be gleaned regarding what policies and actions have been most effective.

This chapter outlines high-level processes that reflect best practices developed through working with dozens of companies to manage online intelligence. But the generic approach presented here is only a starting point—it needs to be customized. Each business has its own unique considerations, and the only constant in the digital world is change. This means that the situation must be continuously reassessed and that processes not only need to be effective, but also adaptable.

Even if you're only monitoring online activity to "keep your finger on the pulse" and have no intention of taking action, you never know when something so egregious will appear that you have to do something about it. Should this situation arise, it is best not to be caught off-guard. Organizations that are prepared for action, with thoughtful, efficient processes, are poised to meet or beat nearly any challenge that arises.

Designing an Effective Approach

The methodology outlined here should provide a starting point for taking the actions necessary to defend the brand. It is also intended to maximize the return on investment that goes into protecting a brand. The approach starts with the prioritization of the intelligence, including:

➤ Determining who is infringing on your brand

➤ Defining the nature of the abuse

➤ Deciding whether or not it warrants action

Next, you need to set up internal procedures, such as assigning ownership, selecting a format and tone for communication, and contacting offenders. The final components involve revisiting the incident and ensuring a satisfactory resolution.

While the model is presented from the perspective of a company defending its brand, a similar process can be deployed to pursue opportunities. In this case, you would substitute the prioritization factors with others more suitable to your goals. For example, if you are identifying new licensees, you could use the criteria outlined in Chapter 6, whereas if you are identifying new partners or customers, you might refer to the criteria presented in Chapter 8.

Any and/or all of the steps outlined can be done in-house or outsourced to a vendor or law firm (see Chapter 9 for vendor outsourcing). Should you decide to do it yourself, the ten-step approach presented should be a good starting point for designing an effective process.

Step 1: Categorize Incidents by Offender

Just as it is important in targeting online monitoring efforts, segmenting who is abusing your brand is the first step in prioritizing incidents and deciding the appropriate course of follow-up action. To achieve this initial segmentation, findings can be categorized according to relationship types.

Some of the potential brand abusers are obvious, such as direct competitors or adult sites that are attempting to divert your customers. Others may not be as obvious: Third-party sites may leverage the popularity of your brand as a search term in an effort to increase traffic; community or fan sites unintentionally misuse your intellectual property; authorized partners display an old logo or broken links to your site.

Some of the parties, such as news sites, could be using your brand name in a page title so search engines correctly categorize their articles, while product review sites could be using your brand as part of a comparison feature. Conclusion? It's important to segment incidents according to who is abusing the brand since some offenders are of greater concern than others.

While it's not necessary to develop a category for all potential relationship types, some of the following categorizations may prove helpful in defining the relationship:

- Authorized Partners/Unauthorized Partners
- Community/Fan/Personal Websites
- Objectionable Content Sites
- Competitors/Noncompetitors
- News
- Product Reviews

Categorizing each site into relationship types such as these is the first step in determining how to prioritize offenses and proceed with the intelligence management process.

Step 2: Categorize the Abuse

Further segmentation of the intelligence generated by online monitoring will allow you to better determine the impact from the activities taking place. In addition to company and industry-specific categories, incidents tend to fall into general groupings, where the brand abuser may engage in activities such as:

- Association of Brands with Objectionable Content
- Customer Diversion Tactics
- Trademark or Copyright Violations
- Claimed or Implied Relationships
- Commentary

Any incident falling into one of these categories can have a significant impact on how your brand is perceived, and it can affect both online and offline purchases. In some instances, it may be beneficial to further segment incidents into subcategories. For example, customer diversion may be broken down into brand presence in the domain (e.g., cybersquatting and typo-piracy), the URL, the metatag, titles, images, or text.

Step 3: Prioritize the Incidents

Determining the priority of the incidents allows you to focus resources and determine the appropriate follow-up activity. The prioritization is generally based on 1) who is infringing on the brand, 2) the nature of the incident, and 3) the potential impact of the activity on the company's brand equity, the customer experience, or revenue.

With regards to who is abusing your brand, competitor offenses are often the most alarming. Incidents related to the activities of online partners are secondary, while brand abuse related to news, product reviews, community/ fan sites, and personal pages are generally a lower priority.

Parties infringing on the brand need to be considered in conjunction with the nature of the incident in order to assess the overall impact. Within this context, the incidents should then be prioritized according to the potential impact of the activity. Some of the general factors that can help assess the priority include the following:

➤ *The Potential for Direct Revenue Impact.* For example, a competitor site with your brand name in the URL or title could have direct revenue impact and should be considered a high priority. It is also important to note whether the site is conducting commercial transactions or appears to be for individual or personal use.

➤ *The Importance of the Audience Exposed.* Sites that reach a specific audience, such as customers, partners, or investors, often demand a higher level of concern than sites that are more benign, such as a personal page. The misrepresentation of a brand on a strategic partner's site, even if the site does not receive heavy traffic, would likely be important because of the audience the partner reaches.

➤ *The Number of Unique Visitors.* A highly trafficked site will, by definition, reach a larger audience, thus it will make more impressions and increase the potential impact. Brand abuse should be prioritized in the same way that advertising is valued—according to the number of people reached and the demographics.

➤ *The Potential to Confuse the Audience of Interest.* Sites that mimic the look and feel of your own website can confuse the audience, influence their buying decision, and even pose a security risk.

➤ *Any Additional Company-Specific Concerns.* These concerns can include a wide range of industry-specific issues or organization-specific priorities. For example, a financial services company might place a higher priority on sites that "deep link" to somewhere other than the company's homepage, which can result in customers bypassing mandatory statements and disclosures.

A matrix, such as the one shown in Figure 10-1, is a useful tool because it gives an initial indication as to the priority of each site. To develop the matrix, the factors assessed to determine a site's priority include those already outlined. To summarize, these prioritization criteria include:

1. Potential for Direct Revenue Loss

2. Nature of the Audience

3. Number of Customers Exposed

4. Potential for Confusion

5. Company-Specific Criteria

To maximize your return on investment, you should also evaluate how you'll take action in response to an incident based on what recourse is available to you and your likelihood of success. If there is no way to contact the offender or you have no legal standing, for example, these obstacles can undermine your efforts.

Step 4: Determine Whether the Incidents Warrant Action

Unless there are legal considerations that dictate otherwise, companies are best served by aligning their priorities with those incidents that merit the investment necessary to reach the desired outcome. In other words, you should weigh the costs versus the benefits. Even an egregious offense may not make sense to pursue if the cost of resolution—either in legal fees or time investment—outweighs the damage the incident may cause.

The next step then is to determine if the activity warrants action and, if so, whether the response should be immediate. Depending on the issue, the site may be held for later consideration if patterns emerge, priorities change, or other considerations are present, such as a change in law or significant court ruling.

If there are a large number of incidents that warrant no action, it may signal the need for a change in the monitoring strategy or process. The incidents may share commonalities, such as the nature of the offenses or where they are found, that could allow collection resources to be redeployed, potentially targeting other online environments or types of abuse.

Who	What	Why	
		Brand Dilution/ Customer Experience Undermined	Lost Customers, Lost Revenue, and Market Share
Competitor	Customer Diversion Copyright Infringement	High Priority	High Priority
Unauthorized Partner Objectionable Content	Customer Diversion Copyright Infringement Claimed Relationship	Medium Priority	Medium Priority
Authorized Partner	Customer Diversion	Medium Priority	Medium Priority
	Claimed Relationship	Low Priority	Low Priority
Fan/Community/ Personal News/ Product Review	Customer Diversion Copyright Infringement Claimed Relationship	Low Priority	Low Priority

Figure 10-1. *Sample prioritization process matrix.*

Resource constraints are another factor to consider. While you may want to be aware of all online incidents, you may only have the staff to take immediate action on the highest-priority offenses. Lesser-priority incidents can be set aside and then revisited later, after you've assessed whether they signal trends or when additional resources become available.

Step 5: Assign Responsibilities for Taking Action

Determining who within your organization will be responsible for reviewing the data, communicating it internally, and taking action is critical. Experience with Internet intelligence shows that there are many different approaches.

For example, some companies will designate a centralized contact to review all data and then parcel it off to another, appropriate person within or outside of the organization who assumes the job of resolving the issue (i.e., taking action). This is not necessarily the same person who is responsible for your online monitoring efforts. For smaller companies with a more limited scope of issues, having a single point person for monitoring, reviewing, and taking action can sometimes work well.

In cases where the same intelligence is relevant to multiple parties, it may work best to allow each individual to directly access the relevant data for their own purposes by drawing from a central database or using a simple, internal distribution process such as e-mail. Cross-departmental, internal communication is crucial at this point, just as it is when collecting competitive intelligence (see Chapter 8 for a discussion of Actionable Information). The more people who can gain value from the intelligence, the better the return on investment will be.

Step 6: Select the Communication

Selecting the form and content of communication with offenders is critical for achieving the desired outcomes. The substance of the communication will largely depend on the nature of the abuse and the desired response. Options to consider are:

➤ Including a "screen shot" or description of the incident

➤ Including the URL or other unique identifying characteristic

➤ Including company letterhead or logo in the correspondence

Appendix F contains a few sample letters for reference purposes only. In general, the most effective letters tend to be succinct and firm but not belligerent. Going overboard can have negative repercussions—potentially making the situation worse. Depending on the circumstances, a hostile letter can cast a company in the wrong light, give the offender ammunition, and even hurt business (for examples, see Figures 10-2 and 10-3). There is nothing like an arguably unjustified, harshly worded cease-and-desist letter to raise somebody's ire. At the same time, a letter that is too weak can be entirely ineffective. It's important to strike the right balance, and in this regard there really is no substitute for good judgment.

In the same vein, the choice of signatory can be interpreted as an indication of how serious your company takes the issue. The best choice for signatory is not mandatorily the owner assigned responsibility for taking action in step 5. It may be a vice president or general counsel.

Hint: A publicly accessible database of cease-and-desist letters for all types of brand abuse, together with a host of other valuable resources, is maintained at ChillingEffects.org. The website is managed by Chilling Effects Clearinghouse, a joint project of the Electronic Frontier Foundation and Harvard, Stanford, Berkeley, University of San Francisco, and University of Maine law school clinics.

In determining the appropriate content for your communication, the following factors may be considered:

➤ Relationship between the company and offending parties (e.g., partners vs. competitors)

➤ Resource constraints (e.g., e-mails and nonlegal correspondence are cheaper and less time-consuming than other alternatives)

➤ Nature of the issue (e.g., legal violation vs. branding)

➤ Effectiveness of the means of communication (e.g., cease-and-desist hard-copy letter vs. an e-mail from a brand manager)

Companies that are monitoring partners for brand protection generally have a more positive response when their initial communication has a friendly tone and is helpful in nature. The same approach is typically effective for fan sites. Cease-and-desist letters, on the other hand, are more effective when sent by counsel. For many companies, the tone of the first communication is amiable, but if a second notification is necessary, the consequences of inaction (e.g., legal ramifications) are specified.

From: "Tom Brazier" <tom@tbrazier.com>
To: <Beattie-Padovano@worldnet.att.net>
Cc: <dwhyte@redshift.com>; <raikins@ctb.com>
Sent: Sunday, April 09, 2000 11:28 AM
Subject: RE: Arai Helmet (Americas), Ltd.

Dear Mr. Holsinger;

Your e-mail, attached, is acknowledged. I also understand that you have sent a certified letter to my home about this matter. We will of course delete immediately all references to Arai helmets in our club website. We will never knowingly advertise Arai helmets in our newsletter and I will make sure the entire membership of BMW riders in California and nationally know of your desires concerning web links to the Arai site, and your litigation threats for so doing. We did in fact have a pointer set to send anyone who uses our website directly to the Arai website so that they could obtain information on Arai helmets. We have done the same courtesy to other helmet, clothing, and equipment manufactures.

Your heavy handed approach to this matter has caused me some concern. I am therefore sending a copy of this response, your letter, and my comments directly to Arai America in Daytona on my law firm letterhead. I am also copying this information to my club, the BMW Riders of Monterey Bay, Northern California BMW Riders, the BMW Internet Riders list; the local advertisers on my club web site, Motorcyclist, the BMW Motorcycle Owners Association Magazine, the BMW RA (OTL); Cycle News and the other national publications to save you the effort of addressing threatening letters to anyone with a pointer to the Arai advertising website. We shall also insure that the rest of the BMW Riders club, which we are in constant contact with, knows not to do this, and will make sure we enclose a copy of your letter to me so that they are appropriately warned. I do fail to see how threats of litigation, for conduct devised to route people to the Arai America advertising website, can be harmful to Arai sales. However I am sure someone at Arai America will set me straight about this soon. For those considering purchasing an Arai helmet, I must suspect that this kind of heavy handed, unfathomable, tactics in the motorcycle community will be long remembered.

I may be reached at the below telephone number on Monday, April 10th if you wish to discuss this matter further.

Sincerely;

Thomas S. Brazier, Esq.
LaMore, Brazier, Riddle and Giampaoli
A Professional Law Corporation
1570 The Alameda, Suite 150
San Jose, CA. 95126
408-280-6900

P.S. Ms. Whyte and Mr. Aikins
Please delete any reference to Arai helmets in the website and from the newsletter immediately. We may wish to consider, when the Board next meets, a ban on the use of the word "Arai" from this point forward in club communications. I will have editorial comments for the next newsletter. Please disseminate this letter and the response to all club members immediately so they may have the benefit of this Arai's counsels letter. I will make dissemination to the magazines, other websites and to the Arai Board of Directors and President/CEO.

Figure 10-2. *E-mail sent to Arai Helmet in response to their cease-and-desist letter.*

Figure 10-3. *A cease-and-desist letter gave this defunct site a new life.*

Step 7: Secure Approval

Before delivering the communication, make sure it is reviewed internally and approved by the appropriate parties. This step may be necessary to ensure that:

➤ The communication meets legal requirements.

➤ The message is consistent with other activities the company may be engaged in.

➤ All relevant parties are aware of the action.

➤ The action is internally coordinated with any other related efforts.

In designing this approval process, the following procedures may be helpful:

➤ Establish which actions and communications are subject to review.

➤ Establish which people/departments need to review and approve the communication.

➤ Designate a point person(s) to shepherd the document(s) through the approval process.

➤ Gain commitments and establish a timetable for completing the approval process.

Step 8: Contact the Offender

Sometimes the communication vehicle is just as important as the content. For example, overnight-mail packages get more attention than correspondence delivered by ground mail or e-mail, especially when accompanied by legal correspondence. And many companies find that sending a physical letter on corporate stationery appears more "official" and therefore is more likely to be taken seriously. The most common modes of delivery include standard mail letter, overnight or priority mail, e-mail, a phone call, or a fax.

Some companies elect to use different approaches depending on who they are contacting and the seriousness of the incident. Partners are contacted by phone whereas other minor offenders are sent a brief e-mail. More "official" and expensive communications are sometimes reserved for offenders that do not respond to a less formal communication.

Whatever method is selected, procedures need to be established to enable efficient response. Also, it is advisable to ensure all actions are recorded for future reference, especially if multiple modes of communication are employed.

When the incident occurs on a website, the site owners can be contacted directly. If the contact information is not provided on the site, it can be taken from the site's registration information, which can be usually be looked up at the registrar's website, which can be identified by using the Whois search of domain names at the website InterNIC.org.

Hint: Spammers can sometimes be tracked down in the same way a legitimate site owner can. You can find the domain name the e-mail links to and then look up the domain owner. Message headers can be forged, but by checking the HTML source of the message, you can often find the domain name.

....

When offenders are unresponsive, brand owners can sometimes get better results by sending notices to Internet service providers (ISPs) regarding illegal activity that they are unwittingly hosting. Depending on where the abuse occurs, this can sometimes be the only effective way to track users down. An example is when an individual is sharing copyrighted content such as software or video games via peer-to-peer (P2P) networks.

ISPs are generally responsive to notices of intellectual property theft. Acting under the provisions of the Digital Millennium Copyright Act (DMCA), the offending parties are promptly shut down. Legislation such as the DMCA in the United States and the European Parliament's directive on privacy in electronic communications has helped compel the cooperation of ISPs.

Step 9: Revisit the Incident

Evaluating the success of your actions requires that you revisit the incidents to see if matters have been resolved. Criteria and procedures need to be developed for determining whether contacted sites have responded appropriately. Depending on your specific situation, the monitoring process may be as simple as clarifying who tracks the incidents and when. For example:

➤ The responsibility for revisiting incidents falls to _____.

➤ Incidents will be revisited _____ days/months after initial contact.

➤ Incidents that remain out of compliance will be revisited _____ days/months later.

Step 10: Take Follow-Up Action

The final step is to determine what action to take when offenders have not responded appropriately to your communication. If the issue has not been resolved, consider the following questions:

➤ Should the offender be contacted again?

➤ If yes, how should the offender be contacted?

➤ Is the content of the original communication appropriate? In most cases, the content will need to be reworded to reflect the delinquency of the offender.

➤ Should a harsher tone be incorporated into the letter? Should reprisals be mentioned?

➤ Should another person/department within the company organization deliver the communication (e.g., legal counsel vs. brand manager)?

Additionally, measurements or metrics should be established to provide a good barometer for evaluating the effectiveness (i.e., compliance or success rates) of current procedures. Establishing target success rates allows you to better judge whether current processes need to be revisited or whether they are working well. Metrics are needed both for online monitoring as well as for acting on the intelligence collected.

Not every offender will comply, of course, so you must consider alternative actions for addressing high-priority incidents. For domain name disputes, arbitrators such as the National Arbitration Forum (NAF) can serve as a neutral mediator. The NAF settled the highly publicized case between Aimster (a file-sharing service) and America Online, citing that Aimster violated the AOL Instant Messenger (AIM) trademark and that the company had to give AOL several domain names, including Aimster.com.

The Internet Corporation for Assigned Names and Numbers (ICANN) has the discretion to shift the ownership of domains based on an arbitrator's findings (see Chapter 3). You can find a list of ICANN-approved dispute-resolution service providers at ICANN.org.

If the offender is engaged in illegal activity, working with law enforcement is another approach that can be effective. As an example, in 2000, DIRECTV's two-year battle against the distribution of pirated satellite access cards resulted in a highly successful sting operation executed in cooperation with U.S. Customs and the Department of Justice.

Best Practices in Action

A large company with a well-known consumer brand has made it a top priority within the organization to defend the brand. The organization has successfully implemented procedures to take action against brand abuse, whether it is through association with objectionable content, cybersquatting, metatagging, logo abuse, unauthorized affiliation, or partner noncompliance.

Objectionable Content

When the brand is associated with objectionable content (namely, pornography, gambling, or hate speech), the legal group sends strongly worded cease-

and-desist letters to all offending websites. The letters demand that the site remove company brand names from metatags, hidden text, or any other text. Almost all sites comply with the company's requests within two weeks.

Cybersquatting

All cybersquatters receive demand letters from the company. The demand letter asks the site to transfer domain ownership to the company; the company, in turn, reimburses registration fees. Almost all sites have complied. One noncompliant site, which is owned by a partner, has asked for unreasonably high fees. The company is working through ICANN arbitration processes to resolve the issue.

Unauthorized Brand/Logo Use

Unaffiliated third parties that are using logos or brand names receive letters from brand managers that respectfully ask whether those sites have preexisting agreements to use the company's trademarked brands. If not, they are asked to remove the logo or brand name. Sites that have formal relationships with the company are asked politely, in a formal letter, to correct improper brand representation. The legal department gets involved if remedial actions are not taken.

Partner Noncompliance

The company's e-commerce group follows up with partner sites that fail to comply with established online guidelines. The group sends a letter encouraging noncompliant partners to remedy the violation (such as improper use of the company logo). If a partner refuses to comply with standards and guidelines, the company's legal department gets involved. A database administrator sends letters to all sites that have broken links to the company, asking them to fix the link.

THE BUSINESS CASE A financial services company estimates that brand abuse is costing the firm more than $2 million annually in lost customers and brand equity. The company implements a plan for monitoring online activity but fails to develop a plan for categorizing and prioritizing intelligence, or for taking action.

The company only has the resources to follow up on 20 percent of the incidents, but instead of prioritizing them, it pursues the first 20 percent of all incidents it finds every month. The lack of a structured approach means that communications are frequently delayed, incidents are not followed up on, and nobody keeps track of repeat offenders. As a result, the company is only able to achieve a compliance success rate of 50 percent. The brand abuse averted translates into a real bottom-line value, as follows:

Percent of incidents tracked × *(Annual brand abuse cost* × *Success rate)*
= *Brand abuse averted*
   20% × ($2,000,000 × 50%) = $200,000

The company decides to overhaul its process for managing intelligence. First, by categorizing and prioritizing incidents, the company is able to direct its limited resources to take action on the 20 percent of the abuses that are causing 80 percent of the damage. Next, it follows up to confirm that offenders respond. When necessary, the company escalates the issue and takes more aggressive action.

A finely tuned, flexible process is followed religiously and, when necessary, it is adapted to reflect changing conditions. This approach allows the company to achieve a success rate of 90 percent, which provides a superior return on the investment in brand protection. Now:

Brand abuse averted = 80% × ($2,000,000 × 90%) = $1,440,000

Figure 10-4 is a flowchart that shows the steps of an effective action plan for improving a company's brand protection efforts.

THE
BOARD
ROOM
SUMMARY

When defending the brand, a well-thought-out plan of attack (see Figure 10-4) will provide the best return on investment in brand and digital asset protection. Brand owners should remember that:

➤ Prioritization of brand abuse incidents is the first order of things, and it depends on the categorization of incidents according to who's abusing the brand and the nature of the abuse.

➤ The costs of taking action can sometimes outweigh the benefits.

➤ Internal processes are most effective when there are clear responsibilities for taking action and appropriate communication mechanisms.

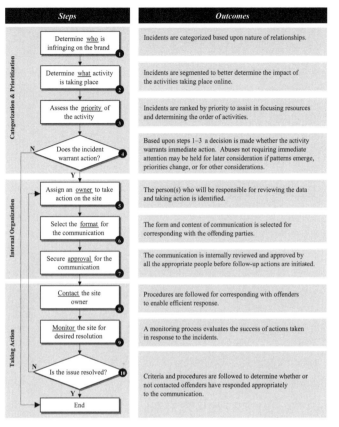

Steps	Outcomes
Categorization & Prioritization	
Determine <u>who</u> is infringing on the brand ①	Incidents are categorized based upon nature of relationships.
Determine <u>what</u> activity is taking place ②	Incidents are segmented to better determine the impact of the activities taking place online.
Assess the <u>priority</u> of the activity ③	Incidents are ranked by priority to assist in focusing resources and determining the order of activities.
Does the incident warrant action? ④	Based upon steps 1–3 a decision is made whether the activity warrants immediate action. Abuses not requiring immediate attention may be held for later consideration if patterns emerge, priorities change, or for other considerations.
Internal Organization	
Assign an <u>owner</u> to take action on the site ⑤	The person(s) who will be responsible for reviewing the data and taking action is identified.
Select the <u>format</u> for the communication ⑥	The form and content of communication is selected for corresponding with the offending parties.
Secure <u>approval</u> for the communication ⑦	The communication is internally reviewed and approved by all the appropriate people before follow-up actions are initiated.
Taking Action	
<u>Contact</u> the site owner ⑧	Procedures are followed for corresponding with offenders to enable efficient response.
<u>Monitor</u> the site for desired resolution ⑨	A monitoring process evaluates the success of actions taken in response to the incidents.
Is the issue resolved? ⑩	Criteria and procedures are followed to determine whether or not contacted offenders have responded appropriately to the communication.
End	

Figure 10-4. *Implementation of an action plan can improve your brand protection efforts.*

➤ Processes for final sign-offs and approvals should be streamlined. These processes should keep proper safeguards in place while minimizing the level of effort.

➤ After the offender is contacted, the incident should be revisited and, when necessary, follow-up actions taken.

Chapter 11

Mobilizing the Forces

A rmed with the knowledge necessary to monitor online activity and take action, some managers will be eager to start aggressively defending the brand. Others will find that their enthusiasm, knowledge, and preparations are not enough to mobilize the forces. As with any new initiative, there can be some substantial issues that need to be worked through before launching a campaign against abuse. This is particularly true for large, established corporations, where you are less apt to find the agility required for rapid response.

The organization may have to clear hurdles such as a broader lack of awareness, unclear internal responsibilities, lack of budget, politics, or good old-fashioned bureaucracy. Brand defense initiatives can be stymied by a culture of apathy that's skeptical of innovation or resistant to change. While clearing these hurdles can be difficult, those companies that step up and meet the challenge will have a competitive advantage over those that fail to take action.

State of Affairs

A Yankelovich Partners/Hill and Knowlton study of 600 midsize to large businesses found that more than 60 percent of CEOs were "concerned" or "very concerned" about negative information about their company on the Internet.[1] This anxiety has not translated into action. According to Continental Research, only one out of every ten businesses makes any attempt to monitor the Internet outside their own site.[2]

It's this lack of corporate vigilance and awareness that has made brands and digital assets easy prey for criminals and unscrupulous competitors that are fighting for revenue. As mentioned, there are numerous reasons for corporate inaction. One of the biggest is the fact that managers and executives remain ignorant regarding the significance and extent of what is happening online. While companies are swimming with the sharks, many don't even realize they are in the water.

Raising Awareness

Raising awareness creates a broader sense of urgency and helps move things forward. The easiest way to facilitate education and demonstrate the importance of defending the brand online is to gather preliminary intelligence through the methods described in Chapter 9. In the words of Mark Twain, "Few things are harder to put up with than a good example." Demonstrating a few real-life cases of brand abuse can help foster an understanding of the implications of the problem and simultaneously light a fire under people.

Build a Business Case

Another effective way to mobilize the forces is to construct a business case and estimate the potential bottom-line impact of abuse, including the return on investment (ROI) of taking action. While many of the benefits of defending the brand are qualitative, it's worth the effort to quantify them whenever possible, if for no other reason than to illustrate the logic behind how the issues translate into revenue. But you also want to be confident that the ROI is real. After all, if it doesn't make fundamental business sense, then it may be time to reevaluate your position or scale back your proposed monitoring efforts.

Manage Risk

In building a business case, it's wise to factor in risk. Remember that the absence of abuse does not equate to the absence of risk—online monitoring may still be financially justified even if the brand in not currently under attack. In fact, such a situation is an enviable one. The absence of abuse may mean that you are in a position to proactively implement a more modest monitoring solution, averting the more exorbitant expense of cleaning up a widespread problem later on in a struggle to regain control.

Brand protection efforts are a form of insurance or security like any other. It's all about managing risk and protecting your assets. People don't wait to put their seat belts on until an accident occurs. And banks install security cameras even if they've never been robbed. Just as intelligence can help to manage offline risks, organizations can benefit from taking proactive steps to monitor relevant online activity for the presence of threats and opportunities. The monitoring efforts that provide intelligence serve as the cornerstone for your brand defense.

Adopt Experiential Learning

In addition to understanding the conceptual implications of defending the brand, you need a personal commitment to learning and an openness to change. And you need to spend some time online. There is no substitute for witnessing firsthand where and in what context the company's brands and intellectual property appear. Try to take a look at things from your customers' perspective, and remember that they may not all be as knowledgeable of business issues or as proficient in online navigation as you are.

Develop a Plan

Beyond understanding and experiencing the landscape, it's also advisable to prepare specific recommendations for taking action (see Chapters 9 and 10). Some companies are aware of online activity that reflects on their brands, but either choose not to do anything about it or don't believe there is anything they can do. The Internet can seem overwhelming at times, and some people see any attempt to curb relevant online activity as futile—you might just as well try to stop the ocean tide. Structuring a clearly outlined attack plan is one way to demonstrate that something can be done. It can also improve your chances of getting adequate resources allocated.

Apathy Is the Enemy

Burying your head in the sand is never a good solution. The problems affect everyone and they're not going away anytime soon. Lethargy in the face of a business case and attack plan does not bode well for an organization—problem solving is never easy.

"How a company reacts to technological change is a good indicator of its inner drive for greatness versus mediocrity."
—JIM COLLINS, AUTHOR OF *Good to Great*[3]

Business is all about fighting the fights worth fighting, even if it's not a sure thing. For example, just because you're convinced that it is impossible to get 100 percent of your customers to pay on-time doesn't mean you don't make prompt invoicing a priority—cash flow is still important. Brand protection is the same way. Just because you can't eliminate all the abuse doesn't mean defending your brand online is not a priority—your brand equity is still important!

Also, the truth is that no company accepts brand abuse in the offline world to the extent it pervades the Internet. Would McDonald's let Burger King put up the Golden Arches in front of all its restaurants to attract customers, only to sell Whoppers inside? Obviously, the answer is no. But on the Web, sites use competitors' brand names or other popular brands to attract visitors, without having a legitimate affiliation. These websites sometimes even sell goods in direct competition to the brands with which they imply an association. Should this be accepted because it takes place on the Internet? If revenue is important to you, the answer is a resounding no!

Who's Responsible?

Another challenge to mobilization is that the consequences of online brand abuse can span many functional areas within a company, including marketing, information technology, business development, legal, and customer service, just to name a few. Not many organizations have a specific individual designated to defend the brand. As such, management of a company's online presence (outside its own domain) doesn't clearly fall within the realm of responsibility of any single individual within most organizational structures.

Also, since the issue is new and doesn't fall neatly under any single department's responsibility, funds are not budgeted. This means that paying for intelligence collection would require a cut somewhere else—a difficult prospect in today's competitive environment where very few items in corporate budgets aren't deemed "mission critical."

The challenge of finding the time and budget for online monitoring can compound a general lack of awareness so that any brand defense initiative immediately has two strikes against it. Oftentimes, companies don't invest in monitoring online activity until something catastrophic or embarrassing happens—maybe the mainstream press reports a heinous incident, or an executive stumbles across an atrocity firsthand.

Few companies remain nimble enough to proactively dedicate staff or resources to an emerging issue that spans many functional departments—even when the return on investment is compelling or the consequences of inaction are dire. Even fewer have the foresight to align brand defense with compensation structures or performance plans. Aligning incentives with brand protection efforts clearly demonstrates commitment at the highest levels. If properly structured, such incentives can also provide added motivation not only to take action, but to do it right.

Hint: Including brand protection in personal and departmental performance objectives can help ensure that managers defend the brand.

Companies that have invested in defending their brand and managing the customer experience outside of their website have seen great returns. Within the travel industry, for example, companies such as InterContinental Hotels Group and Royal Caribbean Cruises have both extended their reach to manage the customer experience on partner sites with a very high degree of success. In each instance, their efforts have resulted in an improvement in the customer experience conducive to attracting, converting, and retaining customers—ultimately improving market share and generating millions of dollars in incremental revenue.

Stepping Up

Some brand owners wonder whether they can afford to protect their brand online. The question isn't whether they can afford to protect their brand; the question is whether they can afford not to. There is no doubt that taking action is financially prudent, but because the effort spans so many departments, the ROI for any individual department will never be as compelling as it is for the company as a whole.

The higher up you go in an organization, the easier it is to recognize the importance of defending the brand, the ROI, and the potential consequences of not taking action. This is because those with broader exposure to company operations are in the best position to recognize how the implications of brand abuse span the entire organization.

For this reason, brand management in the new millennium requires executive-level commitment. But executive support by itself is still not enough. Ultimately, somebody needs to step up and take ownership. Brand defense efforts require a champion—a passionate visionary who can see the big picture yet provide the attention to detail and the cross-departmental coordination that is necessary for successful execution. Even when brand protection is outsourced, somebody within the organization should take ultimate responsibility.

Hint: Large corporations with customer-facing brands should have a senior executive whose primary responsibility is to protect brand integrity.

As Gary Hamel points out in "Strategy as Revolution," his classic *Harvard Business Review* article, "Make no mistake: there are revolutionaries in your company."[4] Uncovering one of these pro-change leaders may be necessary to pierce the layer of cautious bureaucrats and pave the way to taking action. Your success in finding the right person may well determine the ultimate success of the brand defense initiative. The larger the company and more valuable the brand, the more authority the champion must have.

THE BUSINESS CASE

Both online and off, a brand is more than just a name. Businesses invest millions and sometimes billions of dollars building their brands, meticulously studying their markets, and carefully crafting strategies and campaigns to position their product or service as the next Coke, Rolex, or Pentium. For many companies, there is an opportunity to further leverage that brand equity online to reach new customers or build new distribution channels.

The Internet also represents an opportunity for those who seek to exploit, for their own benefit, your investment in building that brand. Profitability pressures fuel bold competitive tactics and desperate attempts to convert sales by all available means. Individuals, competitors, and other companies have every incentive to abuse a respected brand for their own gains, including greater credibility and increased site traffic, or as a competitive tactic.

At the same time, antiquated regulatory and enforcement systems and technological advances such as digitalization have contributed to an environment where online crimes go largely unpunished and where brands and digital assets are easy to manipulate.

When your brand is abused online, thousands or even millions of people can be exposed, including customers, partners, or investors. The abuses can weaken customer loyalty, undermine revenue, and destroy brand equity. The most prescient companies have responded to the situation by taking action to defend their brand, while others choose to look the other way.

Example

A manufacturer of athletic apparel has an established brand name that has become a target for online abuse. In response, the company launches a serious program to monitor consumer feedback and aggressively combat the exploitation of its brand, with a focus on customer diversion. The apparel company also ensures the compliance of online partners with branding guidelines and monitors for gray markets and counterfeiters. The comprehensive approach allows the company to regain control of its brand, capturing revenue while improving customer and partner loyalty. Profitability also improves as a result of a reduction in false warranty claims and customer service costs.

The apparel company's brand protection efforts are in sharp contrast with a competitor. As a result of poor intelligence, this competitor is outmaneuvered online. The competitor's brand equity is severely undermined by unbridled abuse. Costs rise as a result of a loss of control over distribution channels. Rumors of discrimination run rampant and consumer backlash ensues. Problems persist both offline and online until the competitor's losses eventually drive the company into bankruptcy.

THE BOARD ROOM SUMMARY

Challenges associated with mobilizing brand defense efforts can include a lack of awareness, unclear assignment of internal responsibility for the initiative, budget limitations, bureaucracy, or apathy. Those companies that can overcome these hurdles will reap the rewards. Brand owners should remember these key points:

➤ While most executives are concerned about online activity, there are few who take action.

➤ Apathetic views or lackluster responses doom brand defense to failure.

➤ Raising awareness and clearly designating responsibilities are the first two steps needed to mobilize brand protection efforts.

➤ In addition to executive-level commitment, brand defense initiatives require a dedicated champion who can spearhead efforts across the organization.

➤ How well a company defends its brand can ultimately make the difference between success and failure.

Glossary

Ad Web advertisements are almost always a banner or button; a graphic image of a designated pixel-size and byte-size limit. Banners and other special advertising that include an interactive or visual element are known as rich media (e.g., pop-up media).*

Banner An advertisement in the form of a graphic image that typically runs across a web page or is positioned in a margin or other space reserved for ads. Banner ads are usually .GIF images and are greater than/equal to 220 pixels in width, or greater than/equal to 180 pixels in height.*

Blog A type of message board usually found on a personal or noncommercial website. A blog is often dedicated to a particular subject and may be updated by visitors or the site owner. "Blog" is short for weblog.

Browser An application program that provides a way to look at and interact with all the information on the World Wide Web. Microsoft Internet Explorer and Netscape Navigator are the two most common browsers available today.*

Click or click-through Occurs when a visitor interacts with an advertisement instead of simply viewing it. By actually clicking on an ad, the visitor is headed toward the advertiser's destination. (It also does not mean that

*Definitions that are followed by an asterisk are derived from NetRatings. Reproduced with permission. © NetRatings, Inc. 2002. All rights reserved

the visitor actually waits to fully arrive at the destination, just that the visitor started going there.) Click and click-through tend to be used interchangeably. A click-through, however, implies that the user actually received the page.*

Clickstream A recorded path of the pages a user requested in going through one or more websites. Clickstream information can help website owners understand how visitors are using their site and which pages are getting the most use. It can help advertisers understand how users get to the client's pages, what pages they look at, and how they go about ordering a product.*

Cloaking A search engine manipulation tactic where websites display one set of web pages to human visitors and another to search engine crawlers. *See* spoof pages.

Cookie A technology that allows a website to store information on a visitor's computer for future reference and retrieval. The data in a cookie allows a site to maintain information about visitors and their preferences beyond their immediate connection, potentially improving the customer experience by allowing the site to add personalization and features catered to that individual.

Crawler A program that visits websites and reads their pages and other information in order to create entries for a search engine index. The major search engines on the Web all have such a program, which is also known as a "spider" or a "bot." Crawlers are typically programmed to visit sites that have been submitted as new or updated by their owners.*

Cybersquatting Registering a domain that includes a proprietary brand or slogan. It is a common customer capture tactic employed to leverage the power of an established brand, gain false legitimacy, or divert unsuspecting shoppers that bypass search engines and directly type a domain name. It is not uncommon for derivations of a popular brand name to show up in thousands of registered domains that are not held by the brand's legitimate owner.

Deep link A hyperlink to another site that circumvents that website's home page and takes the visitor directly to an internal page. This practice can alter the customers' experience and cause them to miss important information, such as disclaimers or privacy statements. It can also cost companies revenue by bypassing advertising.

Domain name A name that identifies one or more IP addresses. The domain name is intended to be easily user-friendly and identifiable, such as aol .com or ford.com. By using existing trademarks for domain names, businesses attract potential customers to their websites.

File transfer protocol (FTP)   A standard Internet protocol commonly used to exchange files between computers on the Internet.

Framing   A technique for keeping website visitors on a site by "framing" their window while they view content from other domains. An analogy is the picture-in-picture feature available on some television models. The "frame" is sometimes left visible for branding purposes, but more devious sites will purposefully hide the frame so that visitors think they have left, when they are actually still on the original site.

Gray markets   The sale of branded products outside of authorized distribution channels.

Home-jacking   The unauthorized substitution of the shopper's browser "home page" or the unauthorized addition of a site to the shopper's list of "favorites." This tactic automatically returns visitors to a site the next time they launch their browser.

HTML (hypertext markup language)   The set of symbols or codes inserted in a file intended for display in a web browser. The HTML code tells the browser how to display a web page's words and images for the user. HTML is a standard recommended by the World Wide Web Consortium (W3C) and adhered to by the major browsers, Microsoft Internet Explorer and Netscape Navigator, which also provide some additional non-standard codes.*

Impression   The count of a delivered basic advertising unit from an ad distribution point. Impressions are the unit by which some web advertising is sold, and the cost is quoted in terms of the cost per thousand impressions (CPM).*

In-lining   A special kind of link that enables the display of content (usually an image) on one website that originates at another. It is often done without the consent of the rightful owner.

Instant messaging (IM)   A type of communications service that allows a user to create a private, real-time communications path with another individual. Examples include AOL Instant Messenger (AIM) and ICQ (short for "I Seek You").

Internet Relay Chat (IRC)   A system that lets people connected to the Internet join in live discussions through a set of rules and conventions and client/server software. Users can start a chat group (a channel) or join an existing one. Channels where chat sessions take place are sometimes called "chat rooms."

Invisible seeding   The hidden "seeding" of content to optimize search service rankings. This common customer capture tactic involves the unauthorized incorporation of proprietary content, popular brands, phrases, or keywords (unrelated to visible site content) within nonvisible page elements, such as the metatags and nonvisible text, including text hidden through slight variations in color shading. Sometimes referred to as traffic diversion, it is one of the most common intellectual property abuses perpetrated against top consumer brands.

ISP (Internet service provider) A company that provides individuals and other companies with access to the Internet and other, related services such as website hosting. An ISP has the equipment and the telecommunication line access required to have points-of-presence (POPs) on the Internet for the geographic area served.*

Link A highlighted word or picture that can be selected by the user to take him to a different location. In more technical terms, using hypertext, a link is a selectable connection from one word, picture, or information object to another. Clicking on the link triggers the immediate delivery and view of another file.

Link rot A term used to describe the tendency for links to be neglected; such links fail to take the user to the destination they are supposed to. Links that do not function properly are commonly referred to as being "broken."

Link spamming Search engine manipulation tactic where web designers erect hundreds or even thousands of bogus sites that point to the same page. This practice is employed with the intent of fooling search engines that evaluate the quantity of links or the content of the pages linking to a site when determining relevancy. *See also* spoofing.

Metatags Words embedded in the source code of an Internet page that are meant to help search engines determine the nature of the page's content. Brand names are often included as metatags. Recognizing that metatags are frequently abused, search engines now weigh other factors more heavily for indexing purposes, such as links and page titles.

Mirror site An exact site duplicate, with the exception of the URL. Criminals use mirror sites so that if one site is shut down, their business can continue uninterrupted. Mirroring is also used to cast a broader cybersquatting and typo-piracy net. Mirroring also has legitimate uses, such as to reduce or divert network traffic to improve website speed and performance.

Mislabeling links The mislabeling of hyperlinks or use of misleading links that send the shopper to an unintended destination. This common practice is another way that unethical sites sometimes leverage the value of a trusted brand to their own advantage.

Mouse-trapping Manipulation of the browser "back" button, to prevent the shopper from leaving the site, or the deactivation of other browser "exit" or "close" capabilities. Another variation is when the shopper hits the back button and is sent to the wrong location. Redirect pages can also be used to mouse-trap, though they are sometimes present for more legitimate purposes.

Newsgroups A worldwide network of forums or message boards on tens of thousands of different topics. Newsgroups are named using a series of words and periods. The newsgroup environment is also called Usenet.

Page-jacking A search engine manipulation tactic that involves copying an entire page from another website.

Redirects Web pages that automatically forward the visitor to another location. Redirects are considered mouse-trapping when a site skirts good design etiquette and allows the redirect page to enter the browser history, effectively blocking shoppers from retreating from the page they are forwarded to.

Search engine Catalogs and databases containing listings of websites that help you find your way around the Internet. Examples are Yahoo!, Excite, and Google, among others. A search engine has two main software elements:

➤ A spider that goes to every page or representative pages on every website that wants to be searchable and reads it into a program that creates a huge index from the pages that have been read

➤ A program that receives your search request, compares it to the entries in the index, and returns results to you*

Secure sockets layer (SSL) An industry standard security protocol for encrypting sensitive information that is transmitted over the Internet. SSL uses the public and private key encryption system.

(Server) log file A list of all the requests for individual files that people have requested from a website. These files will include the HTML files and their embedded graphic images and any other associated files that get transmitted. The access log can be analyzed and summarized by another program. In general, an access log can be analyzed to tell you:

➤ The number of visitors (unique first-time requests) to a home page

➤ The origin of the visitors in terms of their associated server's domain name (e.g., visitors from .edu, .com, and .gov sites and from the online services)

➤ The number of requests for each page at the site

➤ Usage patterns in terms of time of day, day of week, and seasonal surges*

Short message service (SMS)   The transmission of short text messages to and from a mobile phone, fax, or IP address.

Spam   Unsolicited e-mail, sometimes also called "junk e-mail." The e-mails are often of a shady commercial nature and are sent indiscriminately to mailing lists or newsgroups. The sender may buy or steal mailing lists, gather them from online sources, or randomly generate addresses.

Spawning   A by-product of the online porn industry, spawning involves the automatic launch of new browser windows or the opening of hidden "stealth" windows upon entering or exiting a site, or on delay. Pop-up and pop-under ads have been widely adopted as a somewhat less intrusive variation of this irksome tactic. In some cases, windows are repeatedly launched faster than the visitor can close them, effectively taking over the user's computer screen.

Spider   A program that visits websites and reads their pages and other information in order to create entries for a search engine index. Spiders are so named because they usually visit many sites in parallel at the same time, their "legs" spanning a large area of the "web." *See also* crawler.*

Spoofing   The practice of altering an e-mail message to make it appear as if it came from another sender. This is a common tactic used by people sending unsolicited commercial e-mail.

Spoof pages   Web pages used to optimize search engine traffic. Spoof pages can take various forms, including the use of "doorway" pages or redirect pages tailored to specific search terms and search services; page-jacking of popular site content; and cloaking of a site's actual content when search engine crawlers index the Web. Web designers typically seed their spoof pages with popular brands' slogans, names of personalities, and other content that will optimize their placement on search engines.

Streaming media   The on-demand transfer of audio and/or video content from the Internet to the user's access device.*

Top-level domain (TLD)   The suffix attached to Internet domain names. TLDs can be divided into generic top-level domains (gTLDs), such as .com or .org, and country code top-level domains (ccTLDs) such as .ca and .de (Canada and Germany, respectively.) A list of gTLDs and ccTLDs can be found in Appendix A.

Typo-piracy   Registration of a domain name that is a common misspelling or typo of a popular brand name or slogan. It is a common customer capture tactic employed to leverage the power of an established brand, gain false legitimacy, or divert unsuspecting shoppers that bypass search engines and directly type a domain name.

Unique visitor or audience   Someone with a unique address who is entering a website for the first time that day (or some other specified period). Thus, a visitor that returns within the same day is not counted twice. A count of unique visitors tells you how many different people there are in the site's overall audience during the time period.*

URL (uniform resource locator)   The address of a file (resource) accessible on the Internet. The type of resource depends on the Internet application protocol. The URL contains the name of the protocol required to access the resource, a domain name that identifies a specific computer on the Internet, and a hierarchical description of a file location on the computer.*

Usenet   *See* newsgroups.

Visible seeding   The seeding of visible text that's false or misleading in order to optimize traffic from search engines. It includes the unauthorized incorporation of proprietary content, popular brands, or slogans within visible page elements such as the title, URL, or text. This practice can be damaging to shoppers searching the Web for leading brands since it can also include claimed affiliations and association of these brands with highly objectionable content.

Visit   Occurs when a web user with a unique address enters a website at some page for the first time that day (or for the first time in a lesser time period). The number of visits is roughly equivalent to the number of different people that visit a site. This term is ambiguous unless the user defines it, since it could mean a user session or it could mean a unique visitor that day.*

Web beacons   Tiny graphics inserted in a web page for the purpose of collecting information about visitors without being detected. A server records user information whenever the image is loaded from a web page. Web beacons are commonly used to get an independent accounting of how many people visit a site or to gather statistics on browser usage. While often innocuous, web beacons can be abused and are sometimes perceived to be malicious since they are specifically designed to be invisible.

Weblog   *See blog.*

Website   A related collection of web files that includes a beginning file called a home page. From the home page, you can link to all the other pages on the site.*

Web spamming   Search engine manipulation tactic that occurs when designers copy a web page and embed code that directs a search engine's crawlers to revisit the duplicate but without caching (i.e., storing) the page. The false web pages, disguised as legitimate sites, then appear higher in the search results. *See also* spoof pages.

Appendix A: Top-Level Domains

Generic Top-Level Domains

.AERO	Aviation Community
.BIZ	Businesses
.COM	Commercial
.COOP	Cooperative Associations
.EDU	Educational Institutions
.GOV	U.S. Government
.INFO	Unrestricted
.INT	International Treaty Organizations
.MIL	United States Military
.MUSEUM	Museums
.NAME	Personal Names
.NET	Networks
.ORG	Organizations
.PRO	Professionals (e.g., Lawyers, Doctors)

Country Code Top-Level Domains

.AC	Ascension Island
.AD	Andorra
.AE	United Arab Emirates
.AF	Afghanistan
.AG	Antigua and Barbuda
.AI	Anguilla
.AL	Albania
.AM	Armenia
.AN	Netherlands Antilles
.AO	Angola
.AQ	Antarctica
.AR	Argentina
.AS	American Samoa
.AT	Austria
.AU	Australia
.AW	Aruba
.AZ	Azerbaijan
.BA	Bosnia and Herzegovina
.BB	Barbados
.BD	Bangladesh
.BE	Belgium
.BF	Burkina Faso
.BG	Bulgaria
.BH	Bahrain
.BI	Burundi
.BJ	Benin
.BM	Bermuda
.BN	Brunei Darussalam
.BO	Bolivia
.BR	Brazil
.BS	Bahamas

.BT	Bhutan	.FM	Micronesia,	.IT	Italy
.BV	Bouvet Island		Federated States	.JE	Jersey
.BW	Botswana		of	.JM	Jamaica
.BY	Belarus	.FO	Faeroe Islands	.JO	Jordan
.BZ	Belize	.FR	France	.JP	Japan
.CA	Canada	.GA	Gabon	.KE	Kenya
.CC	Cocos Islands	.GD	Grenada	.KG	Kyrgyzstan
.CD	Congo,	.GE	Georgia	.KH	Cambodia
	Democratic	.GF	French Guiana	.KI	Kiribati
	Republic of	.GG	Guernsey	.KM	Comoros
.CF	Central African	.GH	Ghana	.KN	Saint Kitts and
	Republic	.GI	Gibraltar		Nevis
.CG	Congo, Republic	.GL	Greenland	.KP	Korea,
	of	.GM	Gambia		Democratic
.CH	Switzerland	.GN	Guinea		People's Republic
.CI	Côte d'Ivoire	.GP	Guadeloupe	.KR	Korea, Republic
.CK	Cook Islands	.GQ	Equatorial		of
.CL	Chile		Guinea	.KW	Kuwait
.CM	Cameroon	.GR	Greece	.KY	Cayman Islands
.CN	China	.GS	South Georgia	.KZ	Kazakhstan
.CO	Colombia		and the South	.LA	Lao People's
.CR	Costa Rica		Sandwich Islands		Democratic
.CU	Cuba	.GT	Guatemala		Republic
.CV	Cape Verde	.GU	Guam	.LB	Lebanon
.CX	Christmas Island	.GW	Guinea-Buissau	.LC	Saint Lucia
.CY	Cyprus	.GY	Guyana	.LI	Liechtenstein
.CZ	Czech Republic	.HK	Hong Kong, SAR	.LK	Sri Lanka
.DE	Germany	.HM	Heard and	.LR	Liberia
.DJ	Djibouti		McDonald	.LS	Lesotho
.DK	Denmark		Islands	.LT	Lithuania
.DM	Dominica	.HN	Honduras	.LU	Luxembourg
.DO	Dominican	.HR	Croatia	.LV	Latvia
	Republic	.HT	Haiti	.LY	Libyan Arab
.DZ	Algeria	.HU	Hungary		Jamahiriya
.EC	Ecuador	.ID	Indonesia	.MA	Morocco
.EE	Estonia	.IE	Ireland	.MC	Monaco
.EG	Egypt	.IL	Israel	.MD	Moldova,
.EH	Western Sahara	.IM	Isle of Man		Republic of
.ER	Eritrea	.IN	India	.MG	Madagascar
.ES	Spain	.IO	British Indian	.MH	Marshall Islands
.ET	Ethiopia		Ocean Territory	.MK	Macedonia
.EU	European Union	.IQ	Iraq		(Former Yugoslav
.FI	Finland	.IR	Iran, Islamic		Republic)
.FJ	Fiji		Republic of	.ML	Mali
.FK	Falkland Islands	.IS	Iceland	.MM	Myanmar

.MN	Mongolia	.PT	Portugal	.TM	Turkmenistan
.MO	Macau, SAR	.PW	Palau	.TN	Tunisia
.MP	Northern Marian	.PY	Paraguay	.TO	Tonga
	Islands	.QA	Qatar	.TP	East Timor
.MQ	Martinique	.RE	Reunion Island	.TR	Turkey
.MR	Mauritania	.RO	Romania	.TT	Trinidad and
.MS	Montserrat	.RU	Russian		Tobago
.MT	Malta		Federation	.TV	Tuvalu
.MU	Mauritius	.RW	Rwanda	.TW	Taiwan Province,
.MV	Maldives	.SA	Saudi Arabia		PRC
.MW	Malawi	.SB	Solomon Islands	.TZ	Tanzania
.MX	Mexico	.SC	Seychelles	.UA	Ukraine
.MY	Malaysia	.SD	Sudan	.UG	Uganda
.MZ	Mozambique	.SE	Sweden	.UK	United Kingdom
.NA	Namibia	.SG	Singapore	.UM	U.S. Minor
.NC	New Caledonia	.SH	Santa Helena		Outlying Islands
.NE	Niger	.SI	Slovenia	.US	United States
.NF	Norfolk Island	.SJ	Svalbard and Jan	.UY	Uruguay
.NG	Nigeria		Mayen Islands	.UZ	Uzbekistan
.NI	Nicaragua	.SK	Slovakia	.VA	Holy See
.NL	Netherlands	.SL	Sierra Leone	.VC	Saint Vincent and
.NO	Norway	.SM	San Marino		the Grenadines
.NP	Nepal	.SN	Senegal	.VE	Venezuela
.NR	Nauru	.SO	Somalia	.VG	Virgin Islands
.NU	Niue	.SR	Suriname		(British)
.NZ	New Zealand	.ST	Sao Tome and	.VI	Virgin Islands
.OM	Oman		Principe		(USA)
.PA	Panama	.SV	El Salvador	.VN	Vietnam
.PE	Peru	.SY	Syrian Arab	.VU	Vanuatu
.PF	French Polynesia		Republic	.WF	Wallis and
.PG	Papua New	.SZ	Swaziland		Futuna Islands
	Guinea	.TC	Turks and Caicos	.WS	Western Samoa
.PH	Philippines		Islands	.YE	Yemen
.PK	Pakistan	.TD	Chad	.YT	Mayotte
.PL	Poland	.TF	French Southern	.YU	Yugoslavia
.PM	St. Pierre and		Territories	.ZA	South Africa
	Miquelon	.TG	Togo	.ZM	Zambia
.PN	Pitcairn Island	.TH	Thailand	.ZW	Zimbabwe
.PR	Puerto Rico	.TJ	Tajikistan		
.PS	Palestine	.TK	Tokelau Islands		

Appendix B: Sample Affiliate Guidelines

This appendix includes examples of contractual terms that are commonly used in partner agreements. Sample 1 includes select excerpts from the license and usage guidelines used by a financial institution. Sample 2 gives general guidelines and content requirements for online partners in a retailer's affiliate network.

Sample 1—CreditCard Company Affiliate Agreement

(a) License to Links and Images.

CreditCard hereby grants to you a limited, nonexclusive, revocable license to (i) establish Links to the CreditCard website, and (ii) use, in connection with such Links, each Image (including all copyrighted, trade or service marked, or other protected intellectual property contained therein) solely for the purposes described in this Agreement; provided that you will not add, subtract, or in any way alter or edit any Image (including, for this purpose, any machine-readable code that may be a part of any Image), frame the CreditCard site, or make any use whatsoever of any Image or any other element of CreditCard's intellectual property (including but not limited to CreditCard's name, whether used in a URL, a metatag, or otherwise) other than for the express purposes of this Agreement. By accepting membership in the Affiliate Network, you agree specifically to refrain from (i) originating, authorizing, or participating in any promotion of CreditCard by unsolicited e-mails ("spam"), telephone, offline media, or otherwise, (ii) submitting applications on behalf of another person, and (iii) issuing any press release mentioning CreditCard. Failure to comply with these rules may result in the suspension or termination of your Affiliate Network membership.

(b) Trademark Usage Guidelines.

These guidelines apply to your use of the CreditCard® corporate trademark and other logos, product and service marks belonging to CreditCard. For purposes of this provision, Trademarks shall also mean and include Images and Links embodying the CreditCard® corporate trademark and/or other logos, graphic art, trade dress, product and service marks belonging to Credit-Card.

i. You may not display the Trademarks in any manner that implies sponsorship or endorsement by CreditCard, Inc. of you or any third parties outside of your involvement in the Affiliate Network.

ii. You may not place or display the Trademarks on websites or pages locatable by URLs or domain names that incorporate the corporate names of competitor credit card companies, banks, or financial institutions and/or that incorporate the names of products or services offered by any such competitor entities.

iii. You may not use the Trademarks to disparage CreditCard, its products or services, or in a manner that, in CreditCard's reasonable judgment, may diminish or otherwise damage CreditCard's goodwill in the Trademarks.

iv. You may not use the Trademarks on or in connection with sites or content that, in CreditCard's reasonable judgment, contain: (A) gratuitous, overly graphic, and/or exploitative use of sex and violence; (B) disparaging or sensationalistic treatment of women, ethnic, religious, or political personalities, groups, or icons; (C) inaccurate or distorted presentation of facts to a blatantly partisan advantage; and/or (D) glorified consumption of drugs or alcohol.

(c) License to CreditCard Domain Names and URLs.

Certain Affiliate Network members may elect to establish affiliate websites that are locatable by URLs or domain names incorporating the term Credit-Card®. This provision applies to all such Affiliate Network members.

i. CreditCard Rights. Because CreditCard, Inc. holds federal trademark registrations for the marks CreditCard®, all domain names and URLs incorporating these marks are the property of CreditCard, with respect to which Cred-itCard retains an ultimate right of use and exploitation. CreditCard's property interest extends to domain names in any top-level domain (e.g., .com, .net,

.biz, .cc) and URLs that incorporate the terms "CreditCard, or any confusingly similar variations thereof.

> *Example 1 (domain name): "CreditCard-visa-card.net"*
> *Example 2 (URL): "www.angelfire.com/~CreditCard-platinum.htm"*

ii. License Terms. For purposes of this provision, the term "CreditCard Locators" is used to refer to domain names or URLs incorporating the term "CreditCard," or any confusingly similar variations thereof. The term "Credit-Card Competitors" is used to refer to Providian, First USA Bank, Bank One, Fleet, Capital One, Citibank/CitiGroup, American Express, Chase, MBNA, Discover, Wells Fargo Bank, and any other financial services company that markets or offers credit-related products and services on the Internet.

Sample 2—Retailer Affiliate Guidelines

General Guidelines and Content Requirements

> ➤ Affiliates must submit application through the website. Unsuitable affiliates are identified as follows:
> - Illegal, offensive, infringing, or objectionable content
> - Personal home pages
> - Sites with a model based on posting coupons, promotions, "deals"
> - Third-party payment providers

Links

> ➤ Product lists may appear on affiliate sites, but for each product listed you have to link to that product's specific page:
> - Special link format is required.
> - Company must designate restrictions for time-sensitive offers or limited stock items.
> - Affiliate is responsible for removing outdated links.
>
> ➤ The affiliate is allowed to include a search box for the company's site.
>
> ➤ The affiliate may link to the company's home page (using format approved and graphics supplied by company).
>
> ➤ Framing is permitted.
>
> ➤ Affiliates may NOT:
> - Post sales, promotions, or coupons without written permission.

- Use the company's name (or variations) in metatags.
- Use the company's name in hidden text or source code.
- Use the company's name in the domain or URL.
- Engineer the affiliate site to divert traffic from the company's site.
- Buy product to get the referral bonus.
- List any pricing information on the site.

➤ Referral bonuses are earned when a customer follows a special link (in company's specified format) to the company and makes a purchase:
  - If a customer follows a link to a product, leaves, and then comes back within 10 days through some other way (i.e., not through the affiliate's link again), the affiliate will still get his referral bonus if the customer buys the product.

➤ Referral bonus is paid quarterly through the Affiliate Network, as long as the amount is greater than $100. The referral bonus schedule is as follows:
  - Monthly gross sales (excluding tax, shipping, etc.) up to $4,000 = 2%
  - Monthly gross sales (excluding tax, shipping, etc.) $4,000 to $8,000 = 3%
  - Monthly gross sales (excluding tax, shipping, etc.) $8,000 to $40,000 = 4%
  - Monthly gross sales (excluding tax, shipping, etc.) over $40,000 = 6%

➤ The affiliate must display logo image and the words "in association with [the company]" somewhere on the site.

➤ The company encourages (but won't demand) a link to the company's home page.

➤ Upon termination of the affiliate relationship, all company content and links should be removed from the site.

➤ Affiliate and company are independent contractors and the relationship is not a partnership, joint venture, agency, franchise, sales rep, or employment relationship. Affiliates cannot misrepresent their relationship with the company.

Logos and Trademarks

➤ The affiliate cannot modify (color, font, proportion, etc.) the company's logos and trademarks.

➤ The affiliate cannot display the trademark to suggest company's endorsement of the site or anything else outside the affiliate context.

➤ The affiliate cannot use the trademark to disparage the company or damage brand or "goodwill."

➤ Trademark must be spaced sufficiently away from other graphics or text.

➤ Trademark may appear with competing content (as long as it is spaced appropriately).

➤ Trademark must use the Registered (®) symbol.

➤ The affiliate must include the statement "[Company] is a registered trademark of [company]."

Appendix C: Sample Guidelines for Managing Partner Compliance

These sample guidelines are designed to help a company retain control of its online distribution networks. The examples are taken from the hotel industry. Both franchise owners and individual hotels must comply with the guidelines outlined.

Sample 1: Hotel Franchisee Guidelines

General Guidelines and Content Requirements

➤ Franchisees must have a site, update the content at least quarterly, and cannot share the content with any third party.

➤ Franchisees should support dynamic, real-time sales through an approved centralized database system (franchisees may work with third parties as long as the third party is connected to one of the approved database systems).

➤ Franchisees may not participate in cobranded sites with competitors (though franchisees may participate in noncompeting regionally oriented sites).

➤ Franchisees shall not sell advertising on their sites.

➤ Franchisee sites should be constructed and designed by an approved vendor, or else the website has to be approved by the company. The company will only offer a link from its site to the franchisee site for franchisees that employ an approved vendor.

➤ The designated URL nomenclature for franchisee sites is www.geo graphicdescriptor-brand.com.

➤ Franchisees shall transition any existing site to the new URL nomenclature by no later than December 31, 2003.

➤ The content of the franchisee site shall be in English (additional languages are permitted as appropriate).

➤ Photography and graphics must be done professionally.

➤ Every page on the site should link to the home page.

➤ No "mouse-trapping" or pop-up windows are permitted.

➤ Postings that require users to scroll down three or more pages must have a "return to top" link.

➤ No objectionable content or linking to sites with objectionable content is permitted.

Security, Privacy, and E-Mail Marketing

➤ Franchisees shall not use unsolicited e-mail marketing.

➤ Franchisees shall not collect personal information for the purposes of e-mail marketing unless the consumer has expressly given permission to do so.

➤ Instructions for removing oneself from marketing lists must be conspicuously displayed.

➤ Franchisee shall not collect personal information through e-mail or unencrypted forms.

➤ Franchisees shall not use web beacons.

➤ All franchisees must display the standard privacy statement.

Logo Use

➤ Approved logos must be displayed prominently at least once on every page on the site.

➤ Logos should be copied from the company's press office page.

➤ Franchisees shall adhere to all logo image guidelines for color, font, background, animation, etc.

Links

➤ All franchisees must provide a link to the company home page.

➤ Sales must be made exclusively through a link to the corporate sales page (the company will provide a franchisee-specific link).

➤ All franchisees should display a prominent link to the rewards program site.

➤ Franchisees may link to complementary sites.

Site Operational Guidelines

➤ Franchisees shall not use competitor brands or company brands in their metatags that aren't immediately related to the franchisee.

➤ Franchisee sites should support a 56 Kbps dial-up connection.

➤ Franchisees shall adhere to all file-size and graphics-size restrictions specified.

➤ Franchisee sites shall support Netscape, Microsoft Internet Explorer, and AOL browser versions.

Sample 2: Individual Hotel Chain Guidelines

Customer Diversion

➤ No company trademarks are allowed in the hotel site URLs.

➤ No company trademarks are allowed in a hotel site's metatags.

➤ No company trademarks are allowed in a hotel site's page titles.

➤ No bidding for paid placement on any search services is permitted.

➤ Written consent is required to display the company logo; when consent is granted, the hotel must follow specified standards.

➤ Written consent is required to display the company slogan; when consent is granted, the hotel must follow specified standards.

➤ Written consent is required to display company photos; when consent is granted, the hotel must follow specified standards.

Links and Sales

➤ Hotel sites should not link to any third-party sites. Third-party sites can link to hotel sites as long as the third party has a signed linking agreement.

➤ Hotel information must be pulled from a company-maintained database.

➤ All pricing information should be accessed dynamically from a company-managed database.

➤ Static price points should never be displayed

➤ Hotel sites shall sell at approved rates only.

Relationships with Third Parties

➤ Association with sites that request static hotel information is not recommended. If a hotel has a relationship with a third party in this regard, then the hotel has to designate a person to check the static information site monthly and update it as necessary. A central contact within the company organization must have a list of all sites that need to be updated manually.

➤ Hotels may participate in directory listing programs.

➤ Third-party sites can't sell negotiated or contract rates on publicly accessible websites. They can't sell wholesale rates unless packaged with airfare, car, etc., nor can they break out the hotel fare from the total price.

➤ Information on negotiated rates (such as corporate discounts or local volume account rates) can't be displayed on publicly accessible sites; this information is only for display on sites that are restricted to the people who would be eligible for the rates.

➤ Third parties have the responsibility to update content if negotiated rates change.

Site Operation and Development

➤ Company will build a cobranded rate and booking page for $200.

Appendix D: Overview of Peer-to-Peer (P2P) Networks

This appendix, provided courtesy of the Software & Information Industry Association (SIIA), compares and contrasts three different frameworks for a peer-to-peer network: a centralized framework, a decentralized framework, and a controlled decentralized framework.

Adam Ayer, Internet antipiracy manager for SIIA, and Anne Griffith, SIIA research director, originally developed these illustrative models to help explain how the peer-to-peer frameworks work.

First, let's briefly define some key terms:

1. A "client" is a computer system or process that requests a service of another computer system (a "server") using some kind of network protocol and then accepts the server's responses.

2. The "server" is a computer that provides some service for other computers connected to it via a network.

3. A "servent" is a computer that acts in both capacities on different occasions.

Centralized Framework

A centralized P2P framework is a system that depends on a central server. A user connects to the central server and uploads and/or downloads information to/from it. These users then become clients, requesting information from the central server. The central server controls network access and directs communication between the peers. Without the central server, the network does not function. Figure D-1 illustrates a basic centralized framework.

Centralized frameworks contain anywhere from a single client and a central server, to a million clients and a central server. Whatever entity controls the central server also controls the information—a valuable commodity. The organization that houses the server may be a for-profit enterprise, a university, an individual pirate, or any other group with enough funds to purchase the requisite (and typically inexpensive) hardware. The advantage of centralization is that access is controlled, files may be vetted for viruses (if desired), and the type of file posted can be limited (if desired).

Example: The now-defunct Napster online music service used a centralized peer-to-peer network.

Decentralized Framework

A decentralized peer-to-peer framework is one that lacks a central server. In a decentralized framework, every user acts as a client, a server, or both—a servent. A user connects to the framework by connecting to another current user of the decentralized community. Once connected to the framework, any user then becomes a member of the community, allowing new users to connect to the community through their respective computers.

Clients still exchange information with servers. However, in a decentralized environment, no one entity controls the information that passes through the community. A user has no control over which clients are allowed to connect

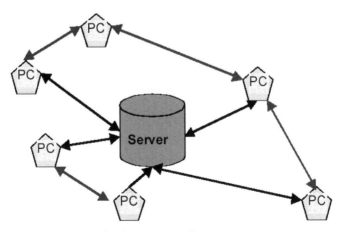

Figure D-1. *Centralized server network.*

to a particular server. Figure D-2 illustrates what a decentralized framework may look like.

When searching a decentralized framework, it usually takes longer to find requested information than in a centralized framework because the request has to travel through a large number of users' computers to find the information.

Example: The Gnutella online file-sharing program is an example of a P2P decentralized server network.

Controlled Decentralization Frameworks

The third peer-to-peer framework takes on characteristics of both centralized and decentralized peer-to-peer frameworks. Within this framework, a user's computer may act as a client, a server, or a servent. However, in this instance, server operators (known as super-peers or super-nodes) control which clients and/or servents are allowed to access a particular server. These operators, therefore, control information much like the operator of the central server of a centralized framework would. Figure D-3 illustrates what a combination of both decentralized and centralized frameworks might look like.

Example: The FastTrack online peer-to-peer network is an example of a controlled decentralized network.

Comparing Frameworks

Each of the three main peer-to-peer models shares similar characteristics—a user may act as a server (hosting files for others to download) or as a client

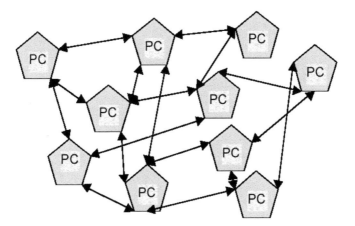

Figure D-2. *Decentralized server network.*

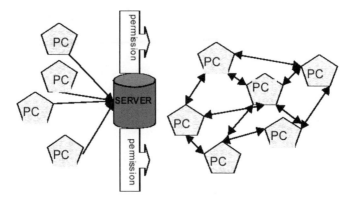

Figure D-3. *Controlled decentralizzation network.*

(downloading files from the hosting servers.) Each model creates an environment that fosters the idea of transferring information from one network node to another with ease.

The differences between the models lie in how each framework is laid out. In the centralized framework, all users surround a central server. The framework has a "star-like" shape with the nucleus (the central server) that has various rays (the end-users) shooting out of it. In the decentralized framework, users, servers, and servents are all connected to each other, creating a "vine-like" shape for the layout of its framework. In a controlled decentralized framework, the framework shape has a unique "web-like" quality.

All peer-to-peer technologies share the same goal of sharing information within the framework. How the information is shared and how much information is shared are the main differences between each peer-to-peer technology.

Appendix E: Sample RFP Scope of Work

These sample excerpts, which are based on actual requests for proposal (RFPs) issued for online monitoring services, are for illustrative purposes only. If your organization is putting out an RFP, you will need to develop a custom version of this sample RFP that reflects your company-specific issues.

Internet Monitoring Services

Background

Company ABC has developed a vision statement that will guide our efforts to ensure the future success of our organization. One element of our vision is the need to aggressively defend the brand. We have invested heavily in building our brand over the past fifty years. As a result of our efforts, the ABC brand has come to represent a level of quality and service that clearly differentiates us from the competition.

A second element of our vision is the need to manage costs and increase quality and service to ensure value to our customers. A key part of our cost management effort is identifying and acting on opportunities to significantly reduce the cost of our needed products and services. Company ABC believes one such opportunity is online monitoring.

The objective of this RFP process is to identify suppliers that can provide the highest levels of service at the most competitive prices to Company ABC. Company ABC also seeks suppliers that are capable of servicing our international subsidiaries and affiliates as the company expands into the global market.

Scope of Work

Company ABC is currently seeking the best solution for online monitoring and brand protection. Specifically, Company ABC is seeking to monitor for online incidents of abuse against Company ABC's name, logo, and slogan.

Types of Abuse

Specific types of abuse of interest to Company ABC include the following:

1. Association of the brand with objectionable content, including:

   ➤ Pornography (any sexual content, including sexually explicit language and/or images)

   ➤ Adult Services (online phone sex operations and escort services)

   ➤ Drugs (sites selling illegal drugs or drug-related paraphernalia)

   ➤ Hate (sites selling products related to the denigration of race, religion, or ethnicity)

   ➤ Violence (sites with grotesque or lurid depictions of violence, murder, and rape, or excess profanity)

   ➤ Extremism (sites promoting terrorist activity, violence, or extreme activism)

2. Customer diversion tactics, including:

   ➤ Cybersquatting and Typo-piracy (unauthorized use of the brand in the domain name, including common misspellings and typos)

   ➤ Metatagging (unauthorized use of the brand name in the site's metatags)

   ➤ Title (unauthorized use of the brand in the page title)

   ➤ Hidden Text (use of the brand name in hidden text)

   ➤ Mislabeled, Broken, and Deep Links (brand-labeled links that go anyplace other than the Company ABC home page)

➤ Logo (use of any logo version other than the one specified by Company ABC)

➤ Claims of Affiliation with Company ABC (other than by those partners that are on a Company ABC approved list)

Please provide a detailed list of which service(s) you, the service provider, would recommend to accomplish each of the above.

Online Environments

Company ABC wants to monitor for association with objectionable content and customer diversion tactics within the following online environments:

1. World Wide Web

2. Usenet Newsgroups

3. Unsolicited E-Mail

Please provide an overview of how your service provides coverage of these sources. In doing so, please be sure to address the following questions:

➤ What do you estimate the current size of each environment to be, and what percentage does your service monitor? How long does this monitoring take?

➤ What are the boundaries of your coverage (i.e., what the coverage includes) and the frequency with which it is monitored? Please define each clearly.

➤ Is there a difference between what you are capable of monitoring and what you recommend be monitored? If so, please explain.

➤ What is your approach to prioritizing monitoring efforts?

➤ What criteria do you use when determining whether to deliver an incident?

International

As stated in the background section, Company ABC seeks suppliers that can service its international subsidiaries as the company expands into the global marketplace. Please address the following:

➤ Do your products provide for international/global monitoring? If so, how?

➤ Which languages do you support? Are there any language constraints?

➤ How do you determine if an incident is present and relevant if the page is in a non-English language?

Prioritization

To get the best return on our investment, Company ABC intends to aggressively take action on the highest-priority incidents. In order for Company ABC to determine the estimated level of effort for follow-up activities, please provide the following information:

➤ Are incidents categorized or ranked by severity of abuse/violation? If yes, please explain how severity is derived.

➤ Are incidents prioritized according to site traffic?

➤ If your answer to the previous two questions was no, are search results categorized or ranked by any particular criteria?

➤ Can the prioritization or ranking criteria be changed?

➤ How are search results delivered to your customers?

➤ How often are reports and/or search results delivered to your customers?

➤ If you provide reports, how are your reports sent to your customers?

➤ Are reports retrievable online? If reports are retrievable online, are there specific hardware or software requirements needed to view/retrieve reports? If yes, please list the requirements.

➤ Does the solution have any alert capabilities?

➤ Can the solution be customized?

➤ What specific information is included in your reports?

➤ Do you include the violator's registration information?

➤ Do you include the ISP's registration information?

➤ Does the monitoring solution also provide workflow capabilities? If so, please provide a detailed description.

➤ Do your clients have the opportunity to verify infringement before notices are sent out?

Appendix F: Sample Cease-and-Desist Letters

These four sample letters are for reference purposes only. They illustrate the form and content of communication directed to parties that may be abusing your brands or intellectual property online. Each letter aims to achieve a different desired outcome.

Sample Letter 1: Enforcement Letter on Use of Properly Formatted Brand/Logo

Date

Recipient
Recipient's Address

Re: Use of _____ Name/Logo on the Internet

Dear Recipient:

The _____ brand and logo are symbols of the quality of products and services we offer to our customers. As you can appreciate, any continual misuse of the _____ brand can destroy this reputation.

It has come to our attention that your use of the _____ brand on your website at http://_____ does not portray our brand in a manner consistent with the quality standards of use as outlined by _____.

   a) A properly formatted brand/logo description of our products and ser-
       vices is available for your use at _____.

OR

   b) A properly formatted brand/logo and description of our products and
       services is attached for your use.

OR

   c) A properly formatted logo and approved description of our products
       and services will be made available to you after you've signed the
       attached use agreement. Please forward the signed agreement
       to _____, or call _____ if you have any questions.

Sincerely,

Name
Title

Sample Letter 2: Cease-and-Desist E-Mail

Date

Recipient
Recipient's Address

Re: Use of _____ Name/Logo on the Internet

Dear Recipient:

It has come to our attention that you are currently using the _____ brand on your website at http://_____. Please be advised that the _____brand is covered by a Federal Trademark Registration, and therefore, all rights to it are held by our Company. You have never received permission to use this mark.

   a) Please cease and desist all use of _____ and confirm your intentions by responding to this e-mail and providing a date on which your use will cease.

OR

   b) Your use of _____ might be acceptable to our Company. Please contact _____ to discuss the possible terms of your continued use.

Please contact me if you have any questions.

Sincerely,

Name
Title

Sample Letter 3: Cease-and-Desist Letter with Notification of Pending Legal Action

Date

Recipient
Recipient's Address

Re: Use of _____Name/Logo on the Internet

Dear Recipient:

_____ is the owner of the trademark _____, U.S. Registered Trademark No. _____, for use in connection with _____. It has recently been brought to our attention that in at least one instance, your company makes unauthorized use of the trademark _____ in connection with _____. Your use of the trademark _____ violates several of _____'s intellectual property rights and is an act of trademark infringement and unfair competition, as it misrepresents and creates confusion as to the association or affiliation between you and _____.

Accordingly, we demand that you immediately cease and desist from using the trademark _____ and confirm in writing within 10 days of the date of this letter that you will cease use of _____'s intellectual property rights. Without a written response, we will proceed with legal action.

Very truly yours,

Name
Title

Sample Letter 4: Cease-and-Desist Letter to Internet Service Provider Regarding Copyright Infringement

Date

Recipient (Internet Service Provider)
Recipient's Address

Re: Digital Piracy

Dear Sir or Madam:

It has come to our attention that you are providing Internet access to and possibly hosting the website piracy.com, which is offering downloads of copyrighted music including such title(s) as: ⎯⎯⎯⎯⎯⎯⎯⎯⎯⎯⎯⎯.

The distribution of unauthorized copies of copyrighted music constitutes copyright infringement under the Copyright Act, Title 17 United States Code Section 106(3). This conduct may also violate the laws of other countries, international law, and/or treaty obligations. We request that you immediately take the following actions:

1) Disable access to this site;
2) Remove this site from your server; and
3) Take appropriate action against the account holder under the terms of your Service Agreement.

By copy of this letter, the owner of the above-referenced website and/or e-mail account is hereby directed to cease and desist from the conduct complained of herein.

On behalf of the respective owners of the exclusive rights to the copyrighted material at issue in this notice, we hereby state, pursuant to the Digital Millennium Copyright Act, Title 17 United States Code Section 512, that we have a good faith belief that use of the material in the manner complained of is not authorized by the copyright owners, their respective agents, or the law.

Also pursuant to the Digital Millennium Copyright Act, we hereby state, under penalty of perjury, that the information in this notification is accurate and that we are authorized to act on behalf of the owners of the exclusive rights being infringed as set forth in this notification.

Please contact us at the address we've listed or by replying to this e-mail should you have any questions. We thank you for your cooperation in this matter. Your prompt response is requested.

Respectfully,

Name
Title

Notes

Introduction

1. "Nintendo Selects Cyveillance to Tackle Unwanted Associations on the Net," *Business Wire* (August 1, 2000).
2. Mitch Betts, "Companies Fight Back Against Internet Attacks," *Computerworld* (October 23, 2000); available at http://www.computerworld.com/news/2000/story/0,11280,52667,00.html.
3. Lisa Gill, "Someone's Watching You: The Web's Secret Police," *NewsFactor Network* (July 15, 2002), available at http://www.newsfactor.com/perl/story/18584.html; also Lori Enos, "Somebody's Watching You: The Web's Secret Police," *E-Commerce Times* (May 22, 2001), available at http://www.ecommercetimes.com/perl/story/9902.html.
4. Graeme Beaton, "Dotcom boom 'just beginning,'" Associated Newspapers Ltd. (March 4, 2002).

Chapter 1

1. Brad Smith, "Will XXX equal $$$?" *Wireless Week* (May 8, 2002); available at http://www.wirelessweek.com/index.asp?layout = article&articleid = CA215523.
2. "TV Advertising Trends Surrounding the Super Bowl," Nielsen Media Research

(January 23, 2003); also "netScore Internet Traffic Measurement Report," com-Score Networks (March 2003).

3. "Zippo Manufacturing Co. Selects Cyveillance to Help Implement Internet Policy," Cyveillance, Inc. Press Release (April 17, 2000).

4. Jennifer Disabatino, "Mattel's Barbie Wins Case Against Cybersquatters," *Computerworld* (July 20, 2000); available at http://www.computerworld.com/news/2000/story/0,11280,47337,00.html.

5. Oscar S. Cisneros, "Mattel: Don't Play with Barbie," *Wired News* (July 27, 2000); available at http://www.wired.com/news/politics/0,1283,37699,00.html.

6. Robert Grove and Blaise Zerega, "The Lolita Problem," *Red Herring* (January 2002); available at http://www.redherring.com/insider/2002/0118/1249.html.

7. Ira Sager, et al., "The Underground Web," *BusinessWeek* (September 2, 2002); available at http://www.businessweek.com/magazine/content/02_35/b3797001.htm.

8. Ibid.

9. "Apple Tells Satanists Not to 'Think Different,'" Reuters (June 18, 2001).

10. Thomas A. Stewart, "Lessons from the Online Gambling Industry," *Business 2.0* (June 6, 2001), available at http://www.business2.com/articles/web/0,1653,12222,00.html; also Henry W. Singer, "High Stakes on a Little Island," *HostingTech*, Vol. 2, 3 (March 2002), available at http://www.hostingtech.com/browser/02_03_island.html.

11. L. L. Bean, Inc. v. Drake Publishers, Inc., 811 F.2d 26, 34 (1st Cir. 1987).

12. Matt Gallaway, "Parody Sites Prevail in Court," *Business 2.0* (February 13, 2001); available at http://www.business2.com/articles/web/0,1653,9452,00.html.

13. Cliffs Notes, Inc. v. Bantam Doubleday Dell Publ. Group, Inc., 886 F.2d 490, 494 (2d Cir. 1989).

14. Jordache Enterprises, Inc. v. Hogg Wyld, Ltd., 828 F.2d 1482, 1486 (10th Cir. 1987).

15. Declan McCullagh, "Osama Has a New Friend," *Wired News* (October 10, 2001); available at http://www.wired.com/news/conflict/0,2100,47450,00.html.

16. "'Muppet' Producers Miffed over Bert-bin Laden Image," CNN.com (October 11, 2001); available at http://www.cnn.com/2001/US/10/11/muppets.binladen/.

17. The Indian Information Technology Act, 2000, Chapter XI, Paragraph 67.

18. Guy Paisner, "Online Porn Goes Mainstream," *Red Herring* (October 1, 2001); available at http://www.redherring.com/mag/issue105/167482.html.

19. Stuart Elliot, "Stars of Pornographic Films Are Modeling in a Campaign for Pony, the Shoe Company," *The New York Times* (February 24, 2003).

20. Demian Bulwa, "U.S. Raids Firms Selling Items Used by Pot Smokers," *San Francisco Chronicle* (February 25, 2003).

21. Leslie Brooks Suzukamo, "Hormel Is Resigned to Use of 'Spam' in Net Slang," *Saint Paul Pioneer Press* (May 29, 2001).

22. Brian Murray et al., "Risk-e-Business" Cyveillance White Paper, Cyveillance Inc. (September 2000).

Chapter 2

1. Jay Lyman, "Cruising Down the Disinformation Superhighway," *NewsFactor Network* (March 5, 2002); available at http://www.newsfactor.com/perl/story/16607.html.

2. Matt Krantz, "Emulex Hoax Suspect Arrested," *USA Today* (September 1, 2000).

3. Johanna Bennett, "Rife with Rumors, Internet Is Growing Problem to Many Firms," Dow Jones News Service (June 18, 1998).

4. Luciano Siracusano, "How Oracle Avoided Getting Emulexed," Individual investor.com (June 6, 2001).

5. Brooke Crothers, "Intel Posts Bug Explanation," CNET News.com (May 9, 1997); available at http://news.com.com/2100-1001-279614.html.

6. Gretchen Morgenson, "The Bears on This Message Board Had Enron Pegged," *The New York Times* (April 28, 2002).

7. Arnaud de Borchgrave et al., "Cyber Threats and Information Security: Meeting the 21st Century Challenge" (Washington, D.C.: Center for Strategic and International Studies, Washington, D.C., December 2000).

8. Ian Fried, "Apple Settles with 'Worker Bee,'" CNET News.com (August 7, 2001).

9. Jim Dalrymple, "Man Arrested for Leaking Apple Documents," MacCentral.com (December 11, 2002).

10. Christopher Locke, et al, *The Cluetrain Manifesto: The End of Business as Usual* (New York: Perseus Books, 2001).

11. Brian Fonseca, "Mining for Opinions," *InfoWorld*, (August 6, 2001).

12. Beth Snyder Bulik, "The Brand Police," *Business 2.0* (November 20, 2000).

13. Oscar S. Cisneros, "Legal Tips for Your 'Sucks' Site," *Wired News* (August 14, 2000).

14. Leslie Goff, "YourCompanySucks.com: Angry Consumers Slam Companies on the Web," *Computerworld* (July 22, 1998).

15. Bally Total Fitness Holding Corporation v. Andrew S. Faber, 29 F. Supp. 2d 1161 (C.D. Cal., Nov. 23, 1998).

16. Goff, "YourCompanySucks.com."

17. Keith Regan, "Building an E-Commerce Community: Friendship Sells," *E-Commerce Times* (June 6, 2002).

18. Hilary Appelman, "I Scream, You Scream: Consumers Vent Over the Net," *The New York Times* (March 4, 2001).

19. Appelman, "I Scream, You Scream: Consumers Vent Over the Net."

Chapter 3

1. Mike Wendland, "Porn Pirates Hijack Surfers," *The Observer-Eccentric Newspapers* (October 4, 1998).

2. "At Risk Online: Your Good Name," *PC Computing* (March 12, 2001).

3. Linda Formichelli, "Brands on the Run," *The Next Big Thing* (April 19, 2001).

4. "Internet Domain Name Disputes: Some Questions and Answers," The World Intellectual Property Organization (2002); available at www.wipo.org/about-ip/en/studies/publications/domain_names.htm.

5. The Dream Merchant Company Kft. and Création Méandres Inc. v. Richard Mandanice d.b.a. Domain Strategy Inc., Claim Number: FA0212000137097, National Arbitration Forum, January 23, 2003.

6. "NPD Search and Portal Site Study," SearchEngineWatch.com (July 6, 2000); available at http://www.searchenginewatch.com/sereport/article.php/2162791.

7. Jim Hu, "Spammer Attacks AOL Search," CNET News.com (June 19, 2002); available at http://news.com.com/2100-1023-937624.html.

8. Lisa Shuchman, "Search and Destroy," *IP Law & Business* (January 2003).

9. Shuchman, "Search and Destroy."

10. Peter K. Yu, "Wrestling with Gator," *IP Law & Business* (January 2003).

11. Postini E-Mail Stat Track (February 2003); available at http://www.postini.com/stats/index.html.

12. Christine Tatum, "Spam Feeding Anger on Internet," *Chicago Tribune* (January 7, 2002); available at http://www.chicagotribune.com/technology/local/chi-020 1070115jan07,0,499999.story.

13. James Gleick, "Tangled Up in Spam," *The New York Times Magazine* (February 9, 2003), Section 6, p. 42.

14. Leslie Miller, "'Mouse-Trapping' Locks Web Users in a Virtual Maze," *USA Today* (May 29, 2001); available at http://www.usatoday.com/tech/news/2001-05-29-mousetrapping.htm.

15. "FTC Halts Internet Hijacking Scam," U.S. Federal Trade Commission Press Release (September 22, 1999).

16. Preliminary Injunction, Re: FTC v. Pereira, et al., Case No. 99-1367-A, U.S. District Court, E.D. VA, Alexandria, September 21, 1999.

17. Brian Murray, et al., "Entangled on the Web: Aggressive Technology Tactics Go Mainstream," Cyveillance, Inc. White Paper (December 2001).

18. Steven Bonisteel, "'Mouse-Trapper' Ordered to Pay Over $1.8M," Newsbytes .com (May 28, 2002).

19. "Washloads and Uploads," *Smart Business* (March 2002).

20. Jim Krane, "Hackers' Next Target? Cell Phones," *SiliconValley.com* (March 10, 2002); available at http://www.siliconvalley.com/mld/siliconvalley/2833740.htm.

Chapter 4

1. Sandeep Dayal, Helene Landsberg, and Michael Zeisser, "Building Digital Brands," *McKinsey Quarterly* No. 2 (2000); available through free registration at http://www.mckinseyquarterly.com/register.asp?ArtID = 860.

2. David Vaczek, "E-Tailers Cross Channels for Sales," *emarketing Magazine* (March 2001).

3. Brian Murray, Rick Grand, and Beth Sanville, "The Customer Is King," Cyveillance White Paper (June 2001).

4. Patricia B. Seybold, *Customers.com: How to Create a Profitable Business Strategy for the Internet & Beyond* (New York: Times Books, 1998).

5. Darren Allen, "Online Shopping: Pry Before You Buy," *eMarketer* (February 6, 2001).

6. Katrina Brooker, "E-Rivals Seem to Have Home Depot Awfully Nervous," *Fortune* (August 1999).

7. Doug Bartholomew, "E-Commerce Bullies," *Industry Week* (September 4, 2000); available at http://www.industryweek.com/CurrentArticles/asp/articles .asp?ArticleID = 891.

8. Bartholomew, "E-Commerce Bullies."

9. Tom Kaneshige, "Avoiding Channel Conflict," *Line56 Magazine* (April 1, 2001); available at http://www.line56.com/articles/default.asp?NewsID=2382.

10. Bartholomew, "E-Commerce Bullies."

11. Brian Murray et al., "Risk-e-Business," Cyveillance White Paper (September 2000).

12. Susannah Patton, "Lip Service," *CIO Asia* (January 2002); available at http://www.idg.com.sg/pcio.nsf/unidlookup/8538D4FEAE5973C348256B4A00300BF8?OpenDocument.

13. Chuck Moozakis, "Strategy Keeps Channel Happy," *Internet Week* (August 13, 2001); available at http://www.internetweek.com/ebizapps01/ebiz081301-1.htm.

14. "Client Spotlight: Polaris Industries Forging an Online Trail in the Motorsport Industry," Digital River Monthly Commentary on e-Business (Fall 2001); case study available at http://drhome.digitalriver.com/livehtml/newsite/dr_success_000.html.

15. Don Tapscott, *e-Business Roadmap for Success* (Boston: Addison-Wesley, 1999).

16. Linda Rosencrance, "Consumers Warned to Beware of Online Disaster-Relief Scams," *Computerworld* (September 13, 2001); available at http://www.computerworld.com/softwaretopics/software/story/0,10801,63825,00.html.

17. Sharon Gaudin, "American Red Cross Warns of Online Donation Scams," *Network World Fusion* (September 14, 2001); available at http://www.cnn.com/2001/TECH/internet/09/14/donation.scam.idg/.

18. "Fraud Fears Over Web Appeals," CNN.com (September 19, 2001); available at http://www.cnn.com/2001/TECH/internet/09/19/gen.appeal.fraud/.

19. Jacqueline L. Salmon, "E-Mail Scam Preys on Relief Donors," *The Washington Post* (October 22, 2001); available at http://www.washingtonpost.com/ac2/wp-dyn?pagename=article&node=&contentId=A23729-2001Oct19&notFound=true.

Chapter 5

1. "Grey Marketing Comes with a High Price Tag," Nortel Networks (2003); available at http://www.nortelnetworks.com/prd/greymarket/enterprise/.

2. "Leading Experts Attack Product Diversion, Fight Fakes, Terrorist Links, and Share Strategies," Anti-Gray Market Alliance Press Release (January 9, 2002); available at http://www.antigraymarket.org/pr010902.htm.

3. David Cho, "A New Formula for Fraud," *The Washington Post* (August 4, 2001).

4. Statement of Mardi Mountford of the International Formula Council during hearing before the Subcommittee on Courts and Intellectual Property of the Committee on the Judiciary, U.S. House of Representatives, 2000.

5. Frequently Asked Questions, Anti-Gray Market Alliance (AGMA); available at http://www.antigraymarket.org/faq.html.

6. "Compaq and U.S. Marshals Seize Counterfeit Computer Products," Compaq Computer Corporation Press Release (February 13, 2002); available at http://h18020.www1.hp.com/newsroom/pr/2002/pr2002021302.html.

7. "Xerox Wins Global Award for Fighting Supplies Counterfeiting," Xerox Corp.

Press Release (February 1, 2002); available at http://www.antigraymarket.org/020102.pdf.

8. Kathleen Haney, "E-Tailers Take Issue with Brand Fraud," *Digitrends* (June 16, 2000).

9. "Hilfiger, Polo, Nike Sue Web Retailer, Alleging Sales of Counterfeit Apparel," *The Wall Street Journal* (March 14, 2000).

10. "About Fraud," The Imaging Supplies Coalition; available at http://www.isc inc.org/info.php.

11. "Lexmark International Files Suit to Stop Counterfeit Toner Cartridges," Lexmark International Inc. Press Release (May 24, 2000); available at http://www .lexmark.com/US/press_releases_details/0,1233,NjY5fDE=,00.html.

12. "Xerox Wins Global Award for Fighting Supplies Counterfeiting," Xerox Corp. Press Release (February 1, 2002).

13. "GenuOne Wins Xerox Contract for Online Brand Protection," GenuOne, Inc. Press Release (February 15, 2001); available at http://www.genuone.com/G1/home/Level0/news/Level1/news_releases/index_html?select_release=Xerox.

14. "New Service Will Help Firms Fight Fake Drugs," The International Chamber of Commerce (November 8, 2002); available at http://www.iccwbo.org/home/news_archives/2002/stories/drugs.asp.

15. Statement of the Honorable John D. Dingell regarding Oversight and Investigations Subcommittee Hearing on Counterfeit Bulk Drugs, June 8, 2000; available at http://www.house.gov/commerce_democrats/press/106st125.htm.

16. John D. Dingell, U.S. Food and Drug Administration Arguments to the Commerce Committee, U.S. House of Representatives Commerce Committee, February 11, 2000.

17. "A Forensic Solution to Combat Counterfeit Pharmaceuticals," *Biocode News*, Biocode.com, (2001).

Chapter 6

1. "Microsoft Intensifies Worldwide Campaign Against Internet Piracy and Criminal Counterfeiting," Microsoft Canada Press Release (April 3, 2001).

2. "Music Downloads for Profit," Forrester Brief, Forrester Research, Inc. (January 31, 2001).

3. "Recording Industry and Online Music Services Battle Over Copyright Laws," CNN.com (May 17, 2000); available at http://www.cnn.com/2000/LAW/05/16/mp3.napster.suit/.

4. John Borland, "Napster, Universities Sued by Metallica," CNET News.com (April 13, 2000); available at http://news.com.com/2100-1023-239263.html.

5. "Recording Industry Announces 2001 Year-End Shipments," Recording Industry Association of America, Press Release, February 25, 2002.

6. Bernhard Warner, "Global Music Sales Fall, Hurt by Consumer Piracy," Reuters (April 16, 2002).

7. "Stop the Music," *CyberAtlas*, (January 15, 2002); available at http://cyberatlas .internet.com/markets/retailing/article/0,1323,6061_955691,00.html.

8. "Cyveillance's Technology Helps ASCAP Lead the World in Internet Licensing," Cyveillance, Inc. Press Release (October 24, 2000).

9. Jonathan Rabinovitz, "Lucasfilm Watchdog Tracks Online Pirates," *Mercury News*, (July 11, 1999).

10. Sarah L. Roberts-Witt, "Branded," *PC Magazine* (April 17, 2001); available at http://www.pcmag.com/article2/0,4149,91780,00.asp.

11. "Web Movie Piracy Up 20 Pct or More This Year-Study," Reuters (May 29, 2002).

12. "The Oscars Get Napsterised," *The Economist Global Agenda* (March 22, 2002); available at http://www.economist.com/agenda/displayStory.cfm?Story_ID = 1049624.

13. Ted Bridis, "Internet Providers Must Help Trace Online Pirates," The Associated Press (January 22, 2003); available at http://www.law.com/jsp/article.jsp?id = 1042568688756.

14. "Valenti Comes to Cannes to Push for Worldwide Alliance on Movie Piracy," *The Mercury News* (May 22, 2002); available at http://www.siliconvalley.com/mld/siliconvalley/3316627.htm.

15. Dan Levine, "Not the Real Slim Shady," Salon.com (June 10, 2002); available at http://www.salon.com/tech/feature/2002/06/10/eminem_mp3/.

16. Declan McCullagh, "Securing the Broadband Revolution," *Wired News* (August 22, 2001); available at http://www.wired.com/news/politics/0,1283,46216,00.html.

17. Dawn C. Chmielewski, "Andreessen: Copy Protection Efforts Are Doomed," *The Mercury News* (April 9, 2002); available at http://www.siliconvalley.com/mld/siliconvalley/3031836.htm.

18. James Lardner, "Hollywood vs. High-Tech," *Business 2.0* (May 2002); available at http://www.business2.com/articles/mag/0,1640,39428,FF.html.

19. "The Oscars Get Napsterised," *The Economist Global Agenda*.

20. Rob Fixmer, "Yes, The Internet Does Change Everything," *Interactive Week* (April 29, 2002); available at http://www.eweek.com/article2/0,3959,9494,00.asp.

21. McCullagh, "Securing the Broadband Revolution."

22. Gordon Kelly, "Piracy Estimates Too Low, Claims MS," *Computer Reseller News* (January 10, 2001).

23. Lizette Wilson, "Shots Fired in Piracy Fight," *San Francisco Business Times* (January 18, 2002); available at http://sanfrancisco.bizjournals.com/sanfrancisco/stories/2002/01/21/story2.html.

24. "BSA Acts Against Software Scams," The Business Software Alliance Press Release (March 21, 2002); available at http://www.bsa.org/usa/press/newsreleases//2002-03-21.993.phtml?type = policy.

25. David Becker, "Piracy May Drive Adobe Out of China," CNET News.com (January 15, 2002); also "Four Out of Every Ten Software Programs Are Pirated Worldwide," Business Software Alliance Press Release (June 10, 2002), available at http://www.bsa.org/usa/press/newsreleases//2002-06-10.1129.phtml?type = policy.

26. "Microsoft Intensifies Worldwide Campaign Against Internet Piracy and Criminal Counterfeiting," Microsoft Press Release (April 2, 2001); available at http://www.microsoft.com/presspass/Press/2001/Apr01/04-02InternetCrimePR.asp.

27. *NACS College Store Industry Financial Report 2002* (Oberlin, OH: National Association of College Stores, Inc., 2002).

28. *Higher Education Retail Market Facts and Figures 2002* (Oberlin, OH: National Association of College Stores, Inc., 2002).
29. Gwendolyn Mariano, "Copyright Fears Make Publishers Wary of E-Books," CNET News.com (October 6, 2000); available at http://news.com.com/2100-1023-246678.html?legacy=cnet.
30. "The Associated Press Selects Cyveillance to Track Web Usage," Cyveillance Inc., Press Release (August 1, 2000).
31. "Internet Study Reveals More Banking and Brokerage Customers Turning to the Web for Key Financial Information," Harris Interactive Press Release (September 21, 2000); available at http://www.harrisinteractive.com/news/allnews bydate.asp?NewsID=149.
32. "Nasdaq Selects Cyveillance's Internet Intelligence Solutions," Cyveillance, Inc. Press Release (November 5, 2001).

Chapter 7

1. "Online Americans More Concerned About Privacy Than Health Care, Crime, and Taxes, New Survey Reveals," National Consumers League Press Release (October 4, 2000).
2. Michael Moon and Doug Millison, *Firebrands: Building Brand Loyalty in the Internet Age* (New York: McGraw-Hill Professional Publishing, August 2000).
3. Jeff Smith, "A Brand New Role for IT," *Optimize Magazine* (April 2002); available at http://www.optimizemag.com/issue/006/marketing.htm.
4. Steve Ulfelder, "Plumb Your Clickstream Data," *Computerworld* (January 1, 2001); available at http://www.computerworld.com/industrytopics/retail/story/0,10801,54809,00.html.
5. Linda Rosencrance, "Toysrus.com Faces Online Privacy Inquiry," *Computerworld* (December 18, 2000); available at http://www.computerworld.com/securitytopics/security/privacy/story/0,10801,552 56,00.html.
6. "Suit Claims Toys R Us Violates Web Privacy Policy," The Associated Press (August 3, 2000).
7. "Online Shopping: Privacy Hazard?" The Associated Press (August 1, 2000).
8. "Toysrus.com Pays $50,000 Fine in Web Privacy Case," Reuters News Service (January 3, 2002).
9. Lisa Gill, "Online Privacy Is Dead—Now What?" NewsFactor.com (March 4, 2002).
10. Mark W. Vigoroso, "Merchants Race to Outpace Online Fraudsters," *E-Commerce Times* (March 4, 2002); available at http://www.ecommercetimes.com/perl/story/16599.html.
11. Saul Hansell, "Visa Starts Password Service to Fight Online Fraud," *The New York Times* (December 3, 2001).
12. Gill, "Online Privacy Is Dead—Now What?"
13. "Online Fraud—Though Victim Percentage Is Low, Fear Is High," *eMarketer* (June 29, 2001).
14. Steven Musil, "Western Union Web Site Hacked," CNET News.com (September

10, 2000); available at http://news.com.com/2100-1023-245525.html?legacy =cnet.

15. Bill Laberis Associates, "Securing the Internet Economy," *InfoWorld* and *Internet Security Systems* (2000).

16. "ingreslock 1524 and the Playboy.com Hack," UseTheSource.com (November 21, 2001); available at http://www.usethesource.com/articles/01/11/21/123212 .shtml.

17. Rachel Ross, "Hacker Exposes Playboy.com Customers," *The Toronto Star* (November 21, 2001).

18. Todd R. Weiss, "Customer Information Exposed by Playboy.com Hacker," *Computerworld* (November 21, 2001); available at http://www.computerworld .co.nz/webhome.nsf/printdoc/77C79F54E967F4FBCC256B0C00074425!open document.

19. Ira Sager, et al., "The Underground Web," *BusinessWeek* (September 2, 2002); available at http://www.businessweek.com/magazine/content/02_35/b3797001.htm.

20. Ann Cavoukian and Tyler J. Hamilton, *The Privacy Payoff* (Whitby, Ontario: McGraw-Hill Ryerson Limited, 2002).

21. Maryfran Johnson, "Follow the (Privacy) Money," *Computerworld* (February 25, 2002); available at http://www.computerworld.com/securitytopics/security/ privacy/story/0,10801,68536,00.html.

22. Patrick Thibodeau, "Profitable Privacy," *Computerworld* (February 18, 2002); available at http://www.computerworld.com/softwaretopics/crm/story/0,10801 ,68354,00.html.

Chapter 8

1. Larry Kahaner, "Keeping an 'I' on the Competition," *Information Week* (September 25, 2000); available at http://www.informationweek.com/805/main.htm.

2. Charles Cooper, "How Tech Delivers for FedEx," ZDNet and CNET News.com (June 3, 2002).

3. Susan Warren, "I-Spy," *The Wall Street Journal* (January 14, 2002).

4. Arik R. Johnson, "What Is Competitive Intelligence?" Aurora WDC (2001); available at http://www.aurorawdc.com/arj_cics_whatisci.htm.

5. Michael Porter, *Competitive Strategy, Techniques for Analyzing Industries and Competitors* (New York: The Free Press, 1980).

6. Liam Fahey, *Outwitting, Outmaneuvering, and Outperforming Competitors* (New York: John Wiley & Sons, Inc., 1999).

Chapter 9

1. "Dow Corning Selects Cyveillance's Brand Management Solution for New E-Commerce Strategy," Cyveillance, Inc. Press Release (May 21, 2001).

2. Julia Angwin and Motoko Rich, "Big Hotel Chains Are Striking Back Against Web Sites," *The Wall Street Journal* (March 14, 2003).

3. Kevin Heilbronner, "Audio Interview w/Eric Pearson," Hospitality Net (December 16, 2002): available at http://www.hospitalitynet.org/transcript/124000346.html.

4. "Unilever Selects NameProtect's VigilActive Service to Protect Its Portfolio of World-Class Brands from Online Abuse," NameProtect Inc. Press Release (June 17, 2002).

5. "Cyveillance to Protect Online Usage of Russell 2000 Index," Cyveillance, Inc. Press Release (July 23, 2001).

Chapter 11

1. Beth Snyder Bulik, "The Brand Police," *Business 2.0* Magazine (November 28, 2000); available at http://www.business2.com/articles/mag/0,1640,14287,FF.html.

2. Brian Murray et al., "Risk-e-Business," Cyveillance White Paper, Cyveillance Inc., (September 2000).

3. Jim Collins, *Good to Great: Why Some Companies Make the Leap . . . and Others Don't* (New York: HarperCollins Publishers, Inc., 2001).

4. Gary Hamel, "Strategy as Revolution," *Harvard Business Review* (July–August 1996).

Index

abortion, 19
actionable information, 165–166
activism sites, 36–39, 46–47
Adobe Systems, 122
AdRelevance, 158
adult entertainment, 9–11
    see also pornography
advertising metrics, 24–26
affiliates, 79–80, 93–94
Agfa Monotype Corporation, 124
Aimster, 202
alcohol, 19
Alexa Internet, 162
Allstate, 87
Amazon.com, 125, 162
Amenita, Chris, 115–116
American Airlines, 86
American Express, 161
American Red Cross, 91–93
American Society of Composers, Authors and Publishers (ASCAP), 114–116
Andreessen, Marc, 120

Ann Taylor, 76
Anticybersquatting Consumer Protection Act, 14–15
Anti-Gray Market Alliance (AGMA), 101
AOL, 47, 48, 115, 146, 202
apathy, 208–209
Apple Computer, 13, 33
applets, 66
appliances, mousetrapping, 69
Arai Helmet, 198
arbitration, 52, 202, 203
ArtistDirect, 11
Associated Press (AP), 127, 128
AT&T, 38
auction sites, 112, 174, 175
audience measurement companies, 161
Australian Competition and Consumer Commission, 66
Authentication News, 103
authenticity of products, testing, 108–109
Avis Rent A Car, 76
Avnet, Inc., 166

baby formula, 99–101
Baer, Harold, 11
Bally Total Fitness, 38–39
Barbiesplaypen.com, 10–11
Barenaked Ladies, 119
Bayer Corporation, 93
BearShare, 112
BellSouth, 143
Berman, Jay, 113
Bernstein, Jodie, 65–66
Berryhill, Melissa, 83
"Bert Is Evil" parody website, 17–18
Better Business Bureau (BBB), 92–93
black markets, 99–101
    see also gray markets
Bongiovanni, Lisa Marie, 11
brand abuse
    cost of, 24–25, 203–204, 211–212
    defining "objectionable" and, 18–21
    impact of, 24–26, 203–204, 211–212
    responding to, 21–26
    risk of, 21
    see also campaign against brand abuse
branding, defined, 135
brand management, in monitoring part-
    ners, 94–95
brand market indexes, 129–130
brand presence, 155–156
brand reach, 156–159
    competitor absence and, 158–159
    competitor brand abuse and, 158
    linking relationships and, 159
British National Criminal Intelligence
    Service (NCIS), 92–93
Broadcast Music, Inc. (BMI), 114–115
Brown, Shona, 39–40
browsers
    "back" or history buttons, 63–64, 65
    changing, 66–68
Bulkregister, 52
Burchell, Katrina, 183
Burger King, 28
Burnett, Andrew, 13
Business Software Alliance (BSA),
    121–123
Business Week magazine, 12

cable modem services, 117
Cable and Telecommunications Associ-
    ation for Marketing, 112
campaign against brand abuse, 21–26,
    190–212
    apathy as enemy in, 208–209
    best practices and, 202–204
    categorizing abuse in, 192–193
    categorizing potential offenders in,
        192
    communication methods in, 196–
        197, 199–200
    designing, 191–202
    executive concerns and, 206–207
    follow-up action, 201–202
    importance of, 3, 203–204, 210–212
    prioritizing incidents in, 193–194,
        195
    proactive licensing of music, 114–116
    raising awareness in, 207–208
    responsibility for, 196, 209–210
capital punishment, 19
Carter, Henry, 30
Cathay Pacific Airways, 90
Cavoukian, Ann, 148
cease-and-desist letters, 56, 197, 199,
    202–203
    cybersquatting and, 51, 203
    for digital copyright infringement,
        118–119
    hate site posting of, 37–38
    for objectionable content, 22–24
cell phones, digital trickery and, 69
Center for Strategic and International
    Studies, 32–33
Chaikind, Bonnie, 11
channel conflict, 77, 82–83
Chase, Larry, 164–165
chat rooms, 112, 117, 118, 125, 162–
    163, 174, 183
Chernin, Peter, 121
Chevron, 11
child pornography, 11–12
ChillingEffects.org, 197
Chrysler, 45–46
Church of Satan, 13
Cipro, 93

Cirque du Soleil, 52
Clausewitz, Carl von, 151
clear GIF, 137–140
click-through rate, 58
cloaking, 54–55
Coca-Cola Company, 20, 181
Collins, Jim, 208
commissions, for referrals, 79–80
Compaq Computer, 101–102
competitive intelligence, 153–168
    actionable information from,
      165–166
    competitor brand presence and,
      155–156
    competitor brand reach and, 156–159
    counterintelligence and, 164–165
    data collection for, 164
    impact of using, 166–167
    Internet as source of, 154–155
    online commentary and, 162–164
    online partnerships and, 159–162
compression technology, 117
Computerworld, 136, 149
comScore Networks, 157–158
confidential information, 32–34,
    135–150
consumer feedback, 34–40
consumer information, 32
Continental Airlines, 11
Continental Research, 206–207
controversial subjects, 19
cookies, 137, 138, 139–140
copier supplies, 103
Coremetrics, 139–140
counterfeit goods, 98, 102–104
    cost of, 109–110
    examples of, 103–104
    online monitoring of, 104–110
    signals of, 105–108
    testing authenticity, 108–109
counterintelligence, 164–165
country code top-level domains (cc-
    TLDs), 50–51, 52
Cranton, Tim, 2
Craven, Julie, 20
crawlers, search engine, 53, 54–55
Cullen, Peter, 149

Curlander, Paul, 103
customer capture, 45–62, 106
    cybersquatting, 45–47, 51, 67, 173,
      179–181, 203
    domain name administration, 50–52
    junk e-mail, 61–62
    mislabeled links, 60–61
    paid placements, 56–58, 177
    search engine manipulation, 52–56
    software utility-generated advertise-
      ments, 58–60
    typo-piracy, 47–50, 51, 67
    see also online monitoring
customer-centric strategies, 76–77
customer diversion, 44–71, 177–178
    bringing the customer back, 45,
      66–68
    cost of, 70
    customer capture, 45–62, 106
    future of, 69
    holding the customer, 45, 62–66
    impact of, 70
    scope of problem, 68–69
customers
    feedback from, 34–40, 46–47
    goodwill of, 7–8
    online monitoring by, 175–176
    online partners and, 75–77, 160
Cyberalert, 40
cybersquatting, 45–47, 51, 67, 173, 179–
    181, 203
Cyveillance, 9, 66–68, 83–84

Davis, Bill, 124
decoys, 119
deep links, 78, 193–194
defending the brand, *see* brand abuse;
    campaign against brand abuse
Delli-Colli, Kevin A., 12–13
Del Monte, Donna, 103
"denial of service" attacks, 119
DesignersDirect.com, 102–103
Deutsch, Sarah, 47
digital clock utilities, 58–60
Digital Millennium Copyright Act
    (DMCA), 118, 201
digital rights management (DRM), 120–
    121, 126

digital subscriber line (DSL), 117
digital watermarking, 120–121
Dingell, John, 104
DIRECTV, 202
Discover Financial Services, 161
distributors, 84–89
  damaging activities of, 84
  managing, 84–89
diversion of customers, *see* customer diversion
Dogpile.com, 175
domain names
  arbitration and, 52, 202, 203
  cybersquatting and, 45–47, 51, 67, 173, 179–181, 203
  domain name administration, 50–52
  online monitoring of, 175, 179–181
  traffic diversion, 53
  typo-piracy and, 47–50, 51, 67
Dow Corning Corp., 173
The Dream Merchant, 52
drugs and drug use, 19

early-warning systems, 31–32
earnings claims, 30–31
e-books, 125–126
EFAM Enterprises, 103
e-mail, unsolicited, 20–21, 61–62, 63, 78, 146–147, 148, 200–201
employees
  online monitoring by, 175–176
  security of information and, 32
Emulex Corp., 30
encryption technologies, 117–118, 120–121, 142
Enron, 31
Epinions.com, 40
Espotting, 56
Estée Lauder, 58
E*TRADE, 30
e-wallet utilities, 58–60
eWatch, 40
Extended Stay America, Inc., 59
extremism, 8, 12–13

Faber, Drew, 38–39
Fahey, Liam, 165–166
false positives, 155, 178

FastTrack, 116
Febreze Fabric Spray, 28–29
FedEx, 59, 160–161
feedback from consumers, 34–40
  activism and "sucks" sites, 36–39, 46–47
  benefits of, 35, 39–40
  types of, 35
file transfer protocol (FTP) sites, 112, 122, 125, 174, 175
financial information, 30–31, 32
financial market data, 129–131
Fiorina, Carly, 133
firearms, 19
Firebrands (Moon), 135
Fischer, Mark, 142
Fixmer, Rob, 121
Flamm, Richard, 1–2
fonts.com, 124
Ford Motor Co., 39
forensic fingerprinting, 108
Forrester Research, 3
framing, 64, 67, 112
Frank Russell Company, 130, 183
fraud, 64, 66, 80, 91–93, 140–141, 143, 144–147, 149
Froogle.com, 108
FTP (file transfer protocol) sites, 112, 122, 125, 174, 175
Fuji Xerox, 46

gambling, 13–14, 70
Gartner, Inc., 140
The Gator Corporation, 58–61, 63
generic top-level domains (gTLDs), 50–51
Gerber, 28
Global Anti-Counterfeiting Group, 103
Gnutella, 116
goodwill, of customers, 7–8
Google, 52, 56, 58, 155, 177, 183
gray markets, 90, 98, 99–102
  combating activity in, 101
  cost of, 109–110
  examples of, 99–101
  online monitoring of, 104–110
  signals of, 105–108
  testing authenticity, 108–109

Grove, Andy, 120
guns, 19
Gursky, Steve, 103

hackers, 32–33, 126, 142–144, 149
Hamel, Gary, 211
Hamilton, Tyler, 148
Harris Interactive, 129, 135, 140
hate, 8, 12–13
"hate" sites, 36–39, 46–47
Helmsley Hotels, 54
Herr, Mark, 140
Hewlett-Packard Company, 101–102
Hill and Knowlton, 206
Hoffman, Donna, 63
Holiday Inn, 57
holograms, 108
The Home Depot, 82–83
home-jacking, 66, 67
Honda, 50
Hormel Foods Corp., 20–21
Hovis, John, 166
HTML, 125–126
Hunker, Jeffrey, 13
Hyatt, 47
hyperlinks
    brand reach and, 159
    broken, 78
    link spamming, 55, 60–61
    mislabeled, 60–61, 67
    sponsored, 56–58

IBM, 14, 31, 50, 85
ibmcasino-one.com, 14
ICANN (Internet Corporation for Assigned Names and Numbers), 51, 52, 202, 203
identity theft, 64, 66, 80, 140–147
Imaging Supplies Coalition, 103
infant formula, 99–101
information collection technologies, 136–140
    cookies, 137, 138, 139–140
    web beacons, 137–140
Information Technology Association of America, 101
in-lining, 64, 112

In Search of Excellence (Peters and Waterman), 76
instant messaging, 112
Intel Corp., 30–31
intelligence, see competitive intelligence
Intelliseek, 40
Interactive Digital Software Association (IDSA), 122–123
InterContinental Hotels Group, PLC, 59, 176–177, 210
Interhack Corporation, 139
internal communications, 32
International Chamber of Commerce (ICC), 104, 109
International Federation of the Phonographic Industry (IFPI), 113
Internet
    as competitive intelligence source, 154–155
    in online monitoring, 173–175
    security of information and, 33
Internet Corporation for Assigned Names and Numbers (ICANN), 51, 52, 202, 203
Internet Relay Chat (IRC), 112, 117, 118, 125, 162–163, 174, 183
Internet service providers (ISPs)
    contact information, 118–119, 201
    pornography licenses of, 19
InterNIC.org, 200
invisible seeding
    described, 54
    managing, 55–56
    popularity of, 67
Ipsos-Reid, 140–141
ISPs, see Internet service providers (ISPs)

Jacobs, John L., 130
JC Penney, 47
Johnson, Maryfran, 149
junk e-mail, 20–21, 61–62, 63, 78, 146–147, 148, 200–201
Jupiter Research, 61–62, 113–114

KaZaa, 112
Kelley, Anne, 122
Kentucky Fried Chicken, 28

Kessler, David, 119
King, Stephen, 126
Kruger, Bob, 122

Lanham Act, violation of, 59
Learmonth, Arthur, 83
legal information, 32
Lexmark International, 103
link rot, 78
link spamming, 55, 60–61
Llewelyn, Beth, 2
Locke, Christopher, 33
logos
    alteration of, 16, 36, 46, 56, 78
    misuse of, 60–61, 78, 203
Lowe's, 76
loyalty discounts, 157
LucasFilms Ltd., 20, 116–117

Maloney, Michael, 64
Mario Bros., 1–2
market data, 129–131
Marriott, 47, 49
Martin, Michael, 9
Mary Kay, Inc., 87–88
MasterCard, 11, 161
Mattel, Inc., 10–11
Maytag Corporation, 83
McCarthy, James, 140
McDonalds, 143
McKinsey & Co., 39–40
Merloni Elettrodomestici, 69
Merrill Lynch, 13
message boards, 162–163, 174, 175
metasearch engines, 175
metatags, 54–56
Metro-Goldwyn-Mayer Studios, 121
Mickey Mouse, 15
Microsoft Canada, 111
Microsoft-casino.net, 14
Microsoft Corp.
    Intel and, 31
    security breach, 32–33, 143
    software piracy and, 2, 121–123
    "sucks" sites, 39
mirror sites, 105
mislabeled hyperlinks, 60–61, 67
MobileStreams Ltd., 9

Monty Python, 20
Moon, Michael, 135
Morpheus, 112
Motion Picture Association of America
    (MPAA), 118, 120
Mountain Dew, 28
Moura, Rui, 130, 183
mouse-trapping, 63–67, 69
Movielink.com, 119, 121
MP3.com, 112–113, 114, 126
music piracy, 112–116
    impact of, 112–114
    proactive licensing and, 114–116

Napster, 112–113, 114, 116
Nasdaq Stock Market, 130
National Arbitration Forum (NAF), 52,
    202
National Association of Broadcasters,
    120
negative impressions, 24–26
NetRatings, Inc., 157–158, 158
Netscape, 120
network administrators, 143
New Balance Athletic Shoe Inc., 102
New Economy, 2
news service piracy, 127–128
New York Times, 31
New York Times Company, 59
Nike, Inc., 39, 100, 102–103, 143
Nintendo of America, 1–2
noise, 164
nonvisible text, 54
Nortel Networks, 99

objectionable content
    in campaign against brand abuse,
        202–203
    cease-and-desist letters and, 22–24
    defining, 18–21
    impact of, 24–25
    nature of, 8, 18–21
    online monitoring for, 173, 178–181
    online partners and, 78
    proliferation of, 8
old economy, 2
1x1 GIF, 137–140

online commentary, 27–43
  consumer feedback through, 34–40
  cost of, 41–42
  as early-warning system, 31–32
  earnings claims in, 30–31
  impact of, 41–42
  product rumors, 28–29, 30–31
  proprietary information and, 32–34
  protest sites and, 36–39, 46–47
  risk management for, 40
  as rumor mill, 28–32
  security threats from, 32–34
  as source of competitive intelligence,
    162–164
  value of following, 39–41
online monitoring, 171–189
  application of, 188
  of counterfeit goods, 104–110
  of domain names, 175, 179–181
  of gray markets, 104–110
  for objectionable content, 173,
    178–181
  of online partners, 93–97, 197, 203
  outsourcing of, 182–188
  resource allocation for, 181
  of search engines, 94, 104–105,
    178–179
  what-where-how approach to,
    172–181
online partners, 75–97
  affiliates, 79–80, 93–94
  benefits of, 77
  as brand ambassadors, 75–76, 160
  channel conflict with, 77
  competitive intelligence and, 159–162
  cost of partner noncompliance,
    95–97
  customer experience and, 76–77
  distributors, 84–89
  impact of partner noncompliance,
    95–97
  managing risks of, 78–79, 80, 81–87,
    90–93
  monitoring, 93–97, 197, 203
  online monitoring by, 175–176
  of online monitoring firms, 187
  privacy issues and, 136

recruiting competitor partners,
    160–162
  risks of, 77–78
  suppliers, 80–84, 94
  third parties, 90–93
Oracle Corp., 30
outsourcing of online monitoring,
    182–188
  company background in, 184–185
  experience of supplier in, 187–188
  factors in decision, 182–183
  partnerships and, 187
  qualifications of supplier in, 187–188
  scope of services in, 186–187
  security in, 185–186
Overture Services, 56

page-jacking content, 55, 64–66
paid placements, 56–58, 177
Paramount Pictures, 121
parody, 14–18
Parsons, Chris, 143
partners, see online partners
password sharing, 112
pay-per-click advertising, 56
peer-to-peer (P2P) file-sharing net-
    works, 111–112, 114, 116, 117,
    119–120, 122, 125, 126, 174, 175,
    183, 201
PepsiCo, 38, 180
personal digital assistants (PDAs), 126
personalization, 135–136, 137
Peter Hart Research Associates, 113
Peters, Tom, 76
Peterson, Martin, 40
pharmaceuticals, 56, 62, 103–104,
    106–107
Pharmacy International, Inc., 106–107
Phillpot, Julia, 121
piracy, 2, 111–132
  cost of, 131–132
  e-book, 125–126
  impact of, 131–132
  market data, 129–131
  music, 112–116
  news service, 127–128
  software, 2, 121–124
  text and image, 125–131
  video, 116–121

Plant, The (King), 126
Playboy Enterprises, 144, 145
Playtex Products, 40
Plevyak, Joe, 173
plug-ins, 66
Pokémon, 1–2
Polaris Industries, Inc., 87, 88–89
Polo Ralph Lauren Corp., 102–103
Pony shoes, 19
pop-up ads, 59
pornography, 8–12
  adult entertainment, 9–11
  brand abuse and, 8–12, 24
  child pornography, 11–12
  cultural differences and, 19
  customer diversion and, 52, 53,
    64–66
  cybersquatting and, 1–2, 45–46
Porter, Michael, 154, 165
Portuguese Instituto do Consumidor,
  66
Privacy Payoff, The (Cavoukian and
  Hamilton), 148
private information, 32–34, 135–150
  corporate risks and, 149–150
  information collection technologies
    and, 136–140
  information security and, 140–147
  managing privacy, 147–149
Proctor & Gamble (P&G), 28–29
product diversion, *see* gray markets
product information, 32–33
product rumors, 28–29, 30–31
Prophet, 9
proprietary information, 32–34,
  135–150
protest sites, 36–39, 46–47
public relations, 31–32
publishers, affiliates as, 79–80

Qwest Communications, 50

Reconnaissance International, 102
Recording Industry Association of
  American (RIAA), 112–113,
  118–119
Red Cross, 91–93
Red Herring magazine, 11

"redirect" pages, 64
referrals, 79–80, 94
Renouf, Brent, 111
reverse lookup, 159, 174–175
Riding the Bullet (King), 126
risk management, 40, 78–79, 80, 81–87,
  90–93, 207–208
Rosen, Hilary, 113
Ross, Terence, 59
Royal Caribbean Cruise Lines, 210
Royal Dutch/Shell, 39–40
Rubbermaid, 82–83
rumors, 28–32

SAFECO, 87
screen captures, 23
search engines
  manipulation of, 52–56
  monitoring, 94, 104–105, 178–179
  obscure, 178–179
  paid placements and, 56–58, 177
  popular, 178
  reverse lookup, 159, 174–175
  spiders/crawlers of, 53, 54–55
SearchEngineWatch.com, 188
Secure Sockets Layer (SSL), 141–142
Securities and Exchange Commission
  (SEC), 162
security information, 32
security of information, 32–34, 140–147
  corporate risks and, 149–150
  information collection technologies
    and, 136–140
  managing security, 147–149
  in outsourcing online monitoring,
    185–186
seeding, 66, 67, 106
  managing, 55–56
  of sites with brands, 60–61
  types of, 54, 67
Sesame Workshop, 17–18
Seybold, Patricia, 80
Shakespeare, William, 73
Shein, Barry, 62
Shenai, Kamalakar, 103
Sherman, Cary, 119–120
short message services (SMS), 69

Siegel, Alan, 68
Siekman, Thomas C., 102
Sigman, Laura, 144
Simon & Schuster, 126
Singapore Airlines, 86
Sinnreich, Aram, 113–114
Smith, Jeff, 136
Software & Information Industry Association (SIIA), 122–123
software piracy, 2, 121–124
software utility-generated advertisements, 58–60
Sony Pictures, 121
source code, 54, 65, 183
SPAM, 20–21
spam filters, 146–147
spamming, 20–21, 61–62, 63, 78, 148, 200–201
    filters for, 146–147
    link, 55, 60–61
    web, 55
spawning, 62–64, 67
spiders, search engine, 53, 54–55
Spiegel, 47
sponsored links, 56–58
spoofing, 119–120
    described, 54–55
    managing, 55–56
    popularity of, 67
Sprint, 81
stakeholders, online monitoring by, 175–176
Starbucks, 180
Star Wars, 20, 116–117
stealth windows, 63
Stinson, Burke, 38
stock market data, 129–131
"sucks" sites, 36–39, 46–47
suppliers, 80–84, 94
Swenson, Scott, 89
Symantec Corp., 147, 148

tamper seals, 108
Tapscott, Don, 90–91
text piracy, 125–131
    e-books and, 125–126
    market data and, 129–131
    news services and, 127–128

third parties
    as apparent online partners, 90–93
    cybersquatting and, 47
Time Warner, 49
tobacco, 19
Tommy Hilfiger Corp., 28, 102–103
top-level domains (TLDs), 47, 50–52
Toyota, 47, 87
Toys "R" Us, 139–140
trade secrets, 32–34
Twain, Mark, 207
typo-piracy, 47–50, 51, 67
typo-squatting, 47–50, 51, 67

unauthorized downloads, 66, 67
Uniform Domain Name Dispute Resolution Policy (UDRP), 52
Unilever, 183
United Parcel Service (UPS), 59, 160–161
United Press International (UPI), 127
U.S. Customs Service, 12–13, 103, 202
U.S. Department of Justice, 92–93, 202
U.S. Federal Trade Commission, 64–66
U.S. Food and Drug Administration, 105
U.S. Justice Department, 19
Universal Studios, 121
unsolicited e-mail, 20–21, 61–62, 63, 78, 146–147, 148, 200–201
URL, 23
Usenet newsgroups, 112, 162–163, 174, 175
utility-generated advertisements, 58–60

Valenti, Jack, 120, 121, 169
VeriSign, 52
Verizon Communications, 46–47, 65, 118–119
video piracy, 116–121
    controlling, 118–119
    copy protection and, 120–121
    digital rights management and, 120–121
    extent of, 116–118
    online file-sharing networks and, 119–120

violence, 8, 12–13
Visa International, 11, 140, 161
visible seeding
  described, 54
  managing, 55–56
  popularity of, 67
Visionary Content Management,
    102–103

Wal-Mart, 83
Walsh, Jim, 154
Walt Disney Co., 15, 22–23, 79
Ward, Jim, 117
Warner Bros., 15, 121
watermarking, digital, 120–121
weather bar utilities, 58–60
web beacons, 137–140
web bugs, 137–140
web spamming, 55
Western Union, 143

what-where-how approach to online
    monitoring, 172–181
  how to search, 175–181
  what to search for, 172–173
  where to search, 173–175
WhenU, 58–60
Williams, James R., III, 128
World Health Organization (WHO),
    104
World Intellectual Property Organiza-
    tion (WIPO), 52
WorldNet, definition of parody, 14
World Wide Web, 173–174

Xerox Corporation, 46, 103

Yahoo!, 11, 31, 40, 115, 177
Yankelovich Partners, 81, 206
Yhland, Tuesday, 139

Zepeda, Phil, 91
Zippo Manufacturing Co., 9